How to Be South Asian in America

How to Be South Asian in America

Narratives of Ambivalence and Belonging

ANUPAMA JAIN

Temple University Press
PHILADELPHIA

Temple University Press
Philadelphia, Pennsylvania 19122
www.temple.edu/tempress

Published 2011

♾ The paper used in this publication meets the requirements of the American National Standard for Information Sciences—Permanence of Paper for Printed Library Materials, ANSI Z39.48–1992

LIBRARY OF CONGRESS CATALOGING-IN-PUBLICATION DATA

Jain, Anupama, 1972–
How to be South Asian in America : narratives of ambivalence and belonging / anupama jain.
p. cm.
Includes bibliographical references and index.
ISBN 978-1-4399-0302-5 (alk. paper)
ISBN 978-1-4399-0303-2 (pbk. : alk.paper)
ISBN 978-1-4399-0304-9 (e-Book)
1. South Asian Americans—Cultural assimilation. 2. South Asian Americans—Ethnic identity. 3. Americanization. I. Title.
E184.S69J35 2011
973'04914—dc22

2010039653

2 4 6 8 9 7 5 3 1

THE AMERICAN LITERATURES INITIATIVE

A book in the American Literatures Initiative (ALI), a collaborative publishing project of NYU Press, Fordham University Press, Rutgers University Press, Temple University Press, and the University of Virginia Press. The Initiative is supported by The Andrew W. Mellon Foundation. For more information, please visit www.americanliteratures.org.

Contents

Acknowledgments

This book has been shaped by a wealth of different people and ideas over the past decade. My family and close friends, professional colleagues, anonymous peer reviewers, acquaintances, and even complete strangers have collectively added to the ways in which I conceive of ambivalence and belonging. While I am technically a first-generation immigrant myself (having moved to the United States at the age of three), I have more in common with my second-generation peers. As a result, I have been concerned with "how to be South Asian in America" for most of my life. This project allowed me to transform that personal question into an exciting and energizing intellectual search. The results can only ever represent an incomplete story but do point to what I consider truly important and revealing patterns.

I owe a debt to the community at my undergraduate alma mater, Bryn Mawr College, where I learned to question everything and to always acknowledge the limits of my own knowledge or experience. I remember Katrin Burlin with much fondness and am saddened that she is not here to track the development of my thinking since she directed my senior thesis so ably. Similarly, my teachers and peers in graduate school at the University of Wisconsin–Madison pushed me to think harder, write more clearly, and always (try) to practice the difficult art of self-critique. Susan Friedman continues to act as an inspiring mentor and one of the best examples of what an academic can and should be; with her passion for teaching, her expectations for rigor and depth in critically rethinking the world, and her excellent scholarship, she represents a standard for which I strive, even though I do not expect to reach it. Craig Werner was a wonderful teacher and reader of my work; I hope for future opportunities to listen to him talk about literature, music, and culture in ways that always leave me feeling more informed as well as energized. It is with sadness that I acknowledge two of my advisers who are no longer with us: Amy Ling and Nellie McKay convinced me that there could be no better dissertation committee available to a graduate student. They trained me in different literary traditions but with a similarly intense commitment to filling in gaps in traditional histories. I am deeply grateful to have known and learned from each of them.

At Union College, I had the support of extraordinary faculty peers, particularly in the humanities and social sciences, as well as receiving multiple internal grants which helped me develop this project. Among others who showed me kindness in the English Department, Harry Marten was an unfailing champion, and I could not have asked for more from a chair; he read every single word I have written and carefully oversaw my development as a teacher. Thank you, again, Harry. Lori Marso is another in a line of inspirational intellectuals in women's studies who encourage me to think differently, both politically and creatively. Her stewardship of the college program, as well as the opportunities she created for junior faculty to get serious writing feedback and the wonderful experience of team teaching with her, dramatically shaped the final product represented by this book. Buying me pastries on my birthday was the least sign of her friendship. As the world's best librarian, who has a passion for Jane Austen and polka dots, I thank Annette LeClair; I think we do make the world better with our efforts, Annette. As for my students, so many of them wowed me with their own desires to understand and give back to their communities; they made classes a true joy to teach as well as allowing me to practice being the lifelong student I consider myself.

The support of a Woodrow Wilson Career Enhancement Fellowship allowed me to devote an entire year to the construction of this manuscript. Along with the peers at the fellow's retreat, I want to thank all the others who have over the years read and commented on work in progress. "The Other G8," which spontaneously emerged at a Savannah conference on postcolonialism, simultaneously encouraged and enriched the project as well as my scholarship more broadly.

During the final phases of this book, the Colby College English Department provided me with truly supportive chairs in Peter Harris and Michael Burke, as well as many colleagues who genuinely cared about teaching and ideas. That they also took the time to keep track of me and my future aspirations was deeply appreciated. Students in my classes were smart, funny, and thought provoking, and they helped me to hone the final drafts of the manuscript as our discussions in and out of class allowed me to refine my ideas and word choice.

The most personal acknowledgments start with dear friends scattered here and there who continue to teach me the power of belonging. I have now known Bob Darcy, Amy Feinstein, Svetlana Karpe, and Lisa Levenstein for more than a decade; these friendships represent years of profound dialogue, emotional support, and just plain fun. Shazia Rahman and I have shared many of the seemingly endless ups and downs of planning, executing, and revising (and revising and revising) research; although our companionship was often necessarily over the phone, I value how we have traveled similar terrain together. Renu Aggarwal and Nalini Lamba Nieves have each experienced some of my most mundane and most epiphanic moments; thank you for listening, for being patient with me, and for always caring. My cousin Seema Jain has done that for me for even longer, ever since one of us mysteriously broke the infamous fish tank.

My extended family in the United States, India, England, Australia, and Vietnam have been very present, even when the distances were great, and I feel lucky to be part of this dispersed clan. Even closer to home, my brother Sanjay has so often stepped in when I was struggling that he truly epitomizes the protective, generous big brother. I want to thank him, Heather, Logan, and Maya for their love. Thanks, too, to the sisters-in-law-in-law and your community in Maine for including me in your wonderful summers. The Stoner family, in Pittsburgh and elsewhere, has made me one of their own and unflaggingly wanted the best for me professionally and personally. They really are the type of "American" family we all hope to have.

My parents, Sudha and Prem Jain, have worked harder than I can imagine, thus gifting me with care, support, and more education than they anticipated I could ever need. That they left behind almost everyone and most everything they knew to relocate us to the United States represents a kind of bravery that fills me with admiration. Mostly, they have been the bedrock that allowed me to push myself past what was easy or familiar. There are not words or any phrases meaningful enough to describe how much I love them and thank them for parenting me.

It means so much to me to share my life with John Stoner. Every day, he makes me want to become the best me I can because his generosity of spirit is so extraordinary. With a fantastic sense of humor, the greatest kindness of any person I have ever known, and a deep passion for justice, he encourages my utopianism. This makes tackling the hard issues—in the classroom, in my writing, and elsewhere—a rewarding rather than seemingly futile endeavor. There are so few certainties in the world that the sureness of his support in the things that really matter is amazing and humbling. Finishing this book would never have been possible without his confidence in me and his forgiveness during the weeks (or months) when I was so engrossed in it that the world receded a little bit. But I always knew he was there.

How to Be South Asian in America

The important thing to understand about American history . . . is that it is fictional, a charcoal-sketched simplicity for the children, or the easily bored. For the most part it is uninspected, unimagined, unthought, a representation of the thing, and not the thing itself. It is a fine fiction.

NEIL GAIMAN, *AMERICAN GODS*

It seemed to [Ralph Chang] at that moment, as he stood waiting and waiting, trapped in his coat, that a man was as doomed here as he was in China. . . . He could not always see, could not always hear. He was not what he made his mind to be. A man was the sum of his limits; freedom only made him see how much so. America was no America.

GISH JEN, *TYPICAL AMERICAN*

Introduction

How to Be South Asian in America investigates assimilation narratives concerned with the ambivalence engendered when accommodating a shifting (and thus elusive) national ideal. The title phrase "how to be" signals this study's central goal of demystifying a purportedly authentic or unchanging American cultural identity. It must immediately be acknowledged that "South Asian" is also a category describing a dynamic "imagined community"[1] of multifarious peoples connected—as conditionally and as meaningfully as any other imagined community—to the Indian subcontinent, in symbolic ways as well as in relation to capital, technology, and movement back and forth. Over the past four decades, the population of diasporic South Asians in the United States, with historical origins in India, Pakistan, Nepal, Bhutan, Bangladesh, or Sri Lanka,[2] has grown beyond two million. Their communities have thus rather recently[3] contributed to American traditions of narrating the nation, a process in which a variety of immigrant groups have participated, admittedly with varied claims to recognized authority. In this book, I look at distinct stories representing the diaspora in the United States which were produced in a shared chronological moment at the turn of the twenty-first century. One of the reasons why studies such as this one are crucial is therefore to update stories of America[4] to acknowledge the contributions of those who have more recently immigrated and thereafter added unforeseen nuances to the national mythology. Reappraising assimilation in relation to this group of relatively new Asian immigrants tells us a great deal about American identities in an age of self-conscious transnationality.

Reading interrelated but distinct narratives reveals that newcomers in America will find themselves confronting the stories of those who came before, both the heartening and the horrifying; in relation to such stories as well as those uniquely made available to or claimed by them in their particular time, immigrants navigate their own paths to belonging. In the future, these stories will be tested and may become familiar and beloved ones through repetition, existing alongside or displacing those that have been foundational in the past. For generations after immigration, these stories may seem more or less fitting for representing certain communities and will therefore undergo their own variations. Diversity among immigrants and differential national responses to them, relating to race-ethnicity,[5] gender, class,[6] diaspora and so forth, produce an array of possibilities for assimilation. The experience of (at least implicitly) having to identify one's narrative among these possibilities, rather than feeling as if one automatically or innately belongs, is perhaps the only characteristic shared by all American immigrants, across all of their many differences. Paradoxically, this commonality in difference replaces the ethnic sameness that has often been considered a necessary prerequisite for "nation."

The sense of renewal represented by repeated cycles of immigration and thus "Americanization" —as I discuss later in this chapter, a term which is used throughout the study to designate complex sets of phenomena rather than whole-scale assimilation—means that processes of belonging are ongoing rather than reaching a conclusion after which there is no more story to be told. The most useful way to read such narratives is not for an anticipated outcome or plot resolution but instead for the style in which they convey meaning. Most readers would probably agree that stories both reflect and shape our realities; tracing *how* such a process works in discrete contexts and with what implications is one of the main tasks of this book. Treating fictional as well as "factual" contexts emphasizes that there is a constant interplay between imagined and lived possibilities, as narratives of belonging concerning history, community, and subjectivity influence one another. How belonging is allocated both materially and imaginatively has serious consequences for individuals and entire communities. Probing the layers of meaning produced through these intersecting stories about contemporary affiliation results in an expanded vision of what it means to be American today. Given dominant symbolism of America, this effort implicates issues such as freedom, democracy, and invention; since my focus on transnationalism complicates exceptionalist narratives of the United States, it has the potential to expose otherwise disguised motivations of power and capital, laying the groundwork for rethinking national assimilation as a more open-ended and therefore adequately flexible process. With these priorities, a study such as this is implicitly concerned with diversity as an important element of social justice. Another way in which this book attends to core American themes—for example, equal representation—is by focusing on a nonwhite immigrant community, whose stories have previously been rather marginal to the study of assimilation, as I describe later.

This approach exposes prominent paradoxes related to "belonging"—being a recognized part of something, being suitable, fitting—which are re-created by the more or less continuous surges of immigration from across the world to the United Sates dating back to the start of European colonization. Each racial, religious, or otherwise distinct group in the country has encountered and continues to encounter these paradoxes. Even as each community repeats some of the patterns for assimilating established by earlier groups, it nonetheless experiences the process as if new because of its own choices about, possibilities for, and limits to being included within existing national narratives. As immigrants engage with assimilation expectations, in both established and novel ways, they add their own versions to the overall story of the nation. Given a history of academic and other disagreement about the definition and import of assimilation, it remains a vital process to examine in American public culture[7] precisely because it impacts every one of the diverse groups that have relocated to the United States. Across the demographic diversity of these groups, one commonality is each group's confrontation with influential ideologies of belonging. These experiences, taken in comparative terms, make visible various "stories of America."

What assimilation to the nation symbolizes, what and who constitutes it, shifts with each group and with the groups' interactions with one another as well as their engagement with immigrant histories that already exist. There are also local and regional instantiations of becoming American, or Americanization. What stays the same is the structure of the process: an existing demographic of people into which a new group is trying—in response to their own unique, firsthand experiences—to become part of the nation. You have coexisting stories by "old timers," often responses to newer stories, which reveal assumptions about what immigration and belonging should mean. These ideologically as well as emotionally laden descriptions collectively cohere in a resulting narrative of America which cannot always be predicted, nor can differing visions always easily be reconciled. Americanization programs have discovered this in the past when they were unable to achieve measurable success in assimilating newcomers. Across variations in accounts of being American, the structural necessity of *having* a story maintains. What also remains the same is that the genre of assimilation narrative continues to serve as a reference point; there are certain aspects of Americanization which are consistent even as the details and the emphases change. As with coming-of-age stories, which can never be universal because of the diversity of human experience, there are nonetheless shared characteristics that make them of a type. Such is also true with stories about Americanization. New immigrants are inevitably responding to older stories in crafting their own and are thus participating in the intertextual evolution required for any genre to be viable into a changing future.

To analyze the genre of Americanization narratives, in this book, I closely read stories from published fiction, independent film, original ethnographic material, and contemporary scholarly theories. Throughout, I insist on a transnational framework for assimilation narratives in order to complicate ideologies of belonging that are too often taken for granted rather than being critically unpacked. I embed my original research and conclusions in intellectual discussions in a number of different disciplines that have addressed questions of belonging in relation to processes of immigration, assimilation, and diasporization. While each of these has been well studied in the humanities, the social sciences, or both, combined attention to them and their relation to one another is a rather new way to approach any of them, since analyses of immigration and assimilation have taken the nation (unsurprisingly but not inevitably) as the subject of most importance, while diaspora studies[8] have tended to focus on a site of dispersal and the possibility of return. Arguing that narratives attendant to nationalisms are no less relevant to understanding transnationalism (and vice versa), as other scholars of cultural studies are also doing today, I work to shift the traditional focus of many previous examinations. This also represents an intervention in postcolonial and Asian American studies, through a simultaneous engagement with each, which historically have tended not to be brought together. In addition to the synthesis of theoretical discourses particularly germane to postcolonial, American, and gender studies, another unprecedented aspect of this book is its sustained attention to Guyanese people of Indian origin, whose informative histories as indentured laborers in the

British Empire have received scant scholarly attention. Adding ethnography to my literary analysis with the chapter on Guyanese Americans, I point out how reading varied cultural "texts" reflects a commitment to diversity at all levels, including in methodology.

Such an approach means that the format of this study is distinctive, even in the context of other scholarship with a similar focus on South Asians. Following prominent scholars such as Rajini Srikanth, who have contributed to the growing "visibility that South Asian American writing enjoys today" (5), it is useful to analyze fairly well-known South Asian literary texts in conjunction with diasporic assimilation narratives which have not received the same degree of attention as others. Therefore, looking variously at narratives which have benefited from scholarly analysis, nonnormative (e.g., queer) accounts, and an original ethnography which was produced through research for this book, *How to Be South Asian in America* synthesizes a number of different discourses to produce a distinctive new form that showcases how the stories take unprecedented shapes which nevertheless allude to repeated themes from the past. This perspective allows for a more expansive view of subjects which are often studied within a single disciplinary framework or have concerned past immigration but have not subsequently been reassessed. The multidisciplinary, multidimensional perspective represented by this study thereby works to deconstruct familiar narratives, names, and symbols in order to examine them anew, to measure their ongoing applicability, to question them; the ultimate goal is to describe what cultural work these narratives, names, and symbols perform as well as what this may mean for the people whose realities are shaped through them.

South Asian accounts of belonging represent another chapter in the ongoing American story, a chapter which is distinctive because, prior to the current self-consciousness about globalism, South Asians were already "global." On the Indian subcontinent, longstanding cultural heterogeneity plus a host of colonial imports has meant that definitions of identity[9] and citizenship were created, reinvented, tested, and challenged over several centuries. In the twentieth century, actual and symbolic transfigurations of boundaries—always dislocating and often accompanied by violence—led to the reorganization of millions of people, whose physical conditions, self-perceptions, and stories about themselves were inevitably changed. For South Asians in diaspora around the globe, often moving due to the machinery of the British Empire, dramatic reorderings of the subcontinent combined with their own migratory journeys consequently result in complicated matrices of identification and affiliation. Even as people in the past were perhaps more global than we might commonly believe (as powerfully narrated in Amitav Ghosh's anthropological history, *In an Antique Land*), the sheer scope is impressive of the diaspora of South Asians migrating along the networks created by the British "Raj." This legacy is the reason why today there are substantial communities of South Asians throughout the world, from North America to Africa to the Caribbean, most often in former British colonies. The national and regional histories of far-flung sites of relocation also became part of South Asian stories, informing national assimilation narratives for those who may have subsequently migrated elsewhere and again. In the context of ever-evolving machineries of imperialisms, this means that dispersal from South Asia to the heart of empire itself (whether the former British or the "new" American one) continues to change the meaning of "the West." It should also not be underestimated the degree to which, previously, supposed citizenship in the British Empire and contemporary knowledge of the lingua franca (i.e., English) has made migration seem possible, in ways that are not as salient for groups other than South Asians.

As diasporans contemporarily categorized according to the U.S. census as an "Asian" group,[10] South Asian American stories are thus uniquely revealing of the ongoing, collective cultural work that produces meanings of Americanization and the nation. By including a relatively new immigrant group in traditions of Americanization stories, this study makes an important contribution to American literary history by allowing us to examine how representations of assimilation have persisted or changed over time and across communities. Throughout the country's history, attitudes about immigrant assimilability have been strongly shaped by prevailing ideologies of nationalism, internationalism, religion, gender, class, sexuality, race, and ethnicity. Every group (e.g., indigenous peoples, the first European colonists, and the latest immigrants arriving from all over the world) has had to negotiate the politics of their historical moment along with different communities across shared spaces. After the creation of an official nation-state, along with individual differences among immigrants, modifications to immigration policy based on particular cultural and material investments continued to result in new stories of national identification. Because of such ongoing processes and also as a result of South Asians' altering their own strategies for inclusion, they were differentially afforded Americanization at the end of the twentieth century than they were at the beginning, a trend toward variable assimilation that has also affected many other ethnic groups.

Among the latest in repeated waves of immigration, South Asian diasporans are no doubt "in the American grain,"[11] but their histories also result in specifically layered narratives of belonging which shape and are shaped by dominant interpretations of assimilation. These narratives are not only relevant in themselves but may well help to clarify the experiences of other immigrant groups, both verifying and challenging versions of American assimilating that have become influential. For example, South Asians re-presence a dialectic that has existed since the United States was first invented. As Simon Schama writes in *The American Future: A History,* "the rumble of anxiety first expressed by the Founding Fathers, that the unwashed might overrun the purity of the political nation they had made, never really goes away. Every time the American economy hits a reef, the last on the boat are usually those whom nationalist politicians want to throw from the decks" (243). In tracing the American story, Schama points out that deep ambivalence about newcomers has always existed alongside narratives of the "social miracle by which the most oppressed peasant or laborer could be transformed in America into a free citizen." Especially in the case of immigrants who seem exotic or unfamiliar to normative Anglo-European culture, repeated questioning about who is more or less acceptable undermines a vision of America's "public image" as "one of the indiscriminate embrace of the unfortunate" (242).

Accordingly, the chapters of this book reflect continuity and divergences over time in the experiences of different American immigrant communities, suggesting shifting meanings for some of the most important personal and collective investments people hold. For instance, even as the familiar association of America with expanded economic opportunities is central to many assimilation stories—as was confirmed in my interviews with Indo-Guyanese Americans, discussed in chapter 4—it was not a primary theme in South Asian American literary and film texts. Another common element in the story of Americanization which is not discussed in the chapters is that of religion; the reason for this is that the stories themselves rarely highlighted it, and subtle references to it did not seem to result in striking patterns for close reading. This narrative gap is potentially worth further exploration but may provisionally be explained by an assumption that South Asian religions—often conflated with Hinduism, which is the religion from the subcontinent most represented in the United States—are "ways of life" rather than theology, as Vinay Lal describes (76). As compared to racist stereotypes associated with anti-Islamic attitudes on the rise since 9/11, some religions have historically not invoked large-scale cultural conflict in the United States, perhaps because they are perceived to be reliably nonviolent and nonthreatening or because they are nonevangelical. As another possible explanation for the seeming lack of salience of religion in the selected South Asian narratives, dreams of religious freedom which may have lured earlier immigrants cannot be considered uniquely North American possibilities, based on ongoing (even if often failed) projects for secularism on the subcontinent and, even more strikingly, the thorough intermingling of religions in Guyana, both of which thwart assumptions of religious orthodoxy.

To connect South Asian American texts with those related to previous immigrant generations is therefore to provide a bridge for extending into the future the story of the United States, which is being (re)written every day. South Asian Americans have received growing attention within the academy only in the past two decades but have often popularly been credited with assimilatory success (usually meaning in a professional, educational, or economic sense). What is not necessarily part of the broader national consciousness is that—like any other immigrant group, in terms that are both localized and national—their population growth, monetary investments, cultural contributions, and political integration all reflect existing and evolving (im)possibilities for assimilation. To trace their contemporary politics of belonging is to deepen our awareness of how members of the national collective continue to contend with varied issues of legitimization (i.e., one's right and ability to belong) pursuant to immigrating. This awareness is no less important for Americans who are descendants of immigrants rather than immigrants themselves, because narratives of belonging implicate all groups in the nation, yoking them to one another even when the relationships are fraught with fears of Otherness rather than predicated on commonality.

Since scholars in multiple disciplines have demonstrated the relative invisibility of Asian immigration stories in U.S. public culture, more studies such as this are necessary and important. Two of Ronald Takaki's influential books which undertook to correct omissions of Asian history from immigration studies point to the type of intervention they represent in their very titles, namely *Strangers from a Different Shore* and *In a Different Mirror.* Contrasted with the "different" stories represented in Takaki's work, Americanization studies historically tended to take Anglo-Americans as the representative figures, which resulted in a poor fit (i.e., no place to belong) for Asian and other nonwhite immigrants. In the past decades, scholarly attention to East Asian American, especially

Chinese American, stories has grown. Contributing to this new tradition of expanding the frame of reference to include "different" stories of immigration and assimilation, *How to Be South Asian in America* provides a counterpoint to familiar narratives. It joins other contemporary assimilation scholarship which has the same goal, including comparative studies, examinations (rather than assumptions) of "whiteness," and attention to Americans marginalized along other axes of belonging and identity in addition to race-ethnicity, religion, or class.

Bearing in mind such diversity, this study exposes how (popular perceptions notwithstanding) *no single narrative* can adequately represent belonging in—often interpreted as "assimilating to"—America. Instead, each immigrant group has had to struggle to identify an intelligible narrative among those available to them. For instance, neither "melting pot" nor any other popular descriptor has collectively been deemed adequate to represent centuries of newcomers affecting and being affected by the nation. The two epigraphs that open this book confirm the unreliability of nonetheless dominant stories about America, especially ones which focus on success, abounding freedom, and limitless agency. Neil Gaiman and Gish Jen both suggest that the "truths" implied by narratives signifying the American Dream require much more careful interpretation than is usual. In fact, by shaping, altering, and sustaining different versions of "Americanness," the circulation of these stories dramatically affects how one interprets the national social order. Feminist critic Susan Stanford Friedman writes that narratives "constitute primary documents of cultural expressivity. Narrative is a window into, mirror, constructor, and symptom of culture. Cultural narratives encode and encrypt in story form the norms, values, and ideologies of the social order" (8–9). Polysemic narrations of nation can thus be read for their influence on identity discourses which, in turn, modify interpretations of Americanization and the narratives describing it. These shifting grounds mean that the import of stories like the American Dream, despite their pervasiveness in immigrant imagination and implicit assumptions to the contrary, cannot be definitively ascertained. Instead, these stories are constantly being rewritten, like any tale worth adapting for a new generation of reader-listeners.

Indeed, as much as immigration policy and attitudes have changed over time, so too has the meaning of the American Dream. Although it is a shared narrative that might seem self-explanatory, it is individually meaningful for people and there are also interpretations specific to different communities which have accrued to the notion. It has tended to signify "better," but "better" in what sense? For laborers across the world looking to expand their economic and work options, those looking to escape famine or conflict, "better" may represent financial stability and security. For refugees without a state—victims of natural disasters or wars—"better" has meant actual safety as well as a place in the world through relocation. For more elite professionals, "better" may have meant temporary sojourn, as has also been true for certain less economically or professionally privileged laborers; in such cases, the American Dream may simply have meant opportunity rather than a desire to become a person identified with a different nation or identity. For South Asian immigrants, the American Dream has been as inchoate as for any and every other group. It has represented expanded opportunities in educational, professional, and economic terms but also the recognition of affiliations which are complicated and layered. In second-generation South Asian stories which I examine, meanwhile, there is an implicit assumption that the American Dream has been achieved; the protagonists are Americans with a degree of financial privilege and with easy access to higher education, whose struggles with assimilation (to both the nation and to their immigrant communities) are most focused on what I call "anxieties of authenticity," as developed in chapter 4. These anxieties are produced because, for the children of South Asian immigrants who are part of the diaspora, there is always another site of identification than the United States which plays a part in their negotiations of national belonging.

Contextualizing contemporary Asian American stories within histories of immigrant narrativity, this study also examines global relationships which coexist with national loyalties, thus adding something distinct to what has routinely been undertaken in studies of assimilation. Transnational analyses have historically been lacking in the way that assimilation was interpreted. As sociologist Monisha Das Gupta notes in *Unruly Immigrants,* similarly to most other immigrant historiography, "the story of South Asian immigration to the United States has not been framed transnationally until recently. It has been narrativized instead within a conventional and nationalist framework of assimilation and cultural pluralism," which she believes has led to an "impoverished" theoretical framework and the posing of only "modest questions" (20). Like Das Gupta, I too am interested in shifting our focus to larger questions concerning ambivalence, capitalism, and (trans)nationalism rather than simply describing identity choices. By doing so, I am able to talk about specific ways that particular narratives of belonging have been transformed because of international, transnational, and globalization ideologies which have pervaded American and other cultures in the past several decades. Such a methodology also allows for a more customized approach to the groups in question because the links that they themselves draw to other parts of the world are foregrounded rather than being either ignored or considered solely as problems for Americanization. For instance, since India was once the jewel in the crown of the empire and a major icon of colonization and imperialism, South Asian narratives are highly revealing about the way belonging and marginalization operated in the imaginary of the Raj, as a backdrop to the American imaginary. Also, tracing how a group of people shift from South Asia to North America, now sites of the two biggest democracies in the world, we find an emphatically (trans)national representation of Americanization.

Furthermore, implicated in "post-'s" including colonialism, modernism, communism—and, some scholars argue, nationalism—South Asians have settled in large numbers in the United States only since 1965, when globalization has often been interpreted as an immanent challenge to nation-bound affiliations. At the same time, global capital's seeming hegemony elicits resistance and suspicion, meaning that globalization can, ironically, be read as shoring up certain models of "nation." The interplay between such challenge and affirmation is worth closely examining, as it is a defining phenomenon in the lives of vastly differentiated people and, if in a largely symbolic sense, makes more porous the line between here and there, East and West, rich and poor, us and them, insider and outsider, and citizen and alien. South Asian communities, with their own internal diversity as well as their noticeable differences from the majority race in the United States, are exceptionally well positioned to represent such "post-"related border crossings. And diasporization itself is one important means for reading our contemporary global cultures and their various investments. Historically in the United States, policy, popular culture, and individuals themselves might have represented essential ethnic identities as a given, whereas now national assimilation has become conspicuously infused with variety because of all the cultural mixing that has reshaped it. It is no longer what it was, with new layers being added all the time; because the story does not end, it is necessary to record it at its moments of articulating and rewriting, looking at its reflection back to history and forward into the future—for the ways it may create new, different, perhaps better, and perhaps no better versions of belonging that are appropriate or adequate to experience, to desire, to practicality.

Instead of affirming American exceptionalist rhetoric, which many previous readings of assimilation seemed to do, this study theorizes that

Americanization is not a measurable or achievable goal but rather a process reflecting the evolving cultural and material investments of different constituencies. Furthermore, my reading strategies reveal that national assimilation is but one among a globalized set of processes representing how people negotiate being part of a collective, whether defined by nation, religion, race, diaspora, or something else. Thus, Americanization represents one of many discourses of authenticity, reflecting a relationship of proving loyalty to earn belonging. Based on these interpretations of assimilation, South Asian accounts of Americanization are best viewed as narrative performances according to which people are rendered legible within specific contexts and in certain moments. Their narratives about America represent (trans)national processes full of contradictions and challenges, with an overall implication that there is a continuing (sometimes urgent) need for diverse and evolving political projects toward cultural and social equality rather than an often celebrated assumption that we have achieved a utopian, new-world American Dream.

Studying assimilation and the American Dream by connecting varied stories, communities, and ideas, the following chapters are concerned with narratives as well as epistemologies of belonging. While the chapters historicize an Asian American group recently immigrating to the United States, they also trouble the possibility of definitively "naming" them. The dialectical tension between confident knowledge and dynamic unknowability is thus one of the important ones maintained throughout the chapter discussions. In addressing such conceptual binaries, I note the particular shape they have taken in narrative or history and ask how they invalidate or make possible different projects for belonging. For instance, the supposed incompatibility of nationalism and diasporic affiliation is very informative in understanding the negotiations required of immigrants attempting to find a role for themselves within narratives of the nation. Similarly, supposedly assimilated versus "ethnic" identities are telling about the assumptions which inform particular notions of Americanization. Paying close attention to the details of South Asian narratives of belonging is therefore a means of deconstructing multiple ideological oppositions and noticing the relationships between supposedly incompatible binary positions.

One of the most significant ways this study works toward its overall deconstructive strategy is by calling attention to pervasive themes that powerfully strain against easy categorical certainties. To start, recognizing that immigrant and diasporic identities are often presumed to be mutually incompatible, I instead consider how processes of diasporization and assimilation are mutually informative rather than in conflict with (or somehow irrelevant to) one another. Related themes include mixing, hybridity, and code-switching: repeated imagery in all the narratives collectively works to gainsay politics of authenticity that limit the types and shapes of stories by which diverse experiences can be narrated. "Authenticity" is a topic implicitly referenced throughout this book which is interrogated in depth in chapter 4. Authenticity concerns about assimilating to both national and diasporic communities result in a thoroughgoing ambivalence, which need not be deemed paralyzing but can instead be interpreted as meaningfully productive because it is a continually negotiated synthesis of seeming opposites. Such motifs are furthermore part of a universal story concerning the ways in which all people necessarily exceed the boundaries of affiliative and other categories simply because there is no one standard configuration that can encompass an individual and his or her life. Instead, all people are only partially able to conform to any *one* category, such as American, Asian, woman, lesbian, or working class, because of all the axes by which people choose and are assigned names for themselves. In chapter 4 the final discussion of my primary texts, I tie together various threads from the preceding chapters in order to point out that it is only in acknowledging the limited fit of any singular narrative that Americans may best be able to recognize diverse stories of belonging, which are as much provisional and performed as they are nonetheless "real."

In light of the often uneven and conflicting forms of these assimilation narratives, I argue that it is more useful to close read them collectively as accounts of "ambivalent Americanization" rather than as stories of total assimilation or ethnic separatism. This inadequate and polarized—albeit common—view of immigration fails to reflect the complexity with which immigrants and other minorities negotiate various affiliations along with those imagined in prevailing national cultures. As an alternative to such simplifications, my overarching interest lies in situating representations of ambivalent assimilation within a tradition of national stories and "narratives of identity" (Anderson, *Imagined Communities* 205) that define America. I examine commonly shared or contested contemporary visions of assimilation as stories that transform, as well as reflect, projects of national belonging. Debates about assimilation energize discussions among sociologists and historians and broadly across the social sciences, offering useful mediations on the subject of Americanization as expressed through art, politics, language, food, and culture. Still, literary studies strike me, with my admittedly biased perspective within an English department, as a rewarding framework within which to analyze assimilation because, as cultural theorist Peter Hitchcock argues in *Imaginary States*, "a good deal of transgressive national critique occurs in the literary" (9). While I adopt strategies and consider insights from multiple academic disciplines, my overall argument is therefore grounded in practices developed within literary studies, even when the texts I read come from ethnographic sources or are stories told in films. The implications of such a study are not "merely" literary, however, as I stress throughout.

Indeed, South Asian narratives are best viewed as part of an ongoing series of opportunities for all Americans to reassess central stories of themselves and their continuing fitness for many (or any) individuals within the nation. Alluding to shared historical experiences on the subcontinent and in the United States, the narratives I discuss commonly pointed out paradoxes of supposed national inclusion versus ethnic exclusion, reflected multiple possibilities for choosing family and community, and highlighted the unpredictable influences of class and gender as well as race on assimilation experiences. As with many other immigrant and ethnic minority groups, South Asian Americanization routinely reflected disappointment in the reality of American "freedom," even as its possibilities framed every story. In the interaction between text and context, individual and community, nation and diaspora, then, unique narratives develop which both define personhood and reshape the way we name things, including the locations in which we reside.

Strategic Readings

My analysis of ambivalent Americanization is an example of "Asian American postcolonial feminist cultural studies" because I integrate scholarly methodology associated particularly with these intersecting disciplinary areas. This interdisciplinary methodology is necessary for substantiating one of my central premises, that just as Americanization is usefully reconceived of as a process through which national belonging is negotiated, diasporization is most usefully approached as a coinciding and coterminous series of strategies for relating to inter-, sub-, or supranational communities. In the following chapters, my joint attention to these unpredictable and creative processes is often precariously maintained because of their dynamism, but I strive to work through the tensions thus revealed. This suits my conviction that responsible theorizing about issues of deep cultural significance means constantly subjecting one's analysis to self-critique to prevent the creation of a new master narrative which will sediment itself and resist future reassessment. I hope to avoid this and related tendencies, such as overstating subversive possibilities suggested by certain important antiessentialist discourses, including hybridity, cosmopolitanism, and diaspora. Instead, by attending to multiple narrative arcs and academic threads which reflect contemporary thinking, I aim for a "thick description" developed from analyzing "densely textured facts."[12] In this specific case, the academic fields of postcolonial, Asian American, and gender studies are most relevant for my study of immigrant communities historically connected to the Indian subcontinent, men and women who are at the same time ethnic minorities in the United States and diasporans indelibly influenced by the former British Empire. Any description of such communities *must* take multiple concerns into account, which is why I synthesize findings from several disciplines.

Furthermore, although all the stories in this book concern South Asian Americanization, there are many significant differences among them, not the least of which are self-positioning, class politics, and hoped-for outcomes. Many of the South Asian stories represent large demographics within the diaspora, namely Indian and Pakistani, while the Indo-Guyanese American ethnographies are part of a less often visible and much less well-represented constituency, especially within published fiction or scholarship. I refuse to consider certain authors, filmmakers, or interviewees as "representative" of South Asians in general; they must be viewed instead as participants in a wide-ranging diasporic dialogue. The media and genres themselves give rise to different types of stories or different emphases within stories, whether because of material constraints, expected audiences, or other reasons, some of which I consider in specific chapters. In each case, I have chosen from available stories that focus on assimilation and that have seemed relatively influential, whether in local or other contexts. By pointing out that the narratives are shaped by multiple, often contradictory impulses—including personal agency,[13] inequalities of gender, race, class, and the like, and conventions of societies as well as genres—I am able to reevaluate tendencies to normalize South Asian American or other experiences. Those tendencies lead to defining immigrants as either completely assimilated to or alienated from dominant culture.

As is common in cultural studies (CS),[14] I examine narratives in different arenas of social production and different media, specifically by pairing literary criticism with readings of popular culture and contemporary historiographies. The first chapter is an introduction to stories of Americanization, the second chapter analyzes quasi-official and personal accounts of recent immigration and assimilation, and the final two focus on fictional interpretations of the same processes. This interdisciplinary approach combines attention to the institutional effects of new types of belonging as well as the imaginative responses that they evoke. Such a methodology ideally allows for a reasonably full representation of communities in relation to ongoing issues of Americanization. This suits my intention of weaving different sets of stories together in a way that appropriately reflects the heterogeneity of South Asian America without settling on any single story as *the* defining one for this large and diverse immigrant and diasporic population.

Analogous types of cultural studies have evolved in multiple directions in the American academy from their Birmingham beginnings and the influence of scholars such as Raymond Williams and Stuart Hall. Rather than considering culture to be innate or invariable, these strategies examine what Fredric Jameson defined as "a vehicle or a medium whereby the relationship between groups is transacted" (34). Across their variation, the proliferation of CS approaches have in common an interest in identifying a core set of issues to be approached through interdisciplinarity when no one discipline or approach seems to suffice. This approach ideally promotes collaborative theorizing and has the benefits of combining multiple perspectives on a singular subject of study in order to develop an understanding of broader cultural patterns.

However, certain aspects of CS and its historical practice have evoked criticism. For instance, interdisciplinary techniques can be a source of great anxiety and can arouse resistance even though the *idea* of them is often lauded in the American academy. Since this type of work occurs between or in the margins of traditional disciplines and often involves "a provocative set of critical interventions," according to Hitchcock (8), CS has raised many questions over the past four decades about the possibility that such intellectual activity can actually satisfy conflicting expectations among academic fields. To engage in "creatively eclectic methodological strategies," as Akhil Gupta and James Ferguson positively describe such a process in terms of ethnography (25), is also to cut across the boundaries between different disciplines without giving a supposedly complete account in terms of any one field, which may mean disappointing many readers rather than fully satisfying anyone. In addition to such anxieties, among earlier versions of CS, there was a tendency to assume a national (rather than global or "glocal") framework, which many critics believe has foreshortened otherwise useful analyses. Yet another criticism that is often levied against contemporary CS is that the central focus on Marxism that accompanied the genesis of the discipline has been lost, although I would argue that, to a greater or lesser extent, most serious efforts at CS retain an interest in "cultural materialism."[15] That is the case in *How to Be South Asian in America*, and parts of my analysis, particularly in chapter 2, are highly attuned to the ways in which interpretations of class influence other cultural outcomes, without my offering a Marxist analysis per se.

What, then, is the value of my cultural studies approach? The value lies in the structure provided for posing theoretical questions in specific moments and places, in relation to particular people. Ideally, the bigger picture (which has been envisioned variously by anthropologists as "collective existence," "an ensemble of texts,"[16] or a "cumulative text"[17]) comes into sharper focus through the answers gleaned in the process, such that cultural patterns become more easily discernible. Even if this process does not quite succeed as a researcher might wish, the cultural work accomplished in doing the analysis both documents and contributes to meaning making. Furthermore, CS befits this type of project because of priorities which have proven valuable across diverse types of scholarly activity, particularly what I consider a tendency to "pluritopic rather than monologic" argument making, as Françoise Lionnet puts it (31). This means investigating how a certain cultural phenomenon or discourse has been generally interpreted, followed by an interpretation of its effects in localized sites or circumstances, without a privileging of one dominant narrative. Interpretations of "culture"[18] may vary in focusing on patterns of behavior, sets of beliefs or shared understandings, human intellectual and artistic work, the use of particular metaphors to describe human experiences, or what anthropologist Clifford Geertz calls "webs of significance" ("Thick Description" 5). In all these cases, CS offers sets of strategies for attending to nontotalizing systems by which humans understand the world around them. By examining how human activity is simultaneously lived *and* symbolic, CS methods have the possibility of doing justice to what Arjun Appadurai imagines are "fundamentally fractal" cultural forms which deconstruct "boundaries, structures, or regularities" (46), for instance, the traditional binary of "popular" versus "high" culture. The implications of such deconstruction are political, as well as literary and sociological, since the focus on localizations of broader patterns may prevent the type of false universalizing, essentializing, or overgeneralizing common to certain projects of the Enlightenment, Western modernity, and other forms of imperialism.

Thus, *How to Be South Asian in America* suggests interrelations between several forms concerned with a shared subject of representation (i.e., assimilation and diasporization) and my discussion moves between different cultural modalities. Unpacking cultural "texts" in "context," adding the concrete, detailed, and precise to theoretical understandings of culture, this method allows for combined attention to the effects of globalizations[19] as well as to particular histories within transnational circuits. With regard to reading literary as well as other texts, Jenny Sharpe for one has convincingly traced how novels represent "possible worlds rather than probable ones," which "stage social contradictions and strive to resolve them" (*Allegories of Empire* 21–22), but obviously there are many things which literary works cannot deliver. Noting the distinct forms of cultural work performed in different types of documents, I call attention to the metaphors and symbols that cathect the idea of Americanization. But I am always conscious of what Ato Quayson calls the "mutual interdependency and antagonism" of the pull toward "discourse analysis" as compared to "the material, social and economic factors" (6) informing assimilation narratives. As demonstrated in debates within feminist, subaltern, postcolonial, Asian American, and cultural studies, these pulls remind us of vexed questions about praxis, or the "real-world" implications of our theories. Nonetheless, as Asian Americanist Anita Mannur usefully reminds, in the study *Culinary Fiction,* literary and material concerns are mutually informative; she writes, "To frame literary analyses anchored in literary theory—structural, post-structural, psychoanalytic—as inimical to the conventions of material analysis . . . is to perpetuate a false divide," and she instead describes her version of literary critique as "an ethical-political project for it recognizes that Asian American literature is aesthetic and political" (16). Similarly, in this book, I view moving between different intellectual registers (e.g., ethical, aesthetic, political, identarian) as a way to acknowledge simultaneously both the metaphorical and the material affects of immigration.

Synthesizing theories developed through a variety of CS strategies, I nonetheless uniquely shift the focus to ambivalence and belonging, while maintaining a political commitment to understanding the materiality of culture. Certain contemporary applications of CS methods, especially in relation to feminisms, have been of notable relevance as I developed these analyses[20] and I find Jigna Desai's discussion of the Indian film industry especially useful for contextualizing my readings of diasporization. Like Desai, I am intent on "forging a fractured and flawed methodology of theorizing transnational cultural politics through difference"

(*Beyond Bollywood* 22). I am also very sympathetic to Mannur's description of her methodology, such that "it is less about understanding what the literature tells us about how and what South Asians in diasporas eat, and more about how food serves as an idiom to imagine subjectivity" (18). Looking at the idioms of Americanization stories, I too see these as "merely one constellation of texts within a wider series of discursive formations that enable us to better negotiate the limits of the knowable, furthering our understanding of how material practices are written about in South Asian" works (Mannur 19). Through various threads highlighted in my argument, I theorize about diasporization and assimilation as a contribution to dialogues sustained by and also initiated in studies such as those described in this section.

(Trans)Nationalism: Reading Americanization and Diasporization

As revealed through my particular deployment of CS, South Asian Americanization narratives illuminate contemporary globalized anxieties about belonging and identity, (trans)nationality, and mechanisms of cultural interpenetration, a palimpsestic[21] set of processes related to diasporization. "Diasporization" refers to the historical dispersal of South Asian Americans from one nation to another, as well as representing ongoing, in-process, extranational networks that connect South Asians across multiple (re)locations. My corresponding use of "(trans)national" both presences and distinguishes related processes. Analyzing the "cultural logics" of transnationality, anthropologist Aihwa Ong usefully elaborates that

> *trans* denotes both moving through space or across lines, as well as changing the nature of something. Besides suggesting new relations between nation-states and capital, transnationality also alludes to the *trans*versal, the *trans*actional, the *trans*lational, and the *trans*gressive aspects of contemporary behavior and imagination that are incited, enabled, and regulated by the changing logics of states and capitalism. (4)

Similarly alluding to multiplicity and changeability within specific fields of power, (trans)national analyses in this book attend to intertwined discourses and, particularly, contradictory systems. For example, since South Asian communities are often perceived to be highly successful in adapting to host cultures, they are labeled and thus treated in particular ways, including as an American "model minority."[22] However, they are also affiliated with a diaspora of peoples throughout the world that serves to prevent absolute or seamless assimilation, which is furthermore hampered by their racial-ethnic difference from their new nation's majority. These are particularly salient aspects of South Asian Americanization that offer us useful insights into the nature of assimilation as a process in general, since they point to the variable and sometimes inconsistent ways in which immigrants have always come to "belong" (or not) in America.

Within the widely distributed—and often polarized—field of possibilities, it is particularly important to define how the terms "assimilation" and "Americanization" are deployed in this book. I reject the interpretation that cultural assimilation is a discrete enactment of homogenization by which one thing conforms to the preexisting character of another. Whereas some interpretations of minority assimilation assume a unidirectional transformation through which newcomers adopt the customs and attitudes of the prevailing culture as they become part of "the melting pot,"[23] my examination highlights multiple valences of immigrant identification. I argue that "becoming American" should be interpreted as a process in which there is always some aspect of volition, adaptation to the country combined with the maintenance of ethnic or other identifications predating immigration, and inevitable ambivalence about transformations that are engendered by migration.

With an emphasis on multiple directions of influence, Americanization, too, can be recuperated from a common association with the casting off of any previous allegiances, cultural practices, world views, or values. Especially as I approach the conclusion of this study, I use the term "accommodation" in order to emphasize how individuals reconcile themselves to their societies through alternative strategies as well as in conjunction with normative ideologies.[24] I am interested in how South Asians "imagine, how they represent themselves, figurally in the visual and literary field, how they position themselves in the narratives of self and society," as theorist Stuart Hall put it in another context ("Living with Difference"). After reading their stories, I conceive of "assimilation" as the processes reflecting how newcomers respond to specific possibilities for belonging to a new community, in this case the nation-state represented by the United States. This opposes an interpretation of total assimilation as an end goal of immigration.

Another way in which studies of assimilation need to be reconceptualized is by focusing on the degree to which transnationalism has become an obvious cultural and intellectual preoccupation, such that we must acknowledge how intertwined investments of nation *and* diasporization influence possibilities for belonging in America. Even though it is true that, as Ong writes, "migration studies has recently shifted its focus from assimilation to take into account the global context of border-crossing movements" (8), it is important to maintain a *simultaneous* focus on assimilation and transnationalism. This allows for continuing dialogues that have been ongoing since the start of European colonizing of America, while also nuancing them in light of contemporary narratives of nation and immigration. To read assimilation from this vantage is, perhaps counterintuitively, to decenter the nation as the proper framework and instead foreground shifting or porous borders.

This observation alludes to one of many academic debates about how most appropriately to parse belonging and identity in the contemporary age. For instance, predictions of a new, allegedly postnational, global order vie for supremacy with descriptions of the "willed merger[s] of nation and dynastic empire," which is how Benedict Anderson glosses "official nationalism" (86). Along this spectrum have appeared conspicuous interventions, such as Anderson's *Imagined Communities*, which dramatically redirected academic inquiry in the 1980s and 1990s with its analysis of nation-building as "the most universally legitimate value in the political life of our time" (3). Anderson's arguments, based on reading the effects of print media, concern the substantial and continuing influence of the concept of nationality on political, economic, and social phenomena of the nineteenth and twentieth centuries; his conclusions have by now been widely discussed and disseminated. According to some readings, the fierceness with which many people continue to defend their sense of national belonging, even when a nation is being "imagined" against material realities, is a defensive reaction to the increase in border crossings of many sorts that seem to accompany postmodernism and postcolonialism. This supports Anderson's claim that official nationalisms are "*responses* by power groups" to historical contingencies rather than proactive assertions (109).[25] Conversely, from the perspective of those without power in a nation-state, many post–World War II strains of "cultural nationalisms," which were often equated with anticolonial and/or minority activism, were projects for disrupting imperialist oppression.

Coexistent with versions of nationalism, diasporas seem to reflect a markedly different ordering of people, characterized as they are by dispersals, sojourns, returns, and settlements of altered kinds in new places. These movements may be read in a variety of ways—as processes which problematically diffuse culture, as confusing rootlessness, as examples of cultural hybridity (whether read positively or negatively), as empowering examples of nomadism à la Deleuze and Guattari, as versions of world-citizen cosmopolitanism[26]—but in every case, attention to transnational diasporas undermines the commitment of nationalisms to being "limited and sovereign" (Anderson, *Imagined Communities* 6). The concept of diaspora is not a new one, but there has been notably energetic intellectual and cultural engagement with it particularly in the past few decades. For instance, Édouard Glissant notes, "The cultures of the world have always maintained relations among themselves that were close or active to varying degrees, but it is only in modern times that some of the right conditions came together to speed up the nature of these connections" (26). Many observers agree that, with twentieth-century (trans)national transformations in technology, capital, and culture, the web which connects discrete and distant sites has been pulled tighter and become more conspicuous than before, even though there have always been migrations that brought diverse peoples into contact.

More recently named diasporas have thus been of central interest in relatively new international academic disciplines such as postcolonial studies, with only three decades of institutionalization, and have also been important in shifting renderings of transnationalism in American public culture. Sociopolitical developments in the United States and diverse global contexts jointly position immigrants in relation to nation, ethnicity, culture, and belonging in specific but dynamic ways. In consequence, diasporic and immigrant identities are often prominently interrelated for many recent arrivals in the United States, and the relationship between nationalism and transnationalism is much more conspicuous than it might have been for earlier theorists of Americanization.

Therefore, as I do with regard to interpretations of Americanization which have been strongly polarized, I challenge discourses of diasporization which focus on one of two major effects of dispersion rather than studying an array of related effects simultaneously. Bifurcated attention has usually been paid *either* to the homeland from which a diaspora is in exile *or* the (frequently troubled) relationship between diasporans and their current places of settlement. Currently, however, diaspora theorists challenge this paradigm by discussing how the transnationalism endemic to diasporization is not served by limited, nation-based investigations that are in clear contradistinction to the continuing *multi*national realities of most dispersals. Ong argues for more careful attention to "complicated accommodations, alliances, and creative tensions between the nation-state and mobile capital, between diaspora and nationalism, or between the influx of immigrants and the multicultural state" (15). Such attention proves that, as a widespread discourse in the early twenty-first century, "diaspora" (which I discuss at length in chapter 1) invites striking metaphors for migratory processes which differentiate individuals or communities at the same time that they connect seemingly unrelated people, since they have in common an experience of self-identifying beyond one nation. A central paradox that is produced is that "to be different in a world of differences is irrevocably to belong,"[27] reflecting dialectics of sameness and difference that probably seem familiar to many contemporary individuals, whatever their responses to this reality.

How, then, does diasporization affect projects of assimilation and narratives of national belonging? In a classic statement, anthropologist James Clifford wrote, "Separate places become effectively a single community" through the continued flow of individuals, information, currency, and products, replacing definitively bounded national territoriality as the primary mapping of "place" such that "diasporic cultural forms can never, in practice, be exclusively nationalist" (303, 307). Diasporas may be more than nonexclusively nationalist and may actually pose "a serious challenge to host societies," in William Safran's view (97), because they can never fully be integrated into the dominant national narrative. To take it a step further, one might theorize that diasporization is *anti*nationalist, a possibility which has invited any number of academic responses. Theoretical alternatives to nationalist assumptions and practices (which cannot claim that nation-states have somehow been transcended in actual time-space) have been imagined as "ethnoscapes,"[28] with narrative-cum-material effects, diffuse "locations of culture" rather than nationally bound ethnic identities and homogeneous communities,[29] and in relation to a number of other metaphors. What these alternative imaginaries share is attention to how transnationality deterritorializes the familiar landscapes of national narratives and nationalisms. Thus, when sociologist Avtar Brah argues that "dispersed across nation states, diasporic collectivities figure at the heart of the debate about national identity" (243), she spotlights communities which have historically been theorized as peripheral to the nation and also enacts a useful strategy of prioritizing diasporization as a key factor in shaping contemporary nationalisms.

Being similarly convinced that diasporas resituate certain epistemologies of human interaction because they transgress geographical and ideological borders, I am particularly interested in complicating our understandings of the relationships *between* communities here and elsewhere. In the contemporary American context, diasporas are a part of the history of immigration which represent the intermingling of waves of diverse newcomers with allegiances elsewhere. The relatively recent diasporic turn in Asian American studies represents intellectual attention to such contingencies.[30] Because of the ways in which racial stereotypes and hierarchies have impeded Asian American assimilation, one corrective that scholars can undertake is to aggressively disaggregate race and nation through a synchronized focus on extranational, as well as national, communities. However, I would argue against *assuming* that diasporization is radically antinationalist, because narratives of "diaspora" are as varied and shifting as national narratives. Nationality, ethnicity, culture, diaspora: each of these expectations of belonging may meet with conformity, as well as resistance, especially for people implicated in multiple narratives.

Reading Ambivalence

Accordingly, in this book, I engage *multiple layers of ambivalence* in South Asian American narratives of belonging, particularly in relation to nation, assimilation, diaspora, cultural identity, race-ethnicity, class, and gender. Maintaining a simultaneous focus on aspects of affiliation which historically have often been analyzed separately, I address questions of community and belonging while inspecting a spectrum of ideas about assimilation and diasporization. The concept of ambivalence emphasizes the range of possibilities available to individuals contending with both Americanization processes and transnationalism, as well as signaling the variability of stories. The concept is also quite appropriate for a book such as this, which offers a "reckoning" with the American Dream, which Jim Cullen concludes has long been marked by ambivalence, because "for much of our history, [Americans] could never quite decide whether we finally regarded immigrants as a blessing or a burden" and immigrants "themselves have been unsure about whether to stay" (7, 188).

Ambivalence—simultaneity paired with difference, having mixed responses, feeling genuinely torn between seemingly opposite choices—also seems the most suitable means to characterize issues which are hotly debated and in which disagreements people invest so much. These issues concern the displacements of particular subjects and the often ambiguous ways that nations incorporate them in the collective imaginary, even when it is as outsiders. Attitudes toward assimilation implicitly raise questions about divided loyalties and the answers are so important because they get at the very heart of who "we" think we are and who we are *not.* Given these stakes, it is not surprising that major binaries—for example, assimilated/alienated, us/them, insider/outsider—persist. In this context, "ambivalence" is a vehicle for deconstructing binaries (following Jacques Derrida and Gayatri Spivak, in particular) and examining active interconnections between supposedly oppositional processes and realities.

I am certainly not the first scholar to argue that reading "ambivalence" suits poststructural practices which challenge master narratives. Many of the best-known contemporary theorists in both postcolonial and Asian American studies have invoked the concept. Homi Bhabha's theories about contemporary migrations and "gatherings" (*The Location of Culture* 139) have been particularly suggestive; for example, he touches on specific themes also relevant to the present project when he writes that "the conceptual ambivalence of modern society becomes the site of *writing the nation*" (146). Bhabha here emphasizes that nation-states are constructed in engagement with theories of the ideal; furthermore, it is in discourse, through words and language, that national communities are most clearly realized. The ambivalence he locates in the process is produced by the contrasts between narratives of what the nation ought to be and how people within the nation live out their interpretations of what it *is.* In prominent discussions which also focus on ambivalence but offer other types of cultural interventions, Timothy Brennan critiques intellectual cosmopolitanism, Paul Gilroy interrogates exile and homecoming in *The Black Atlantic,* Lisa Lowe describes Asian unassimilability in *Immigrant Acts,* and Edward Said analyzes colonial discourse in *Orientalism.*[31]

A particularly important precedent for this book is *Ambivalent Anticolonialism: The United States and the Genesis of West Indian Independence, 1940–1964,* a historical study by Cary Fraser which includes a discussion of South Asians. When Fraser argues that American goals for decolonization projects warred with Cold War imperatives for national power, the book's title and his analysis both speak to processes which are inevitably mixed and can thus seem self-contradictory. In a similar fashion, I argue that even pluralistic imperatives for immigrant assimilation clash with unacknowledged hierarchical global ideologies of race and gender. Just as post-"independence" colonial situations required reimagining the relationship of communities to one another, so do immigrant desires to belong in a new country resituate ethnic identifications. A historian, Fraser devotes two chapters to what was formerly British Guiana and thus contributes to a relatively small body of scholarship about Guyana; chapter 2 of this book likewise outlines some of the history of Indians in Guyana. Finally, unlike many other historians of the Caribbean, Fraser asks how American policies as well as British imperialism combined to shape the fate of certain postcolonial countries. He can thus draw connections between different (trans)national histories that are not always understood in relation to one another. His goal, like my own, seems to be to understand postcolonial communities in light of the mutual influence of national and international histories, and by looking at global contingencies that affect local possibilities.

With the prevalence of theoretical interest in the notion of ambivalence, rather than considering it a problem, I find it an invaluable tool for exploring cultural meanings. For theorizing "betweenness" as a scholarly metaphor, I am particularly indebted to Amy Ling's recovery of Asian American writing "between worlds" and Shirley Geok-lin Lim's notion of the "ambivalent American" in *Reading the Literatures of Asian America,* as well as how Deepika Bahri and Mary Vasudeva situated South Asians "between the lines," or borders, of multiple identities. More recently, Françoise Lionnet and Shu-mei Shih, in their introduction to *Minor Transnationalism,* usefully describe how the "minority and the immigrant are constitutive of the national in its status as the object of interior exclusion, integral to what the national means and how citizenship is defined," and they also invoke "the ambivalence of identification" (12–13). Synthesizing various theoretical narratives like these has been a parallel process to my readings of fictional, ethnographic, and film texts concerned with the same important issues.

As a last point, ambivalence is a concept that suits certain themes presented in the following chapters—that is, mixing, hybridity, and code-switching—which prove to be as informative about texts as people. It was while completing my doctoral dissertation that I first confronted in practice the challenges of what Mikhail Bakhtin famously described in *The Dialogic Imagination* as heteroglossia,[32] or the notion that there are always multiple voices in any kind of utterance. In an informal dissertation group, despite the different literary traditions with which we were individually engaged (e.g., Jewish, Irish, South Asian), each of us discovered that authors whom we believed to be largely critiquing a certain type of representation nonetheless often reinforced it. For instance, if Gertrude Stein caricatured anti-Semitism in various moments in her writing, she seemed at other instances to negatively stereotype Jews. As we advised each other on dissertation revisions, we returned again and again to the challenge of providing clear-cut evidence for our claims about how authors made use of various tropes. What I learned in that situation about the more general phenomenon of heteroglossia was that our political investments in our academic writing made it difficult for us to acknowledge when stories, which seemed to offer what we believed to be progressive possibilities, were inconsistent and ambiguous. This was a good lesson for me in taking care to differentiate what a text implies from what I might wish it to transparently assert, due to a particular ideological interest of my own. As a result, rather than searching for proof of a singular reading, I instead work to identify and contend with the frequent equivocality of narratives concerning truly complex and dynamic aspects of human cultural activities.

Chapter Overview

In chapter 1, "Reading Assimilation and the American Dream as Transnational Narratives," I describe the key discourses which inform my analyses of ethnography, film, and literature. My goal throughout the chapter is to examine how notions of nation, narration, and diasporization intersect in shaping the experiences of South Asian Americans. This discussion allows me to interrogate the ways in which diasporas alter our perceptions of the global and the local. Tracing how diasporic and immigrant positionalities might influence one another, I call attention to layered constructions of national identity, in particular by historicizing the concept "South Asian" and its implications for reading assimilation. Narrowing the focus from theories of nationhood and selfhood to the case of the United States in particular, I offer a broad discussion of Americanization as represented in dominant stories and influential ideologies, particularly the American Dream.

In chapter 2, "They Came on Buses: 'GuyaneseOpportunities' as a Contemporary Americanization Program," I engage in what can be considered "microethnography."[33] I discuss an initiative through which people of Indo-Guyanese descent were recruited—by means of bus tours originating in Queens—to live in Schenectady, New York. My reading of the motivations underlying, and the impact of, this Americanization project considers how assimilation processes relate to transformative migrations both within and beyond national borders. Adopting an ethnographic methodology which involves gaining "exceedingly extended acquaintances with extremely small matters" (Geertz, "Thick Description" 21), I examine local community and city officials' responses to the increased presence of a South American (Caribbean) South Asian community in a small city in upstate New York. These perspectives are complemented by narratives from Guyanese Americans, who narrated their own interpretations of Americanization. What "GuyaneseOpportunities" reveals is that expectations, particularly concerning class status, continue to create contested and unpredictable versions of assimilation, such that government and local efforts, immigrant choices, and informal reactions to immigration combine to evoke both belonging and exclusion simultaneously. In particular, the "racial economics" associated with Americanization complicate two dominant stories about the nation: both the utopian vision of America as legitimately a land of opportunity for any hardworking newcomer and the "melting" of Old World ethnicity into New World nationality.

Chapter 3, "'Stretched over Dark Femaleness': Three South Asian Novels of Americanization," discusses creative responses to assimilation processes. These South Asian American narratives engage with the same complicated questions concerning Americanization which are taken up in the first two chapters, but the published fictions develop literary metaphors of belonging and alienation that are often startlingly different from other stories. In novels which concentrate on assimilation, Meena Alexander, Bharati Mukherjee, and Bapsi Sidhwa tell distinct but related stories about South Asian women in diaspora immigrating to the United States. As represented by the "dark femaleness" described in Meena Alexander's *Manhattan Music,* the narratives portray displaced and marginalized protagonists who eventually create unexpected families or communities based on other modalities for belonging than the expected ones. While situating them within novelistic traditions, especially American bildungsromane, I describe the authors' unique literary projects: interpreting Americanization through activism, advocating for immigrants to be "maximalists" when responding to normative scripts, and learning about assimilation from the Parsee experience of a diaspora within diaspora.

Looking at a different medium, in chapter 4, "'How to Be Indian': Independent Films about Second-Generation South Asian Americans," I focus on a particular type of independent cinema and analyze the anxieties of authenticity which come into play when narratives of belonging are grounds for contestation or confusion. Viewing selected films by and about South Asian Americans, I describe children of immigrants constructing a sense of both "Indianness" and "Americanness" through imagining diaspora and engaging popular culture, as particularly befits film narratives. In *Chutney Popcorn, ABCD, American Desi, and American Chai,* the stories highlight the dialectic of authenticity and "invention" rather than emphasizing the classic diasporic binary of homeland versus host country. Practices of performativity that are inherent to cinema make these films a useful site for examining Americanization within a (trans)national framework. Major themes discussed in this chapter include invented identities, code-switching, ethnic loyalty, and "drag" as a discourse of belonging.

The chapters collectively represent various processes of South Asian Americanization which implicate nationality, race-ethnicity, diasporization, and other politics of belonging. These narratives have an important place among the many stories of assimilation in the United States. Americans' current levels of engagement with globalism and transnationalism—marked by the continuous transgression of national boundaries through militarism, refugee and migrant displacement, popular culture, big business, and political endeavors such as environmentalism—invite sustained dialogue about the relationship between national and global identifications. Furthermore, in increasingly "mixed" (with regard to discourses and cultures) sites across the planet, rife with discord as well as (trans)national promise, it is crucial to scrutinize processes of immigration and assimilation with an eye to how they contribute to contemporary affiliation possibilities. This book systematically confronts and adds to our understanding of these phenomena, offering insights into issues of concern to all people while, at the same time, investigating the immigrant experiences of a relatively new American community.

In each chapter, even as I approach this field of issues from a slightly different perspective in addition to looking at a different medium for narrativity and a sub-demographic of South Asians, the overarching concern is with the nature of "belonging." To belong is to be a member of a group, to be suitable or fit to be part of something, usually described as a feeling or experience. To belong or not to belong has serious consequences for people's abilities to enter or remain in certain places, to call on particular resources, to have a sustainable sense of home. Approaching these complexities through an intersectional analysis seems the most promising way both to better understand issues related to Americanization and diasporization and to acknowledge that my story in this book is but one among many still to be read and heard.

1 / Reading Assimilation and the American Dream as Transnational Narratives

In 1782 a French immigrant, Hector St. John de Crèvecoeur, published Letters from an American Farmer, one of the most influential meditations on what it means to be an American. In his letters, Crèvecoeur portrayed America as a magical place free of the encrusted beliefs, customs, and traditions that had disfigured European society.

GARY GERSTLE, "LIBERTY, COERCION, AND THE MAKING OF AMERICANS"

Relation informs not simply what is relayed but also the relative and the related. Its always approximate truth is given in a narrative. For, though the world is not a book, it is nonetheless true that the silence of the world would, in turn, make us deaf.

ÉDOUARD GLISSANT, *POETICS OF RELATION* (TRANSLATED BY BETSY WING)

As described in the introduction, in light of South Asians' dispersal in multiple countries, it is necessary to read their assimilation stories within a sustained (trans)national framework that can be sensitive to both postcolonial and national histories, in order to supplement cultural analyses that would otherwise be incomplete. Given this imperative, my discussion of ambivalent Americanization enters an ongoing academic dialogue, involving many different voices with diverse preoccupations, about the meanings of "ethnicity," "culture," "nation," and "diaspora." Each of these concepts symbolizes an often cherished marker of belonging that is conventionally felt to be rooted in a common history and innate similarities shared by certain individuals. By contrast, in the present study, they are interpreted via theories of invention, self-fashioning, and performance, which expose how politics of identity are diversely inflected. Without overlooking their material implications—"the world is not a book," after all—we must still attend to names for belonging as *narratives* through which we imagine and enact who "we" are, because it is in narrative form that truth (admittedly always approximate) is conveyed, to quote Édouard Glissant from the second epigraph to this chapter.

In order to set up the scaffolding for my focused interrogation of South Asian narratives as represented in selected ethnography, literature, and film, in this chapter I track several imbricated narratives of Americanization which are foundational. In what may seem a counterintuitive development, I begin this section with theories of diasporization which shed light on the types of national assimilation stories produced by South Asians. This methodology enacts a shift in focus from a purely national framework, as has been typical of traditional assimilation scholarship in the United States, in order to presence transnationalism as an obvious (if often overlooked) theme within any American story. Within this framework, I then outline Americanization as a discrete discourse of national assimilation, emphasizing disagreements and debates about its meaning rather than assuming a cohesive and timeless narrative appropriate for all groups and eras. Pointing out how Americanization is itself part of a larger story about the changing meaning of "nation" is the next step in contextualizing South Asian American experiences. Since many historical conclusions about assimilation focused primarily on Anglo-European immigrants, the chapter then offers as a necessary counterpoint a discussion of how Asian immigrants—largely barred from immigrating for the first two-thirds of the twentieth century—complicate some familiar Americanization stories. Finally, the chapter concludes with an analysis of the American Dream as a preeminent example of stories which represent assimilation possibilities, limits, and transformations.

Separating (and organizing in a teleological fashion) the different histories which are all simultaneously represented by the category "South Asian American" is an impossible (and likely misleading) activity. Pointing to layered genealogies and irreversible transformations, Bill Ashcroft has written that the story of Indian independence and partition from Pakistan is a "narrative in which time and space, history and geography meet. . . . The catastrophic construction of India, so contingent a demonstration of imperial power, is nevertheless an engagement in which the effects of change work dialectically" (107). Speaking of temporality, spatiality, and historical contingencies in relation to South Asia, Ashcroft here points to the complicated narrative threads that cannot quite be untangled when one attempts an analysis of identities produced within multiple dialectical systems. For instance, if one focuses on "cultural" as a type of belonging often associated with "Indianness," then one has to ask, how exactly should we define "culture"? Which cultures should be considered national, familial, ethnic, class based, and so on? What variations are allowable within a paradigm of collective identification? If the nation, a relatively recent invention, has come under attack from a number of late twentieth-century perspectives linked to progressive politics, so too have seemingly alternative concepts such as diaspora and cosmopolitanism. These analogies for understanding cultural identities have run the risk of themselves becoming prescriptive rather than descriptive as they attract figurative and material investments, such that questioning their validity may be viewed as a threat by those who name themselves in those ways.

We may well wonder, what exactly does ongoing contestation about how to label identity or community reveal? Since there seem to be mutually existing contradictions between what nation, diaspora, and ethnicity denote or connote, what should we do about the variability of interpretations that seem increasingly available to us? How should we integrate related analyses based on distinct models, for example, of the neologism "cosmopolitics" (Cheah and Robbins), the idea of a "Brown Atlantic" (Desai, *Beyond Bollywood*), or "new" cosmopolitanisms (Rajan and Sharma)? Beyond a limited readership of academics trained in these topics, what are the broader implications of these important interventions?

To address such questions, my interdisciplinary strategy is to juxtapose histories related to regional reorganizations on the Indian subcontinent, British colonialism, Americanization, and evolving global ideologies that come into play as a backdrop to stories told by South Asians in America. I ask, if nations are "imagined" (as per Benedict Anderson's seminal construction) and diasporas are unbounded, then how do these imaginaries inform one another? Answers to such questions in relation to South Asian communities have resulted in a growing body of scholarship, which is reshaping notions of belonging even as scholars are describing ethnic communities, literary texts, consumer practices, and social movements. In the humanities, two influential projects concerned with mapping similar terrain to this one are Rajini Srikanth's exploration of "the world next door" and Inderpal Grewal's deconstruction of "transnational America." Images in their respective book titles pointedly signify both the national and transnational, with each naming a study which develops its arguments by enmeshing what have historically been artificially separated modes of analysis. There are also a number of investigative studies in the social sciences which help to give us a fuller picture of South Asian demographics.

In many of these and other scholarly analyses, authors often show how identities are created through particular narratives; I would further argue that such narratives are no less important than the materiality of territories, people, and capital for structuring (trans)national belonging. Any "nation" is in large part a story told over and over again, developed through naming cultural practices including the social, juridical, economic, political, and medical. Popular narratives of belonging in the United States have emphasized icons of welcome, such as the Statue of Liberty, and imagery of newness, as in the "New World," collectively symbolizing freedom, progress, and individualism. These have had an enduring impact on notions of national community that have themselves been transformed through many developments, importantly including assimilation histories. This type of iconography has at least implicitly marked the connections between "American" and other populations—of immigrants, aggressor states, and international allies, for instance. Analyzing one type of transnational connection, Desai points out in her project focused on South Asian film that "diasporas and homelands are produced and constructed through narrative"; she also asserts, as have many other contemporary cultural critics, that "diasporas and nations produce *each other*" (*Beyond Bollywood* 20, emphasis added). Although certain narrowly defined nationalisms might wish to maintain an absolute sovereignty, fulfilling that desire is usually based on obscuring or eliding traces of internationalism that intractably shape even the most self-focused of national narratives. And the reality that national stories can never be interpreted in one incontrovertible or even static manner remains hard to deny; a famous example of this is American "melting pot" imagery that was once celebrated and is now often rejected for its homogenizing implications, responses which are arguably equally based on misreadings of Israel Zangwill's coining of the phrase.[1]

Immigrants in Diaspora, or "Fluid Equilibrium"

Specific stories about South Asians in America suggest generalizable insights regarding other communities in the United States and around the world, communities which are also affected by the continual interplay of the local and the global.[2] Writing about Creole and other language diasporas in *Poetics of Relation,* Glissant outlines a number of key effects related to such globalism. Offering a narrative theory for perceiving these effects, Glissant imagines that "fluid equilibrium" might resist "normative decrees" by representing a "shimmer of variety" and a "radiant sparkle" (98). Images of shifting intensity such as these accompany his theories of "relation," through which he posits that each of us recognizes the Other within us, which shapes how we understand ourselves and the world. Glissant suggests that processes such as diasporization represent inherently hybrid frameworks within which to interpret identities, epistemologies, and theories. When he writes that transformations in diasporic contexts will produce paradoxical results such that "fixity would lie in change," Glissant describes dynamic and often unpredictable processes by which contemporary individuals in diaspora interact with others (27).

Tellingly, while confronting central questions concerning subjectivity (what defines identity? how will individuals reconcile themselves to socialization? which is *truly* one's community?), South Asian American narratives portray paradoxical and ambivalent trajectories by which diasporans may "become American." As Srikanth points out, "South Asian American writers' not insignificant contribution to American literature and to the American imagination is the delineation of narratives and spaces that enable the conception of a nation as simultaneously discrete *and* entwined within the fold of other nations" (11). In short, South Asian American stories inform us of the ways in which people retain as well as reinvent identities when immersed in new cultural configurations. In an example of what this community's unique stories expose, the ability of South Asians to sustain both global and national identities implies that conventional notions of belonging and home[3] are inadequate to describe the experiences of many contemporary individuals. Anannya Bhattacharjee calls for a new reading of "nation" to reflect these realities, clarifying that she does not mean "the nation as a bounded geographical unit but the nation as an ideological force" (229).[4]

As evidenced by the need for new definitions of this sort, South Asian Americans challenge one's ability to name[5] populations neatly and definitively. Analyzing this effect is clearly the impetus behind the academic work *A Part Yet Apart: South Asians in Asian America,* edited by Lavina D. Shankar (who has a piece in the collection on the "limits of (South Asian) names and labels") and Rajini Srikanth. This collection of essays concerns the diasporic positionality that has often made South Asians a poor fit for nation-based Asian American identities and political activism. In the preference for the term "South Asia" rather than "India" in the American academy, scholars such as these remind us that India has historically included what are now other nations on the subcontinent. Independence and partition in 1947 had momentous, life-changing material effects on the lives of people throughout the subcontinent.[6] Still, one cannot simply obscure or erase the past histories of communities who have not been consistently associated solely with "Hindu India" or "Muslim Pakistan," even though some officials on the subcontinent have attempted to do so. Discussing South Asian writing, Cicely Havely rightly observes that "in the case of the Indian subcontinent, so widespread, so complex and multifarious, so to-and-fro has been the Diaspora that there is a danger of rendering 'inoperative' the majority of those English-writing authors" who are recognized in Commonwealth canons. As Havely continues, "what claims of birth, cultural inheritance or residence entitle you to a place has never been—nor probably can be—clearly defined" in relation to the subcontinent (61).

South Asian writers around the world repeatedly narrate this complexity of identification; it is memorably represented in a scene from Amitav Ghosh's novel *The Shadow Lines*, in which one of the characters wonders if she will be able to see the physical border that has been created between Pakistan and India. Short of such a separation, she cannot imagine how one country could suddenly be two or what difference it makes to claim such a boundary. Bapsi Sidhwa also represents this dilemma in *Cracking India*, when the child narrator, Lenny, tosses down a plate and wonders if one can similarly and so easily "crack" a country. Remarkable reinventions of nation on the subcontinent are thus part of what South Asians bring to their stories, wherever they are set. All communities implicitly contend with the need to name themselves, but the relevance of these concerns is therefore especially apparent in the case of contemporary South Asian diasporans in the United States.

Attending to communities such as South Asians, which are spread *across* and *beyond* national or regional borders, scholars in a wide range of disciplines have theorized about the broader implications of such "cracking" and other types of diasporization. In actual, historical migrations as well as in what Salman Rushdie aptly calls "imaginary homelands," diasporans seem to invite alternative narratives of belonging to replace dominant, nation-based ones that modernity and its empires engendered. Across the differences and debates, there are certain kinds of questions that most theorists pose about diasporas, regarding lived experiences, creative responses, and contested ideas. Stéphane Dufoix offers a well-regarded overview of the history that has lead to this "ancient word," initially referring only to religion, being "applied to most of the world's people" (1). His discussion is suggestive about the ways in which responses to diaspora have reflected the overarching concerns of particular historical moments. It is also useful to remember that, across variations, all diasporic trajectories reflect both spatial and temporal migrations through which we might better understand human behavior, movements, identities, and histories. One also has to ask about diasporic relationships with various nation-states and nonnational institutions in terms that are both horizontal and vertical. Should diasporas be framed by the "homeland" from which people were dispersed, by the host countries in which some members currently reside, or by some other paradigm that accounts for multiple sites of belonging? Is the past of more, or less, relevance than the present in shaping identities? Broadly put, how should we understand the meanings of multiple cultural influences?

Even as particular diasporas have been interpreted in unique ways, there are also common themes to be noted. Prominent diasporic stories have included "classic" cases of the Jewish, Greek, and Armenian diasporas, the pan-African international formation that Paul Gilroy differentiated from these in terms of "The Black Atlantic,"[7] and newly emerging analyses of overseas East Asian communities representing extremes of access to resources. South Asian diasporas within this context are themselves distinctive; they can be differentiated from some of the other cases mentioned because there is no central exodus or return myth, South Asians' are often voluntary rather than forced migrations, and there are discrete diasporas within the diaspora (as I discuss with regard to Parsees in chapter 3). What South Asians share with other diasporans is a positionality that is, in theory, explicitly extranational. Yet, aside from the demands of every modern nation-state for individuals to document clear citizenship status, there are also many ways in which South Asians are no less bound to particular identities than any other group.

Some specific reasons why the South Asian case has nonetheless been viewed as distinctive in evolving discourses about diaspora are that the size of the population on the Indian subcontinent speaks to a more critical mass than many other places of origin; colonization by the British resulted in opportunities for somewhat unusual crossings of the globe in the wake of empire; and the sympathetic correspondence between American and Indian versions of the bourgeoisie allowed South Asians to fit narratives for successful minorities. Even with this correspondence, the question of what the diaspora should represent still haunts South Asian communities in the United States, as a consequence of their racial differences from the majority as well as of the extensive networks that have been built between nonresident Indian (NRI) communities and the subcontinent. Paradoxically, these connections officially establish South Asians *as* Americans with capital to invest in the "homeland" but also mark them as Americans for whom there is always a sense of belonging *there* as well as *here*.

In light of such complexities and a proliferation of interpretations of "diaspora," it is necessary to clarify one's terms and offer a specific articulation of the cultural work diaspora performs in particular contexts. The nearly twenty-year-old journal *Diaspora: A Journal of Transnational Studies* offers a useful reflection of the evolving range of topics now under the purview of "diaspora," in that the editor (Khachig Tölölyan) and the review board represent the most recognizable contemporary theorists and debaters in diaspora studies. The journal is described on its website as being "dedicated to the multidisciplinary study of the history, culture, social structure, politics and economics of both the traditional diasporas—Armenian, Greek, and Jewish—and those transnational dispersions which in the past three decades have chosen to identify themselves as 'diasporas.'" The journal's distinction between traditional and "newer" communities is important because it points to the dramatic shifts represented by current interpretations of diasporization. The use of the term "transnational"[8] in the journal title signals an interest beyond particular dispersals to metaphors for other kinds of border crossings; the journal editors also privilege self-definition as the criterion for being recognizably in diaspora, rather than conformity to a checklist of historical attributes. The range of groups which are represented in the journal, and in contemporary diaspora studies more generally, spans the globe and represents decidedly different types of global migration, including voluntary as well as forced, elite as well as subaltern, and sometimes in much smaller numbers than former analyses of dispersal. Thus, diaspora studies might include communities which are Arab, Chinese, Italian, Japanese, Latino, or Vietnamese, groups which were in the past not always considered in relation to processes of diasporization. Religious diasporas are again garnering focused attention, particularly the Muslim *umma,* with the rise of international debates in public culture about the meaning of Islam today. Also, diasporas based on, for instance, sexuality are under examination as sources of transnational group identity, along with continuing interest in global language communities.

In contrast to some historical descriptions of diasporas as unmoored communities with a near-mythic homeland from which they were expelled, theories of diaspora within postcolonial studies have tended to shift more and more toward politicized interpretations of what diasporas do or should signify. That so much of this intellectual conversation takes place within literary and cultural studies means that diasporas have been analyzed particularly in relation to "texts" such as literature, films, and performances. For some textual scholars, diasporas are among a set of models for articulating difference and posing it against hegemonic nationalisms (in chapter 3, I discuss another such model: hybridity). If the "post-" in "postcolonialism" seems like a premature designation for many people in the world still oppressed by (neo)colonial state apparatuses, then "diaspora" may name a way both locationally and more metaphorically to evade confining expectations. In this type of reading, scholars leverage theories of diaspora as interventions into dominant ideologies, for example, to challenge various sorts of cultural or racial essentialism.

Evolving instantiations of "diaspora talk" such as these have provoked another spectrum of academic responses in a continuing dialogue about the import of diasporas for contemporary understandings of individual and community belonging in relation to and beyond nationalism. Many theorists have made the case for reading "diaspora" as "a critique of the notion of an origin and homeland," in the words of Desai (*Beyond Bollywood* 20) or, as Brent Hayes Edwards puts it, as "an ambitious and radically decentered analysis of transnational circuits of culture and politics that are resistant or exorbitant to the frames of nations and continents" ("The Uses of *Diaspora*" 52). And yet, as Edwards himself acknowledges, such analyses are "open to ideological appropriation in a wide variety of political projects" including "versions of nationalism or racial essentialism" (54); thus, they may fall prey to the very types of thinking which others perceive of "diaspora" as resisting. If "diaspora" became central to certain progressive politics because it suggested theoretical models for evading the over-monitored borders of many nationalisms, what can we make of its unpredictability in verifying or testifying to antiessentialism?

Rather than choosing between a seemingly positive or more pessimistic interpretation of "diaspora," I would direct attention instead to analyzing diasporization and its effects, thereby to ambivalence and multiple possibilities related to the same processes. In this, I am following thinkers such as Pnina Werbner, who—in an essay published in the journal *Diaspora*—described a "new concept of diaspora" developing at the turn of the twenty-first century, in which transnational communities should be read as "both ethnic-parochial *and* cosmopolitan ("The Materiality of Diaspora" 6). What is important to glean from such observations is that, while a theoretical model can provide us new avenues for reconceptualizing systems of inequality, it is in and of itself merely one analogy by which to understand the world around us, rather than actually existing in some static condition to serve our political or ideological purposes. "Diaspora" is neither inherently empowering and resistant nor disabling and unrooted; associated processes are more appropriately interpreted as series of movements of diverse kinds with many varied motivations by which people end up being located differently than before. What the difference of location means will also vary from case to case, although some broad patterns do emerge when examining large numbers of people in diaspora and the narratives they construct to describe their experiences and identities.

Just as the local and global significances of "diaspora" will inevitably be more unpredictable than any theoretical model we might develop, the adaptation of the term for so many different types of globality is both intellectually valuable for, say, drawing connections and offering comparative analyses of previously unpaired phenomena, and problematic in potentially stretching the meaning of the term beyond pragmatic use. Particularly at this juncture, when debates about the meaning of "diaspora" may not always be intellectually generative, scholars need instead to specify the material and cultural conditions of transnational communities. The elasticity of any term is not endless, and evolution in diaspora terminology begs the question of what individual thinkers are really interested in with regard to particular people engaged in particular types of dispersal. Properly historicized, "diaspora cannot become a master trope or 'figure' for modern, complex, or positional identities, crosscut and displaced by race, sex, gender, class, and culture," James Clifford warns ("Diasporas" 319). If it is to have explanatory or predictive value in representing multifarious global realities, then "diaspora" must instead be as provisional as any other concept via which one analyzes communities and cultures.

To *presume* a binary opposition between nationalisms and diasporization is to reinstate older polarized and unrealistic orders of structuring which postcolonial theories of "diaspora" have tended to deconstruct as political lies serving particular agendas, such as discourses of Eurocentrism, Orientalism, and sexism. Gilroy suggests that a more productive intellectual stance which is antiessentialist would represent

> a webbed network, between the local and the global [which] challenges the coherence of all narrow nationalist perspectives and points to the spurious invocation of ethnic particularity to enforce them and to ensure the tidy flow of cultural output into neat, symmetrical units. . . . This applies whether this impulse comes from the oppressors or the oppressed. (29)

With the last line, Gilroy reminds us that "narrow nationalist perspectives" have not only been associated with imperialism but also, seemingly ironically, with anti-imperialist freedom movements, such that many postcolonial nations have developed anticolonial cultural nationalisms which created different but potentially no less harmful hierarchies. This passage is also worth looking at closely because Gilroy anticipates several themes that continue to be central to "diaspora talk" currently: webs of connection; simultaneous theorizing about the local and the global, rather than one or the other; and the ways in which ethnicity can be reified as easily and problematically as nation. Evelyn Hu-Dehart recently revisited these themes and provided a gloss on the ways that diasporas may seem to represent "newer" human taxonomies, but there are nevertheless dynamic ways in which "modern diasporas seem to emerge, unfold, move, change, and fade within . . . colonialism, slavery, new world plantation, free market capitalism and imperialism, state or monopoly capitalism, and currently, late capitalist or neoliberal globalization" (435). Contemporary diasporization thus means that constantly shifting formations develop as fields within which individuals and their communities negotiate belonging to multiple constituencies, including nations.

All histories of dispersal should not be collapsed into one, lest we create an alternative master narrative of belonging, which would serve just as certain nationalisms do to cover over diverse and often conflicting experiences of migration, whether meaning literal or more figurative relocations. Many scholars have further pointed out that not enough acknowledgment has been made of material limits to the proliferation of effects ascribed to diasporization.[9] If Clifford argued over a decade ago that the model of diaspora was "being appropriated" and suggested shifting attention away from an over-emphasis on homelands ("Diasporas" 306), what often followed in "diaspora discourse" was no less focused on one particular interpretation of the meaning of dispersal—that which coincides with celebrations of cosmopolitanism as a paradigm for overcoming provincial localisms or nationalisms. Instead of interpreting diaspora in this way, I would argue that it is more informative to examine what theoretical work the term "diaspora" seems to accomplish such that it has been invoked across so many types of difference rather than in studying sameness. Fittingly, David Palumbo-Liu writes about his interest in "the ideological purchase different articulations of the term allow," advising that we should read the "narrative form" of diaspora rather than seek a uniformity of meaning (355). Similarly, in my study, processes of diasporization (and related transnationalisms) are emphasized, instead of diasporas as clearly identifiable and discrete collectivities. But I must acknowledge that such a strategy is not without its risks. It speaks more to theoretical possibilities of dispersion and may seem to bear the cost of a concise description within finite disciplinary boundaries. This risk seems worth it, however, for several reasons, not the least of which are the rewards of a cultural studies approach, as I discuss in the introduction.

Within the framework of reassessing Americanization, what most interests me is how diasporization becomes one way to take the pulse of our times. Diasporas are implicated in major historical, global shifts and help to mold understandings of other types of affinities, political structures, and communities. Diasporization—in addition to being a metaphor for figuring displacement and naming the Other—starkly exposes the limits of national borders, in the sense both of policing crossings and of the inability to entirely prevent them. Thus, South Asian and other diasporic narratives both mark and transgress borders of national belonging, since communities read as transnational inevitably also engage national narratives. It would be hasty, however, to assume that this is either necessarily positive or negative. Diasporization may invite more pluralistic modes of nation-building based on recognizing difference, but of course we cannot forget that conditions of national liminality and marginalization—such as those also experienced by minorities who are women, immigrants, and Americans of color—often compel full-scale assimilation or otherwise result in insularity, invisibility, or exclusion.

Assimilation as a Contested American Ideal

Simultaneous with reflecting the influences of global identities and ideologies, immigrant narratives contribute in large measure to consolidating meanings of the nation-state. In the United States, continuing waves of new immigration repeatedly bring to light inconsistencies and paradoxes. For one example, stories of America have usually prioritized individual autonomy, which strains against submission to state power, family, and community. Yet the process of assimilating to a national collective (to some degree at least) is an inescapable element of contemporary citizenship; migration experiences merely amplify one's recognition that this is so. "No taxation without representation," the rallying cry for the new American republic, itself announced that reciprocity is considered a central aspect of the state-citizen relationship, if one that is inconsistently rendered. Cycles of (different types of) immigration continue to resurrect related questioning and debates that Americans have faced beginning with European colonizers.

Upon a review of a broad spectrum of interdisciplinary studies, Americanization actually emerges as collections of choices made by ethnicized groups within contexts delimited by national, regional, and local authority, as well as contemporaneous popular sentiment, meaning that multiple interpretations of assimilation remain in play simultaneously. In historical and cultural terms, processes of Americanization have varied widely, depending on the community in question, historical imperatives, and differences within groups, such as generation, gender, and class. Exclusionary national policies, combined with the seeming pressure to reject one's ethnic community and ancestry by "melting" into the prevailing culture, can lead to a determination that the outcome of assimilation is harmful and to be avoided. Conversely, assimilation can seem a very positive process if it affords a means for cultural integration despite ethnic differences from the majority, something that America seemingly offers but that most host countries do not or cannot.[10]

Thus, "America" has often come to be defined through what "Ameri*canizing*" of immigrants has meant in a particular place, at particular moments, for particular people. "Already assimilated" Americans often seem to laud the American dream, for instance, but immigrant narratives have frequently portrayed Americanization as being related to orthodoxy, normativity, and chauvinistic ideologies about race and gender differences, without actual representation of minority groups. On the one hand, then, assimilation may seem a reasonable exchange for supposedly expanded opportunities and thus a pragmatic expectation required of all new groups. On the other hand, Americanization plans have often proved coercive and have been shaped by various intolerant attitudes, especially toward those with notable variations from the current majority, thus implicitly preserving the status quo and serving those with national seniority. For many immigrants, assimilation representing national belonging may always seem like an elusive and impossible dream. What else, then, can we expect of immigrant stories of Americanization but ambivalence toward the process?

As noted in the introduction, due to such shifting perspectives, assimilation is best approached as a set of *processes,* rather than outcomes, of newcomers engaging possibilities for belonging to an already established national community. From as early as 1860, "Americanization" came to signify assimilation as an allegedly unique national project.[11] Furthermore, according to sociologists Richard Alba and Victor Nee—the authors of a recent influential study that marks a scholarly return to the topic of Americanization in social sciences—assimilation was "once unquestionably the foundational concept for the study of ethnic relations" (1). Alba and Nee point to highly contested ideological terrain by historicizing variations in thinking about assimilation over time, such that assimilation might now be considered a "worn-out" concept (1). As they show, while assimilation has been a major topic in American scholarship in certain eras, such as in the aftermath of wars and following the civil rights movement, it is now considered by many scholars to be a rather anachronistic concept that does not correspond with (neo)liberal projects of cultural pluralism.

Into the twenty-first century, scholars continue to disagree about assumptions associated with Americanization. Some have argued that U.S.-style assimilation problematically presumes that all immigrants will, given enough time and the ability to adopt mainstream attitudes, lose their ethnic particularity in order to blend into the national culture. Such critiques are usually pointed responses to previous visions of Americanization, as happened with the image of the "melting pot" from Zangwill's 1909 play of the same name, which was commonly interpreted to promote wholesale assimilation. Historian Russell A. Kazal summarizes similar ideologies in this manner: "Before the mid-1960s, the concept [of assimilation] often presupposed a rather static, Anglo-Saxon 'core' American society to which one was presumed to assimilate" (470); with historical conjunctures such as the civil rights movement, there have since been many challenges made against "core" assumptions of Americanization, but they certainly persist.

Since discussions of assimilation have been taken up again with a renewed vigor in the past decades, scholars have exposed the staying power of such ideals of assimilation as well as explored alternate stories of belonging. As many historians have noted, an enduring assimilationist myth was first promulgated in the eighteenth century in writing, by individuals such as Hector St. John de Crèvecoeur (described in the first epigraph to this chapter); this interpretation subsequently coalesced into a story that resembles the American Dream, a motif which I discuss later. For example, the historian Gary Gerstle writes, according to this myth, "immigrants eagerly became American, making themselves over into a new breed of people—liberty loving, fiercely independent and proud, and increasingly prosperous" (525). By the middle of the twentieth century, however, backlash against such an interpretation of assimilation led many scholars to decide that "Americanization was an alienating rather than emancipatory experience" or, even more critically, to condemn it as "exploitative rather than alienating" because it is a "a coercive process forced on the newcomers" (526). Such disagreements in public culture about Americanization not only had an important effect in shaping myths associated with the nation but also resulted in variations to immigration policy.

When comparing historical efforts at assimilating newcomers to the nation—for example, Americanization projects, such as those I discuss in chapter 2—it is clear that people have meant varied things when they speak of "Americanization" and have interpreted the process with incompatible ideological premises. Some Americans have celebrated diversity, while many others have implicitly rejected cultural qualities that seem too different from the existing national demographics. This speaks to broader tensions, since, as Simon Schama describes it, "the American story has always been a dialogue between Jefferson's unbounded faith in heroic individualism and the obligations of mutual community voiced by Lincoln and Franklin Roosevelt" (367). Who deserves to be part of the community of heroes is an ongoing question in the nation, while, even today, institutional language continues to create categorical separations between "legitimate citizens" and "aliens," suggesting that many Americans assume the occurrence of a transparent, transformative process in which immigrants overcome being "foreign." Accordingly, sociologist Sharmila Rudrappa writes that Americanization "entails a self-conscious replacement of older selves with a new American identity" (147), which gainsays readings of identities as layered and intersecting that I encourage throughout this study.

Indeed, interpretations of the assimilability of different groups in the United States have been inconsistent, resulting in particular sets of symbolism for distinct communities. During World Word I, for example, there were heightened tendencies to view new immigrants as suspect foreigners due to fears of divided loyalties for European Americans, resulting in policies intended to ensure conformity rather than ones that might encourage unique identities for ethnic groups. Versions of Anglo-conformity[12] have been prevalent in American policy during certain other periods and many observers attest to these patterns rising again after 9/11. At specific historical conjunctures, institutions such as schools, medical practitioners, and law enforcement became agents for assimilating particular groups to American culture. Short-term experiments in Americanization from earlier periods included many ethnic groups; in 1913, for instance, the Commission of Immigration and Housing began to develop strategies for converting immigrant values and easing the integration of such groups as Mexican American women into labor markets in places such as California (see the context for this effort in chapter 2).

Particularly under the mantle of Progressivism, many such attempts were made to assimilate newcomers to the United States through systematic programs that would allegedly aid immigrants in gaining the skills and knowledge needed to succeed in the United States, while also ideally "managing" distinct groups. Gerstle offers a representative overview of such efforts:

> Confronting immigrants seemingly walled off in ghettos who spoke foreign languages, adhered to strange customs, suffered the effects of impoverishment, and appeared indifferent or antagonistic to the United States, Progressive reformers responded with Americanization campaigns on a scale not seen before. In schools, at workplaces, at settlement houses, and in politics, they taught immigrants English, the essentials of American citizenship, skills useful in getting decent employment, and faith in American values and institutions. (530)

Although rarely as concentrated in chronology or effort, such programs of Americanization have reoccurred throughout U.S. history; they seem to have led cyclically to raging debates about how much assimilation is necessary, positive, or fair in exchange for the rights and responsibilities most associated with citizenship, both symbolic and legal. The "GuyaneseOpportunities" plan discussed in the next chapter is a recent index of such debates, reminiscent as it is of Progressivist schemes from almost a century ago.

Over the past century, such Americanization projects have helped to define national identity—whether they have resulted in assimilation or alienation, been ad hoc or official, or been pluralistic or overtly racist and sexist. For instance, in the 1920 study *Schooling of the Immigrant* (which was part of a series intended to solve problems related to socializing immigrants by providing systematic information and advice), educator Frank V. Thompson examined government initiatives to raise money and create programs for Americanization. In his assessment of assimilation campaigns undertaken in 1915, Thompson admitted to a curious paradox: "to democratize our newer brethren we must resort to autocratic procedure" (15), which to him meant compelling immigrants to assimilate rather than counting on persuasion. Thompson was sympathetic to the foreign-born; he declared it was the responsibility of all Americans to encourage the citizenry to be better educated and more democratic. Yet he bemoaned the difficulties of properly training adult "aliens" who had not profited from an American education from the beginning. What his account of assimilation most clearly exposes is that Americanization as public policy or private initiative always runs the risk of becoming mandate, rather than an inclusive (and admittedly utopian) vision in which the nation and its newcomers mutually influence one another. In any case, most Progressivist projects, like many Americanization schemes in general, were short-lived. Gerstle describes Progressivism as "a spectacular failure" (530) in achieving the intended control over social processes associated with assimilation, attesting to the degree of unpredictability associated with Americanization.

I would argue that there is never likely to be a sole, agreed-upon measure of "successful" assimilation to the United States precisely because the meaning of Americanization is contested and immigration continues to evoke ambivalence. But this does not mean that there are no patterns to be discerned or meaning to be made from processes of assimilation; in fact, the expectations of different Americanization ideals reveal central political priorities of the "America" to which particular groups of immigrants are relocating in specific historical moments. Additionally, as individuals tell varying tales about their nation, they are also inevitably developing stories about their own personal identities,[13] since national narratives have the effect of "delineating the cultural practices through which personhood is defined," as literary scholar Priscilla Wald puts it (2). National knowledge begets and is begotten by self-knowledge, affirming that (trans)national politics of identity are important to examine when describing Americanization.

Narratives of Americanization as Narratives of Nation

Contradictory visions of Americanization complement the ways in which the meanings of "America" are unstable and regularly contested, especially by newcomers and minority groups. The repudiation of British reign, the Civil War, the real and perceived threats to nation figured by the Cold War, and the divisive political climate of the Vietnam War era or post-9/11 all confirm that the construct "America" has undergone numerous challenges. Furthermore, there have been waves of migration both external as well as internal, such as the Northern Migration of freed slaves during and after Reconstruction, which have reshaped the country. Similarly insisting that there are multiple "Americas" depicted in Asian American literature, Rachel C. Lee lists some of the most prominent (and inconsistent) of these visions, including "a utopian space of possibility, a violent exclusionary society, a series of assimilationist narratives, a fantasy of wealth and privilege projected onto movie screens, and a center of financial speculation and faddish consumption" (3). The broad spectrum of possibilities suggested by this list are worth the careful attention Lee and others pay it, because they prove the lie of a unitary or universal experience of belonging in America. As Homi Bhabha observes in *Nation and Narration,* for all nations, there "is a particular ambivalence that haunts the idea of the nation, the language of those who write it and the lives of those who live it" (1).

In historical narratives about nation, however, not enough attention has consistently been paid to various types of heterogeneity as they imbue Americanization with a similar sort of ambivalence. Normalizing discourses imply that patterns of assimilation are identical among immigrants, as if there is no significance to racial or other hierarchies and realities on the possibilities for belonging to a national community. Many assimilation studies have reified such discourses by assuming Eurocentrism, a set of ideologies which cultural studies theorists Ella Shohat and Robert Stam insist needs active rethinking rather than passive multiculturalism. Gerstle concurs that Eurocentrism overdetermines assimilation iconography: "It is hardly accidental that the nation's greatest monument to the immigrant—the Statue of Liberty in New York Harbor—affirms the Eurocentric tradition and marginalizes the experience of those who came to the United States via the Pacific or across the Rio Grande" (548). In response to such associations and elisions in the American national symbolic, many ethnic studies scholars collectively attempt to de-center the notion that normative whiteness and a European heritage alone define Americanness, a notion which is institutionalized at the expense of other paths to belonging.

As noted earlier, a standard story of Americanization to which many writers and thinkers have responded is the potential elimination of all ethnic differences. Zangwill's "melting pot" has usually—if too simplistically—been interpreted as the national vision of an amalgamated whole best representing the dominant group (i.e., descendants of European immigrants who may rather ironically claim primacy through nativism)[14] and processes of "conversion" through assimilation. It has been one among a host of related metaphors invoked to describe a process of incorporating new immigrants into familiar narratives, but it is also a useful marker of the dynamic nature of such stories since they have from their inception been questioned and critiqued by generations of Americans. Accordingly, Wald explores a literary tradition of "constituting Americans," meaning authors from many ethnic backgrounds who have historically exploited rather than bemoaned the ambiguity and ambivalence of not fitting major narratives of America. Ongoing dialogue among Americans in literature, politics, and other arenas means that there is always resistance as well as conformity to dominant or institutionalized versions of how one defines being American. While this resistance may well suggest empowering alternatives to hegemonic notions of Americanization, I explore in chapter 4 how, when immigrants face a false binary of assimilating (of tacitly affirming normativity or being marginalized or even excluded from (trans)national narratives), there are accompanying anxieties of authenticity. If Wald posited an "anxiety of identity" faced by the American writers she discusses, in this study I extend this idea to identities emerging in multiple media.

Such accounts in varied media affirm that America is manifestly a country with many stories rather than one grand narrative. Interpretations of American belonging have always been shaped by multiple agendas, which are at times in tension with one another. Analyzing this tension, Asian Americanist Patricia P. Chu concludes that "the American literary canon has come to function as a site for debate about the nature and proper boundaries of American identity itself" (10). There are, for example, stories from "official"[15] sources as well as from those interested in constructing specific politically liberal or conservative models of "We the People." Clearly, the stories that are told about the nation change as sociopolitical conditions change and are revised in direct response to altered patterns of immigration, so that literary representations of constituting America also reveal contradictory emphases in distinct historical moments. Contemporary stories of America and Americanization in public culture more and more often include representations from both (ethnic) majority and minority communities, representations which collectively testify to the continuing variation in interpretations of national identity.

Competing stories about America confirm that, from the seventeenth century forward, immigrants have grappled with questions of how, how much, and with what consequences to consider themselves new or different people upon migrating. Werner Sollors aptly writes, "Works of ethnic literature—written by, about, or for persons who perceived themselves, or were perceived by others, as members of ethnic groups—may thus be read not only as expressions of mediation between cultures but also as handbooks of socialization into the codes of Americanness" (*Beyond Ethnicity* 7). Such socialization was not a seamless process even for early British immigrants, who could not take for granted their assumption of

American identities. Although later immigrants, especially those from non-European nations, are more often viewed as temporary sojourners who actually continue to belong elsewhere,[16] it is nonetheless the case that letters, diaries, and fictions from the earliest decades of the new American nation disclose a sense of alterity and anxieties about cultural belonging.[17] British colonialists might seem to have faced rather easy integration into the evolving American society; however, despite "ethnic" similarities, class, gender, and other axes of difference still presented obstacles and required transformations before belonging was proffered. For indentured servants emigrating due to poverty, for example, class divides from the Old World proved more rigid than utopian narratives might suggest. Furthermore, earlier immigrants, through their own stories, defined what it meant to be American for those who immigrated even shortly afterward, sometimes creating what were to be enduring divisions in the national community.

Among other contributions to public culture, literary texts have importantly shaped the "America" to which newcomers may be expected to assimilate. In fact, James Craig Holte argues, "The American literary tradition is . . . an almost obsessive inquiry into what it means to be an American" (25). This inquiry has consistently taken racial identity as one of the starting points for understanding belonging to the American nation. As a consequence, Walter Benn Michaels describes literary investigations of "What is America?" as cultural texts which turned "Americanness into a racial inheritance and culture into a set of beliefs and practices dependent on race" (141). He illustrates how these ways of understanding the nation have had lingering effects on contemporary configurations of identity, race-ethnicity, and culture. They are furthermore evident in contradictory and paradoxical visions of the nation (officially democratic but exclusionary; allegedly classless but as economically divided as the Old World, or even more so, according to recent studies;[18] antiauthoritarian in its inception but poised as the new Empire in the twenty-first century). As a result, varied projects for constituting "our America" continue today and with as much diversity as among ethnic groups. Such literary metaphors are not "merely"[19] culturally important, but they also perform important ideological work by projecting national identity in conjunction with other practices and possibilities.

Across many differences of immigration, history, and chronology, literary texts about Americanization have portrayed the process in a wide variety of ways—as hope and disappointment, accommodation and resistance, and gratitude and rage, in complex relationship to one another. As if writing back to attitudes like that expressed in Thompson's contemporaneous *Schooling of the Immigrant,* authors such as Abraham Cahan were outspoken critics of assumptions that immigrants would discard their cultural practices and belonging in favor of new American identities. Ethnic-minority writers continue to grapple with this topic in the early twenty-first century, even if it is not as prevalent a theme in Anglo-American literature. Literature by American Indians as well as African, Asian, Arab, Latin, Caribbean and other Americans attests that, even when assimilation plans are not as systematic or rigid as in earlier periods, many aspects of immigrant and racial-minority Americanness continue to be tested by "real Americans"—including accents and linguistic practices, culinary habits,[20] and work ethics.

Literary explorations of "Who is American?" such as the famous case of *The Autobiography of Benjamin Franklin* have been an important part of spelling out American identity, along with narratives from less "authorized" individuals within the United States which destabilize dominant accounts. In an argument about the latter, Donald E. Pease offers a model of "multiple interpellations" to describe various versions of Americanness that resist a national meta-narrative; he imagines that figures "surge up" at "internal divides, as unintegrated externalities" and "expose national identity as an artifact rather than a tacit assumption, a purely contingent social construction rather than a meta-social universal" (3, 5). Pease elaborates related concepts within "postnational narratives," such as "resistant materialities," "revisions," and "provisional strategies." His discussion potentially invests too much in the notion of the "postnational," but it is nonetheless helpful in resisting simplistic assumptions about the ways that assimilation narratives must inevitably reinforce exclusive nationalisms. It would be hard to deny that, along with assimilationist and nativist interpretations of America, there have always been and continue to be those stories that present alternative views. An important question is how much attention and credence we give to these other narratives of national identity. Focusing on narratives imagined by people at the margins of the hegemonic national symbolic, it is obvious that many works of American literature confound categorization according to previous models of Americanization. This certainly invites the creation of alternative literary histories.

Alternative Americanization stories are especially important for exposing how migration results in a heightened awareness of negotiating national invocations, which has universal implications for engaging pivotal questions concerning contemporary "nationhood." As Anderson has influentially noted, for most individuals, national belonging is a primary means to contemporary political and social positioning even if/as theorists reject insidious aspects of ideologies related to it. Aamir Mufti and Ella Shohat posed an important question that points to what needs deconstructing: "How do we rethink [the nation] as a means of identification and mobilization, as the 'home' of critical consciousness, given its clear discriminatory history, its inability to mobilize men and women, gays and lesbians, and ethnic and religious majorities and minorities on equal terms?" (4). Ideally, a postcolonial studies approach like mine, in conjunction with Asian American theories, offers specific methodology for rethinking "nation." Offering a potential answer to Mufti and Shohat's question in relation to just such a methodology, Gayatri Gopinath maintains that "the home as national *and diasporic space* is continuously created and consumed within the realm of transnational public culture" (188, emphasis added), meaning that "rethinking" nation is happening all the time in contested spaces of cultural production. In the contemporary context, it is crucial to recognize that a powerful nation-state such as the United States is irrevocably implicated in national and transnational circuits of oppression as well as in encouraging "the pursuit of happiness." In other words, rather than naturalizing the phenomenon of national identity or allowing national pride to silence criticism of the nation-state, it is more important to critically analyze the consequences of competing narratives of national assimilation.

Hardly symbolizing unity or certainty, the dynamism and disputation surrounding *all* national stories showcase multiplicity of meaning, official and unofficial versions of knowledge, and the ambiguity that accompanies intellectual pursuits for the "true story." Institutional or officially sanctioned versions of national history tend to reiterate claims of ethnic purity, cultural homogeneity, moral superiority, or exclusive entitlement to an identifiable territory. Indeed, historians of the novel tie the dissemination of nationalism as well as imperialism to the canonization of literary texts, such as when Englishness was promulgated by teaching British literature throughout the colonies. This reinforces Edward Said's claim in such pieces as "Permission to Narrate" that disciplinary apparatuses de-authorize certain narratives of nationalism and reify others. Yet, even as some stories of the nation may seem more authoritative than others, Bakhtin convincingly argued that nation and novel are both formed through heteroglossia, or a variety of languages in collaboration and tension, rather than a singular type of speech. Combining these various insights exposes the interrelatedness of nation and narrative, with changing implications that storytellers (including historians) cannot predict or control.

The significance of "nation" has therefore invited rereading and reinterpreting throughout the past century, even if reports of the nation's demise have sometimes been exaggerated.[21] Since global capitalism reaches beyond national territories, such that borders seem highly porous and the value of nationalism is routinely up for debate, what should and does "nation" now represent? Postcolonialist Anne McClintock emphasizes the symbolic nature of the collectivity when she writes that nations are "systems of cultural *representation* whereby people come to *imagine* a shared experience of identification with an extended community" (89, emphasis added). Similarly, classicist Artemis Leontis characterizes a nation as an "abstract" community, describing a chosen common cause rather than innate sameness of character or action:

> conceived when a heterogeneous group consents to three basic assertions about the essential identity of its constituent parts: that there exists a social body with an explicit and peculiar character; that the interests and values of this social body take priority over all other interests and values; and that this social body must be as independent as possible, attaining at least political sovereignty. (143)

Even as modern nations are dissolved and rearranged in what some observers would describe as continuing escalation, when ethnic and national belonging are in (often armed) conflict around the globe, Leontis's abstract community continues to be an overriding factor in most individuals' lives. Major themes include enfranchisement, taxation, and citizenship, as well as more symbolic registers, such as representation and inclusion. Notwithstanding globalization, we must continue to contend with (re)deployed nationalisms that inform contemporary experiences and identities, sometimes resulting in "commonsense" master narratives of exclusion attributable to ethnocentric or xenophobic renditions of affiliation.

However, dialogue and debate about the meaning of the nation are not only inevitable but also generative and arguably in the best interests of diverse communities "united" by the nation-state. Anthropologist Thomas Eriksen claims, "If one accepts that national identity does not have to be founded in common ethnic origins, the disruptions and conflicts surrounding [nation-building] rituals may actually have strengthened national cohesion by making a wider participation possible" (146). How to imagine solidarity—that is the dilemma for any multicultural/

multiethnic nation and it is through interaction between different narratives and discourses in the public culture that a shared sense of cultural identity may well be effected. If we follow literary critic Bruce Robbins in analyzing "domains of contested politics" (12) in relation to nation, diaspora, *or* cosmopolitanism, we might resist equating nationality with essentialized identities and instead focus on negotiations of positionality with certain kinds of social or political goals. If nations are constructed in dialogue, then cultural identities are usefully perceived as reflections of and influences on intersecting sets of contradictory as well as affirming processes.

As with many versions of nationalism, there are competing narratives of Americanization, but only the passage of time and the presence of multiple generations of a particular group in the United States seem to have allowed their stories to take a more acknowledged role in defining what America and being American signify. The catch-22 is that the generations after the immigrant one stand in a different relationship to the national body, for example, if they are born to official citizenship. Also, their firsthand experiences of assimilation may not directly involve a geographical "there" prior to being "here." Thus, this further elaboration of the broader community's story of assimilation needs to be traced back to immigration, an examination that does not always happen. This is because the second generation is usually more readily allowed a claim to America than the generation before; being educated in the United States also means being institutionally Americanized, for instance. Maxine Hong Kingston dramatically depicts how the children of immigrants must "translate" America for their parents in *The Woman Warrior* when the narrator becomes an unwilling and humiliated go between for her mother and a neighborhood pharmacist with whom the family has a misunderstanding. What gets lost in translation is how being "new" to America represents a vantage point from which assimilation is differently, if as ambivalently as, experienced for later generations. For Asian Americans, one of the continuing stories of Americanization concerns inscrutability and "the unassimilable alterity of racialized cultural difference," in the words of Lisa Lowe (44), but it is also the story of generation gaps which are potentially part of all immigrant histories.

Counterpoint: Asian Immigration after 1965[22]

South Asians, like immigrant groups before them, have found that becoming American is not merely a matter of geographical relocation but requires identifying narratives that are appropriate or accepting ones imposed on them. As described in the preceding sections, varied and even paradoxical visions of the nation mean that projects of constituting America have changed with time and for different groups—so much so that narratives of Americanization have sometimes taken dramatic turns within the same immigrant group. By the civil rights era, some South Asian community leaders transitioned from self-naming as "East Indians" to lobbying for the designation "Asian Americans." South Asians collectively pursued a different strategy than before for national inclusion by calling on the perceived value of an official minority status, an example of Gayatri Spivak's theoretical paradigm of "strategic essentialism."[23] This shift was prompted by the political necessity of combating repeated bans on Asian immigration to the United States and resisting the perpetuation of racialized ideologies about essential differences between European and "Oriental" immigrants. Historicizing the development of this panethnic narrative for Americanization reminds us once again about the importance of contextualizing ethnic groups in relation to a panorama of identities instead of in simple contrast to the majority group. Rather than a claim of sameness to white America represented in certain early twentieth-century prerequisite citizenship cases, for South Asians, it was a protected minority status based on pan-Asian identification which became the legal grounds on which rights might be earned and injustice overcome.

Thus far, intertwined diasporic and immigrant stories of communities such as South Asians are still recent enough that they have not become familiar in American public culture. Sociologist Bandana Purkayastha summarizes, "A key factor in the lives of South Americans is that [they] are, for the most part, relatively new immigrants to the social landscape of the United States, due to earlier restrictions on Asian migration" (17). Even though South Asian Americans have becoming increasingly visible in the United States—especially in metropolitan areas of dense settlement such as New York City, Chicago, or the San Francisco Bay Area—many others in the country may be unaware of their immigration experiences as they are similar to or different from other groups. It is unusual for Americans to be formally educated or otherwise well informed about the diasporization that has resulted in immigrant communities of more than two million South Asians. South Asians are sometimes included in national narratives, but it is often as an afterthought or results in an uncomfortable fit. Perhaps the heightened media attention, beginning in the first decade of the twenty-first century, to India's rising economic prowess will alter this situation, but inconsistent cultural and political attention is currently one of the continuing experiences of South Asian Americans. Combined with this lack of attention, the nonstatic nature of immigration policy and the varying narratives of belonging available to heterogeneous groups means that South Asian Americanization has signified differently depending on historical timing.

Variability in South Asian assimilation experiences thus matches the vicissitudes in American immigrant history more broadly; in some periods, certain types of immigration and assimilation have been encouraged and at others, these very same trends have been strongly resisted. South Asians' particular routes to Americanization mean that certain themes have been prominent in South Asian American narratives, as occurs with Asian American communities in general: namely, themes including race-based exclusion, cultural stereotyping, and politics of identity and ethnicity. South Asian American stories of belonging help expand our understanding of these phenomena in contemporary terms, contributing to narratives of the nation while also exposing realities particular to immigrants who are part of diasporic communities. This is one of the significant ways in which South Asians contribute to "quintessentially American" stories of assimilation.

As revealed in their narratives, among multiple scripts of belonging and identifying in the United States, racial-ethnic difference persistently induces ambivalence and continues to be one of the most significant factors determining assimilation possibilities.[24] In *Playing in the Dark: Whiteness and the Literary Imagination,* Toni Morrison identifies how, even if as a subtext, race has always critically shaped the manifest plot in canonical American fictions, which repeatedly defined Americanness as whiteness. Because of a black/white paradigm in which American national identity was historically posited as the opposite of blackness, African Americans narrate among the most ambivalent stories of belonging. And even though mainstream assimilation theory has not consistently confronted the role of racism in Americanization, putatively "white" Americans also faced challenges to assimilation due to racializing assumptions that promoted certain hierarchies—they, too, had to prove their ethnic suitability.[25]

Especially in Anglo-conformity models of Americanization, distinctive difference and assimilation are interpreted as being in direct conflict with each other. Thus, in complicated and sometimes unpredictable interaction with gender, class, and other identities, ethnicity continues to affect Americanization and Americanization continues to define ethnic groups. This is the case even though ethnicity is confusingly equated with racial or national heritage, ancestry, culture, language, or religion, in varying combinations. Assimilation narratives have repeatedly upheld traditional understandings of "a primordially rooted collectivity, or one sharing a sense of peoplehood" (Kazal 439). Although scientists remain unable to provide conclusive defenses for the validity of racial differences, commitments to them persevere, and ethnic essences seem "real" to many people, a tendency which certainly works to shape assimilation options and experiences. This is apparent when one closely reads the processes by which ethnicities are named, symbolically positioned within a nation, and regulated. However, these tendencies have been challenged by many thinkers prior to and throughout the twentieth century. In a notable example, Sollors argues in his introduction to *The Invention of Ethnicity* that ethnicity is "not so much an ancient and deep-seated force surviving from the historical" but instead "a process—and it requires constant detective work from readers, not a settling on a fixed encyclopedia of supposed cultural essentials" (xv). Persistent debates within Americanization studies have involved such variations in reading ethnicity as one among a series of affiliations with significant sociopolitical implications.

To presence Asian patterns of immigration and narratives of identity within these fields of possibilities requires a more concerted effort of imagination than is true for some other immigrant groups, whose stories may be more frequently repeated in our institutions and through popular culture. Despite the heightened visibility of Asian American assimilation experiences at particular historical junctures and a few stories which have become canonical—such as Kingston's *The Woman Warrior*, discussed briefly earlier—they remain underrepresented in mainstream national discourses.[26] It is a fairly recent practice for American educators to regularly include Asian American history within their lessons about "our" past. Migrating to America from across the Pacific Ocean or the Mexican border is often interpreted as a wholly dissimilar story to the heroic landing of European pilgrims, partly because of concerns about foreignness and "illegal" immigration. Asian immigrants, who were viewed as "strangers from a different shore," were at times invited into the nation as useful labor—to build the railroads, for example—but were not necessarily viewed as desirable future citizens.

Lowe has been prominent in theorizing about why informative and even moving stories about Asian America have not usually penetrated mainstream culture. In fact, Asian immigrants often continue to be deemed ultimately unassimilable, although they have contributed materially and culturally to America for centuries. Lowe explains that "the project of imagining the nation as homogeneous requires the orientalist construction of cultures and geographies from which Asian immigrants come as fundamentally 'foreign' origins antipathetic to the modern American society that 'discovers,' 'welcomes,' and 'domesticates' them" (5). Such troubling contradictions are reiterated not only in public policy and popular culture but also in stories by Asian Americans themselves. What Lowe concludes about Asian American "cultural politics," therefore, is that Asian American experiences displace conventional models of assimilation precisely because certain immigrants have in the past and continue in the present to operate primarily as Others to (white) American selves. That this historical attitude has been reinforced by a lack of systematic inclusion of these immigrant communities into stories of the nation leads Kandice Chuh to posit that we must wait for "the next moment in Asian American literature . . . when Asian American subjects and their stories will be read as 'American'" (187).

Instead of such an interpretation, a stereotype for being exotic and inscrutable has influenced how other Americans—of multiple races—have responded to immigrants from Asia and furthermore has strongly shaped international relations, as powerfully depicted in *M. Butterfly,* David Henry Hwang's award-winning play. Relations between nations combined with long-established systems of managing ethnic difference within the country continue to shape how Asians, immigrants as well as more established communities, are positioned in the United States. The alterity so long associated with Asians within the American nation is represented by drastic measures such as the first of many bars to Asian immigration, the Chinese Exclusion Act of 1882. Even though ideologies of race today are not identical to those over a hundred years ago, previous policies enshrining ethnic alienation or belonging continue to haunt understandings of American identity. Such problems of narration are ones that have had dramatic and telling effects on the construction of Americans' stories about themselves.

Some recent, notable efforts at recovering Asian American history help to bring us to Chuh's "next moment," however. One of these is the restoration of the immigration station at Angel Island, in San Francisco Bay. As narrated in Felicia Lowe's 1988 documentary *Carved in Silence,* the discovery of poems carved into the wood of a ranger's station halted its destruction and led to the preservation of rather unique narratives from American immigration history. Many groups of children in

California are now being taught on school trips that, until 1940, several decades of Chinese immigrants were detained at Angel Island and "examined" before either being allowed to immigrate or being deported. Collected in *Island: Poetry and History of Chinese Immigrants on Angel Island, 1910–1940* (Lai, Lim, and Yung), the poems speak of isolation and despair as Angel Island became a sort of purgatory, when the hopeful travelers were stuck between countries. This story is now more familiar to Americans in general, but we have long permitted collective amnesia about these histories of Americanization or, as often, the rejection of Asians from the nation. And yet Lisa Lowe notes that Asian immigration "is fundamental to understanding the racialized foundations of both the emergence of the United States as a nation and the development of American capitalism" (ix). The disjuncture between the deep significance of such stories which have constructed that new possibility—Asian America—and the lack of broad familiarity with these stories speaks to one of the many reasons why "ambivalence" is such an appropriate way to conceive of Asian Americanization.

A pattern of exclusion from dominant national narratives is common to varied groups of Asians in America, but since South Asians have come to scholarly and other attention relatively recently, their case has exposed distinct patterns of negotiating that exclusion. Making an important move to incorporate South Asian America within Asian American studies, Shirley Geok-lin Lim argues, "Writing by South Asian immigrants . . . exhibits similar dialectical relations between the U.S. and an Asian homeland or point of origin as in the Chinese American texts, but the best known of such . . . writing tends toward diasporic versions of identity that exceed the notion of exile" (303). Even though attention to "diasporic versions of identity" has become more common in Pacific Rim studies, Lim is correct that South Asian American stories do particularly deconstruct nationality, since their identities historically, as well as currently, transcend master narratives of nation as *the* framework for belonging. This is certainly not to imply that all South Asian American immigrants conceive of or narrate their identities in these ways, for many of their stories reproduce normative, assimilationist readings of Americanization. Nevertheless, "the historically shifting, heterogeneous processes of identity-formation and identity-politics thematics in the works of first-generation and second-generation Asian American writers" potentially prevents oversimplification of national narratives (Lim 307). Similarly to earlier examples of Chinese, Japanese, and Korean American accommodation to the nation, South Asians struggle to belong in the United States even as they continue to engage with an enduring transnationalism that yet again alters the meaning of "America."

Due to the history of the subcontinent which engendered unique paths of immigration, South Asian narratives of the United States make manifest the ongoing interplay of national and transnational narratives for belonging. As early as the 1890s, immigrants in the United States who would "define the Indian polity . . . were global in their mission and outreach long before *globalization* had become common parlance," according to Sucheta Mazumdar (228). Meanwhile, colonial and postcolonial transformations throughout the twentieth century continue to inform contemporary diasporans after relocation. Experiences of broad incorporation under a new ruling body are not new to South Asian populations, as is immediately recognizable in the changes wrought by the Mughal Empire throughout much of the subcontinent between the sixteenth and the eighteenth centuries. Islamic rule produced lasting cultural as well as religious transformations, radically altering regional power structures. This was followed by European rule and the imposition of yet other languages, religions, and laws—centrally through British imperialism from the seventeenth to the mid-twentieth centuries but also with other, usually more localized, influences such as that of the Portuguese in Goa from the sixteenth century on.

On the South Asian subcontinent, group names and configurations were therefore both sustained and rearranged. As Gita Rajan and Shailja Sharma document, even if South Asians in American public culture "are constructed as a homogeneous group despite their religious, national, class, and ideological differences, within this imposed group identity, the schisms are deep indeed" ("New Cosmopolitanisms" 18). Through interactions between highly diversified groups of people—including "original" inhabitants of the subcontinent, Mughals, and Europeans, as well as others such as members of the Parsee diaspora who relocated from Persia—India was created, became independent and partitioned simultaneously in 1947, and was further divided when Bangladesh achieved autonomy in 1971. As mentioned in the introduction, the redrawing of various types of borders resituated people in dramatic ways. These histories of changing territorialities certainly bear out "nationalism's undivorcible marriage to internationalism" (Anderson, *Imagined Communities* 207), since one nation could become multiple overnight and make former co-citizens into foreigners to one another.

South Asian Americans are collectively related to communities of people on the subcontinent who were also interpellated as certain kinds of "natives" through Mughal and European imperialism. One "benefit" of the major thrust of colonization was that, until 1947, to be a colonial subject made it possible for South Asians to migrate to other British colonies, often as laborers (called "coolies") or for educational advancement for those of certain socioeconomic groups. Another "inheritance" that has had a tremendous impact on South Asian dispersal through to today is the imposition of British English, especially for elites who can claim relative fluency in an international language deemed critical for "high" culture and commerce. From other parts of Asia to the Caribbean, to Africa, to South America, and to Fiji, there are communities of people descended from Indian diasporans whose journeys would not have been imaginable in such great numbers without the network built through the British Empire.

And yet, even as there were remarkable colonial influences such as these, other measures of belonging have persisted in South Asian communities, including tribe, caste, religion, and regional language. Grewal therefore concludes that, "given the heterogeneity of the Asian and South Asian populations in the United States through the 1990s, it is important to examine the various forms of transnational connectivities that enabled these subjects. In these connectivities, discourses of race, gender, class, caste, and nationalisms all came together to create some divergent versions of postcolonial cosmpolitanisms" (*Transnational America* 37). If in the early twentieth century, the United Kingdom and the United States passed legislation limiting Asian migration, at the beginning of the twenty-first century, both countries have become hosts to large numbers of South Asians, who bring their layered histories with them when they migrate. In the future, comparative studies that pay attention to the specificities of assimilation experiences in other sites where South Asians have dispersed may offer us some rich material for analysis about how the diaspora has interacted with various national narratives. Pallavi Rastogi's recent *Afrindian Fictions: Diaspora, Race, and National Desire in South Africa* represents a major move in this direction, with its attention to Indian South African narratives of belonging.

In the United States, South Asian immigrant communities have experienced a gradual rise in numbers only over the past few decades, following the dramatic immigration reforms concerning quotas for Asians after 1965. Although South Asians have been present in the United States for over a century, national policy and international developments resulted in a long gap between earlier and later phases of immigration. The first significant waves of South Asians began arriving in North America in the early 1900s, represented primarily by agricultural laborers from the Indian area of Punjab who attempted to leverage their status as subjects of the British Empire to relocate to Canada in search of economic prosperity. As depicted in the 2004 film *Continuous Journey,* by Canadian director Ali Kazimi, some of these Indian sojourners were blocked from landing their ships, which exacerbated tensions already present in colonial relationships. Barred from entry into Canada, Indian immigrants subsequently attempted to migrate to the United States. However, public policy and popular sentiment increasingly opposed nonwhite immigration in both the United States and Canada such that the South Asian populations remained low until midcentury, composed mostly of male bachelor communities whose family members were not permitted into North America.[27]

By contrast, there are the members of the second major immigration wave, who are commonly referred to as "post-1965" South Asians. These immigrants relocated to the United States after the Hart-Cellar Immigration Act,[28] which eliminated previous quotas based on national origin and through which certain categories of South Asians came to be seen as welcome additions to America.[29] After 1965, South Asian immigrants benefited from the civil rights movement in the United States and immigration preferences shifting to prioritize professional and educational status. In addition, public policy came to advocate a family-reunification model for immigration to the United States, which led to a significant increase in the size of South Asian American communities. By the end of the 1990s, the community was further transformed by a bifurcation between middle-class professionals and working-class South Asians, who filled different labor needs in the United States, from Silicone Valley software programmers to New York City taxi drivers and many others perhaps less visible to the public eye. Monisha Das Gupta attends to some lesser-known stories in a study of "unruly" immigrants, describing queer, feminist, and labor South Asian organizations that have to "struggle for rights in the face of their formal/legal and popular codification as noncitizens" (4). Her goal is a shift in focus on South Asians from what is highly familiar in public culture to what requires more careful theorizing; chapter 2 of this book represents a similar effort.

Over a decade ago, when there was less scholarship concerning South Asian Americans than there is today, Deepika Bahri and Mary Vasudeva offered a useful historical marker in their reading of the various valences of these communities "between the lines," which is worth quoting at length. They theorized that the label was being

> deployed in Anglo-America for various purposes: to gain visibility in the sociopolitical arena; to speak against racism and misrepresentation from a position of collectivity; to initiate social action for the economically depressed and systematically alienated among the group; to open an avenue for the exploration of lost or receding cultural ties with the country of origin; to provide a forum for expressing and investigating experiences and feelings of displacement, alienation, and other forms of cultural anxiety; and to gain a more equal footing, perhaps even an advantage, in market value and economic opportunity. (Introduction 7)

What immediately stands out in this rich description are words such as "deployed," "speak against," and "to gain," which all emphasize immigrant agency. Furthermore, there is an acknowledgment of the heterogeneity of meanings associated with South Asian identities and also the ways in which these are invented identities which serve particular purposes, rather than supposedly innate ethnic similarities.

Prior to the contemporary period, however, the use of the label "South Asian" for such purposes was not consistently applied either by immigrants themselves or in American categories. In fact, many immigrants from the Indian subcontinent previously hoped to be recognized for their "Aryan," rather than "Asian," heritage.[30] In 1923, for example, in a landmark Supreme Court case, Bhagat Singh Thind failed to convince the courts that, as a member of the Caucasian race, he met the existing criteria for American citizenship. The verdict in such prerequisite cases as *U.S. vs. Bhagat Singh Thind* had a major, if sometimes forgotten, impact on processes of redefining race and Americanness. At the conclusion of deliberations in Thind's case, the judges decided that Asian Indians were not eligible for citizenship since they were not considered "free white men" according to "the understanding of the common man," regardless of their arguable Caucasian ancestry (Haney-López 1–36). It was another twenty years before Indians became eligible for U.S. citizenship and another twenty after that before strict quotas on their naturalization were lifted. Attesting to a similarity between South Asians and established residents was therefore a failed tactic for Americanization in the early part of the twentieth century. In chapter 4 of this book, which is concerned with performances of ethnicity in South Asian films, the question of shifting readings of identity is considered further.

Confirming that processes of Americanization are neither invariable nor interchangeable—even among groups similarly categorized as "Asian"—possibilities for self-naming were uniquely tied to the (trans) national journeys that brought South Asians to the United States during historical conjunctures that made certain identity narratives legible. As is true of other ethnic-minority groups, South Asian American experiences of assimilation expose racial oppression, but for many among the post-1965 generations, class and other types of cultural privilege may have allayed some material and cultural obstacles to assimilation. As a result, becoming part of America as an alleged "model" minority invited complicity with racist projects of nation-building. Despite repeatedly documenting, in fiction and nonfiction, racial discrimination in the United States (or precisely because of such experiences?), South Asians have developed their own versions of American "exceptionalism"[31] to differentiate themselves from other, less "successful" minority groups. For instance, as members of a supposedly ideal minority, South Asians may choose to accept interpretations of assimilation which privilege individual success through hard work and thus disregard the barriers to assimilation-through-upward-mobility faced by other ethnic groups. Such phenomena have led to ongoing struggles in immigration and critical race studies to find methods to draw connections between ethnic-minority groups rather than merely asking about Americanization in relation to a dominant group, in light of the overdetermined vertical relationship between minority and majority cultures in terms of opposition or assimilation. This overdetermination means that "horizontal communication amongst minorities is made invisible" (Lionnet and Shih, "Introduction" 7).

Rendered visible, collaboration or tensions between different minoritized communities attest to the unrelenting way in which racialized groups differentially claim and are granted versions of American belonging, no matter the pretensions of those who advocate "color blindness" in a post-affirmative-action era. There are common processes of assimilation experienced by all American ethnic groups, but there may be (mixed) benefits resulting from certain stereotypes associated with one's own ethnic and cultural group. Such stereotypes then influence choices made within American media and publishing industries, which can limit the variety of stories available in public culture. Some scholars argue that model-minority types of collusion with the dominant ethnic group helps to explain the expanding niche market for South Asian stories in America, as the subjects of these stories seem culturally distinct (thus interesting) but still assimilable (thus nonthreatening). It is clear that racialized understandings of the "right sorts" of minorities have pitted Asian and African or Hispanic Americans against one another. And although Americanization stories across panethnic Asian groups are varied, the rubric of "Asian America" which has come to include South Asians has often been defined in opposition to other ethnic-minority identities. Historian Vijay Prashad sums up problematic interminority conflicts as a narrative in which "the immigrants are good; the blacks are bad. Punish the latter. And many South Asian Americans applaud" (*The Karma of Brown Folk* 3). As Prashad documents, South Asian communities have sometimes negotiated paths to assimilation by explicitly opposing themselves to other ethnic groups, leveraging their "cultural capital for success" (6) and accepting a version of Americanization that perpetuates racial intolerance.

Recent scholarship about South Asian America appropriately notes the complicity with racist ideology in some historical strategies for assimilation, but the status quo and individuals made powerful by it are most served by alienating ethnic-minority groups from each other. As Lowe describes, reading Fanon, "bourgeois assimilation and bourgeois nationalism [are] conforming to the same logic, . . . being responses to colonialism and reproducing the same structure of domination" (73). One can trace some of these processes at work, for example, in tensions between Irish and Chinese railroad laborers in the late 1800s. As they competed for grueling, often unpleasant work that other Americans did not seem willing to do, their employers were able to exploit racial suspicion (sometimes leading to violent conflict) in order to decrease wages and increase profits. However, the ambivalence produced by supporting bigotry against one group that might just as easily be applied to oneself—because it is based on similar premises related to white superiority—is undeniable. As in colonial circumstances around the world, American assimilation of immigrants has reflected hierarchies of race and caste that assign value, power, and identity to different human groups differently.

In the context of the contested history of assimilation that has influenced policy, popular culture, and narratives of America throughout the twentieth century, Asian stories of more recent Americanization present themselves as a striking counterpoint to more familiar Anglo-European stories. Part of a constructed "ethnicity" often conflated with Indian because that is the most numerous population among South

Asians in America, the majority of these immigrants and their children have "become" American (if they have) in the glare of the dot-com and Silicon Valley tech phenomena, and after other Asian groups, usually East Asian, have come to occupy particular national niches over multiple generations. As such, South Asian stories are highly suggestive about the continuing evolution of national narratives—in particular, that most famous of stories, the American Dream.

Ambivalent American Dreams

The American Dream is one of the most familiar and persistent narratives of Americanization. This is the rags-to-riches, pull-yourself-up-by-your-bootstraps story of a strong (Protestant) work ethic. Few people would argue that this "dream" is not one of the most recognizable signifiers for allegedly unique immigrant possibilities in the United States. Indeed, Anne Sexton's ironic poem "Cinderella" acknowledges that we all know this story:

> You always read about it:
> the plumber with twelve children
> who wins the Irish Sweepstakes.
> From toilets to riches.
> That story.
>
> Or the nursemaid,
> some luscious sweet from Denmark
> who captures the oldest son's heart.
> From diapers to Dior.
> That story.
>
> Or a milkman who serves the wealthy,
> eggs, cream, butter, yogurt, milk,
> the white truck like an ambulance
> who goes into real estate
> and makes a pile.
> From homogenized to martinis at lunch.
>
> Or the charwoman
> who is on the bus when it cracks up
> and collects enough from the insurance.
> From mops to Bonwit Teller.
> That story. (53–54)

However, this part of Sexton's poem makes "that story" seem both unbelievable and ridiculous with an irreverent tone, absurd-seeming juxtapositions, and mixed allusions to both high and popular cultures. For instance, the alliteration that pairs the elegant and rich (Dior) with the degraded and mundane (diapers) sets the reader up for the ending of the poem, in which the American Dream is as frozen in time and as separated from "real" life as dolls in a museum case. Meanwhile, happiness is represented by fake smiles which are impossibly "pasted on for eternity" rather than being genuine expressions of emotion (57).

Despite many efforts at demystification, such as Sexton's poem, narratives of the American Dream pervade national culture, even though the meaning of the dream remains as troublingly elusive as its attainment is for many Americans. This was brought home to me several years ago, when I taught an introductory survey at Union College called "Major American Authors," which focused on twentieth-century literature in the United States. Each of us in the department independently selected the reading list for our own class. In making selections, I found myself stumped about how to create an appropriate syllabus for a fleeting ten-week trimester. What logic should I apply? How would I limit the extensive field of possibilities? How much should my scholarly specialization influence the design of a survey course? What, in the end, did I want to teach the students? Faced with so many questions, I resorted to a familiar technique of "close reading" the title of the course, and in the process of unpacking the phrase "Major American Authors," I found that I was inevitably questioning what constituted an appropriate American literary canon. As a result, the course description looked something like this:

> We will be reading literature by American authors from the late nineteenth century to the latter part of the twentieth century. In doing so, we will ask what makes these authors "major" (or not) and "American." Taking as our starting point a central motif of the United States—"The American Dream"—we will interrogate how American literature responds and contributes to this narrative of the nation. Questions we will attempt to answer together are: What is the American Dream? Who says so? Who has been able to achieve this dream, and why? How do race, class, gender, sexuality, and other types of difference modify who dreams of what?

In conversation with colleagues, I developed a list of assigned works based on a belief in introducing students to multiple genres, a personal interest in rereading certain texts, and, most important, a commitment to establishing multiethnic and postcolonial writers within American literary traditions. (This latter goal led to some highly negative comments on student evaluations about not being taught "real" American writers.) By choosing a central theme, I believed I would provide a useful focal point while giving students a nuanced entry into reading "major" American literature. The collection of texts meshed well, I thought, and I was generally satisfied with what the class achieved.

Among the usual disappointments for any professor imagining an ideal course, however, was one which was completely unanticipated: the theme that was intended to offer us a common lens for reading the literature proved to be a major stumbling block. The jumping-off point that I assumed would lead to debates and deeper analysis about its applicability (i.e., what is the American Dream?) was almost impossible for us to describe with any specificity. When analyzing the topic in various texts, students never defined what the American Dream actually signified for them. When I pushed them to say something specific about the theme before developing arguments regarding particular works of literature, they responded with rather vague notions of achieving "freedom" and "independence," especially in relation to Old World immigrants in the New World. They were able to generally agree that it was a dream of being successful, but defining our national credo as a belief in materialism perhaps seemed ignoble. And this definition was brought up only to be criticized, while the word "better" was a mainstay.

Over the course of the term, we gained some insight into our central motif as represented in a selection of literary sources, but I found myself increasingly amazed at the paradoxical situation that we all *knew* what the American Dream was but that no one in the class could point to the sources from which he or she had gained this knowledge. The "pursuit of happiness" championed in the Declaration of Independence was the most specific many of us could be, but contemporary ways in which this rhetoric was reproduced were harder to identify. I mentioned this reaction to friends and colleagues, who admitted that they had also taken for granted what this ubiquitous trope signified; however, when trying to describe its evolution and articulate its meaning, they were hard-pressed to answer more thoroughly than the class did. To provide students with a clearer history, when I taught the course for the second time, I revised the syllabus by assigning different literary works and by including some of the founding texts of the United States, in addition to recent analyses of the American Dream by famous historians and political scientists. These contemporary thinkers often bemoan the contemporary interpretation of the dream as primarily or solely an opportunity to garner money or luxuries, which seemed to match what was happening in my classroom. Yet few of these writers offered any more specific a definition of the dream than we were able to achieve in my Major American Authors class.

Bemused that everyone seemingly knew this narrative but few were able to name the source(s), I began to examine paradoxes associated with the American Dream and traced the popularization of the phrase to the conclusion of a 1931 historiography, *The Epic of America,* by the prominent scholar James Truslow Adams.[32] It is useful to date the American Dream to this usage because, prior to that point, the phrase was considered so unfamiliar and off-putting that Adams's publishers persuaded him not to use it for the book's title as he wished to do (Cullen 3). Even without it as the title, Adams's book succeeded in instructing readers about the American Dream; he wrote, "If we are to have a rich and full life in which all are to share and play their parts, if the American dream is to be a reality, our communal spiritual and intellectual life must be distinctly higher than elsewhere, where classes and groups have their separate interests, habits, market, arts, and lives" (422). In thus describing the shared national narrative of an improved, less divided, and spiritually elevated future for all Americans, Adams put into words what my students and I could not name but which we, too, considered a central part of the American "epic." Adams believed that what distinguished Americans was their exceptional ability to work collectively, with regard to hard realities such as markets and also to the intellect, in order to overcome the problems common to all societies. He further described the American Dream "as a dream of a social order in which each man and each woman shall be able to attain to the fullest stature of which they are innately capable, and be recognized by others for what they are" (415), rather than being judged by their ancestry.

In the near century since Adams penned those poetic lines, the American Dream has consistently been interpreted to mean that Americanization offers hope for a better future, with the communal (and even socialist) origins of the dream often forgotten. Whether describing the achievement of the dream or a failure to achieve it, many people in the nation measure Americanization and belonging with implicit reference to this looming ideal. It was a shared assumption that implicitly shaped many of the narratives in fiction, film, and interviews that are presented in the following chapters; these narratives too imagine Americans "being able to grow to fullest development as man and woman, unhampered by the barriers which had slowly been erected in older civilizations, unrepressed by social orders which had developed for the benefit of classes rather than for the simple human being of any and every class" (Adams 416). What it means to belong in or to America is certainly affected by a utopian vision of this sort at the heart of the national imaginary, central to founding documents and memorialized on treasured monuments. Putting it in clear and rousing words of his own, Adams imagined an "unhampered" and "unrepressed," thus free, citizenry able to exist in newness and extend humane treatment to all by posing itself against Old World exploitation. Although many Americans may not be able to cite a source for this dream narrative, it is one that every American will find familiar.

In contemporary public culture, there are ongoing attempts to define and understand the American Dream, collectively representing the continued hold it has on the national imagination. For example, there have been such articles published recently as political journalist Ronald Brownstein's with the title "Is the American Dream a Myth?" and an essay about baseball and "the anxiety of the American Dream" by Ron Von Burg and Paul E. Johnson. There are also recent books with titles such as *American Dreaming: Immigrant Life on the Margins* (by Sarah J. Mahler) and *The American Dream: A Short History of an Idea That Shaped a Nation* (by Jim Cullen). In a review of another book on the subject (Simon Schama's *The American Future,* which is mentioned earlier), David Leviatin offers a fairly representative summing up of what many people perceive the dream to be: "Diversity of thought and of person, the product of constant immigration, . . . innovation, improvisation, and tolerance. In a society in which curiosity and inquiry are encouraged, toleration rather than coercion will flourish, creating an environment in which truth will be sought after and prized" (300). Leviatin affirms familiar interpretations that immigration to America leads to the transformation of individuals and ideas, thus resulting in an unorthodox newness.

In diverse texts and across disciplines, many scholars interrogate these familiar tropes, posing similar questions to those I confronted when teaching the class on the American Dream. It is as if the American Dream is so ubiquitous as to go unremarked, so obviously true that it does not require analysis, or so clearly a fantasy that it is not worth thinking about. In a literary and cultural analysis, Demetrios J. Lallas further reasons,

> When the phrase "the American dream" graces the titles of laws, is deployed in op-eds and political speeches, exploited by

> advertisements, played with in sitcoms and on cinema screens, don't we always already know essentially what's being referred to? Symbolically, perhaps, but not in any manner that would pass the degree of rigorous scholarly analysis we expect for countless less important discursive devices and theoretical terms. (5)

For Lallas, "longstanding neglect" in examining ideologies associated with the American Dream has obscured an original use by the reporter Walter Lippman as a "far from congratulatory" concept (6, 9). Indeed, the very word "dream" is a suggestive distinction from "reality." Lallas critically assesses how the meanings of the American Dream have changed over time, concluding that asking hard questions about the dream (as in the case of Martin Luther King Jr.) has at times been deemed "un-American" or unpatriotic, but he insists that such a tendency is "true" (243) to the tradition of Lippman in resisting anti-intellectualism, laissez-faire economics, and plutocracy disguised as democracy. Lallas might therefore appreciate how anthropologist Mahler recaptures some of the original tone of the American Dream; she describes her book about Salvadoran and South American immigrants as "a narrative of disillusionment" and a "chronicle of the hopes and desperation experienced by a group of undocumented immigrants . . . [whose] portrayals of their lives in 'America' are full of deceit, dejection, marginalization, and exploitation" (3). In contrast to Leviatin's summary of toleration and truth, Mahler portrays a type of hope that is repeatedly dashed.

Despite similarly bleak narratives emerging from all groups of Americans, Lallas, Mahler, and many others concur that American Dream imagery is pervasive. This is despite the reality that, as Brownstein points out, there is a greater tendency to economic continuity than to near-mythical upward mobility in the United States. Yet even those who do not seem to be living the dream "play an important ideological role in American culture" by maintaining hope in the self-uplift narratives (Mahler 5). The dream is maintained through generations of immigrants who are driven "to achieve despite the obstacles they encounter, and though most fall short of realizing these dreams, they do not see their efforts as vain" (Mahler 5). One of the implications of continued American dreaming of this sort, even in the face of evidence to the contrary, is that an idealized vision of succeeding is so persistent that it seems to be entirely a matter of individual effort and determination. As Mahler acknowledges, such

> utopian fantasy . . . may seem naïve, even incredible in this day and

> age, though it captured the imaginations of earlier generations of immigrants. . . . But beliefs held by fresh waves of immigrants to U.S. shores are not so surprising when understood as one of many manifestations of the material fetishism that erupts when people from commodity-poor societies enter consumptive, industrial ones. (83)

The very contrast between countries of origin which may not seem to promise materially comfortable lives and arriving in one of the world's wealthiest superpowers is hard to overlook, as Mahler points out. Furthermore, "information people receive about the United States is almost exclusively by two sources: earlier migrants and the media. Both sources offer much biased information and foster unrealistic dreams" (Mahler 84). What may seem like wishful thinking is instead constantly reinforced in American society and has thus become a central means to defining belonging for immigrants.

Even though the origins and specific meaning of the phrase "the American Dream" are often less than clear even for those who invoke it, there are still a series of assumptions that are most often associated with it. Jim Cullen provides a focused examination of the evolution of the phrase in his history of "an idea that shaped a nation," beginning with Adams's introduction of it into the public culture. In a representative statement, Cullen summarizes that the American Dream has been "enshrined as our national motto," and "the term seems like the most lofty as well as the most immediate component of an American identity, a birthright far more meaningful and compelling than terms like 'democracy,' 'Constitution,' or even 'the United States'" (5). Cullen describes the dream as part of a long tradition that continues to speak to contemporary longings, as well, such that "in the twenty-first century, the American dream remains a major element of our national identity" and "becomes a kind of lingua franca, an idiom that everyone—from corporate executives to hip-hop artists—can presumably understand" (6). Cullen cautions, however, that we must reckon with the dream as "neither a reassuring verity nor an empty bromide but rather a complex idea with manifold implications that can cut different ways" (6–7). Throughout his analysis, Cullen emphasizes ambivalence and ambiguity, arguing that there is no one dream but instead American *Dreams* that variously emphasize upward mobility, agency, and freedom. Usefully explaining what may otherwise seem paradoxical, he concludes that "a sense of dissatisfaction, a belief that the nation we inhabit isn't quite right—but *could* be—represents [the American Dream's] most important legacy"

(40), along with its shared nature that binds a heterogeneous population together into a nation. Ending his examination on a hopeful note—his own American Dream—Cullen writes, "what I would hope is that the American Dream could serve as a rigorous standard that we can use to ask a series of searching questions. . . . To ask and begin to answer such questions can transform the Dream from a passive token of national identity to a powerful instrument of national reform and revitalization" (189). Although it is often the case that the dream becomes a weapon to punish those who are not highly successful or, alternately, is dismissed as a false lure for immigrants, Cullen's vision of what it *might* be certainly continues the tradition of America being associated with possibility, with something "better."

Contemporary South Asian stories represented in this book revisit the prevalent theme that has long inspired American writers and so strongly shaped notions of Americanization. Even as they mark their particularity, South Asian narratives also invoke famous literary heroes who confronted adversity when trying to belong and who nonetheless strove for success, as in Horatio Alger's *Ragged Dick* (1868), Upton Sinclair's *The Jungle* (1906), Willa Cather's *My Antonia* (1918), and F. Scott Fitzgerald's *The Great Gatsby* (1925). Prominent responses to the American Dream from the perspective of racial minorities are reflected in works such as Carlos Bulosan's *America Is in the Heart* (1946), Ralph Ellison's *Invisible Man* (1952), and Paule Marshall's *Brown Girl, Brownstones* (1959). Current scholarly attention to *America Is in the Heart* is one example of the crucial work accomplished through the recovery of literary texts and enlarging the canon to include important writers who were historically overlooked due to their minority status. Since the civil rights movement and in part because of greater attention to previously marginalized stories, we have works which are now canonical (as evidenced by their regularly being excerpted in anthologies of American literature) such as Toni Cade Bambara's *Gorilla, My Love* (1972), Maxine Hong Kingston's *The Woman Warrior* (1976), Frank Chin's *Donald Duk* (1991), and Julia Alvarez's *How the Garcia Girls Lost Their Accents* (1992). Novels in this tradition that are by South Asian Americans and that are discussed in chapter 3 are Meena Alexander's *Manhattan Music*, Bharati Mukherjee's *Jasmine*, and Bapsi Sidhwa's *An American Brat*.

Like foundational narratives about the American Dream, South Asian assimilation stories depict the hardships of immigration but may also engage a vision of unlimited opportunity. The stories portray immigrants who have had to confront possible exclusion in response to their very bodies (i.e., "dark," female, or just visibly different) and their origins in the "East" but who may also have enjoyed certain types of privilege[33]—notably, socioeconomic advantages prior to migration and, often, functional fluency in English. Broadly speaking, Bandana Purkayastha writes about South Asians that

> based on their education and training *in other countries,* these migrants were able to move into white-collar occupations and buy homes in the suburbs during a time when native racial minorities were still contending with a series of structural impediments, especially regarding education and housing, that prevented them and their children from "achieving" similar patterns of integration. (18)

Purkayastha here ironizes the "achievement" of integration,[34] suggesting how South Asian Americans may themselves rehearse the exceptionalism common to narratives of belonging and succeeding in the United States. Thus, their immigrant histories are best appreciated as paradoxically shaped by group privilege despite racial minoritization, at least for many of those in the first cohort after 1965,[35] such that they "appeared to fulfill the American dream" (Purkayastha 1). And yet seemingly triumphant Americanization[36] in South Asian narratives is often accompanied by great ambivalence about personal identity and an inability to feel at home in any community. This self-contradictory story of assimilation is like earlier stories about the American Dream that portrayed a simultaneous instinct for participating in the dominant national narrative and misgivings about that very narrative, especially in response to experiences of exclusion or oppression.

Ambivalence associated with assimilation is thus inevitably part of the layered history of the American Dream; this is not a realization to be bemoaned but instead to view as both inevitable and incredibly productive for an evolving narrative "in which *all* are to *share* and *play their parts*" (Adams 422, emphasis added). That the American Dream will be an often-inconsistent narrative of assimilation is no surprise, since Adams himself emphasized that it was "not the product of a solitary thinker. It evolved from the hearts and burdened souls of many millions, who have come from all nations" (428). Teasing out the contradictions inherent to Americanization even more explicitly many decades after Adams, Vijay Prashad writes in a recent review that "Rajini Srikanth's *The World Next Door* is a beautiful and thoughtful exploration of the imagination of South Asian America. . . . Desi[37] texts for her are not just about themselves, but they are also a riposte against the stereotypes of citizenship that engulf us" (publisher's website blurb for Srikanth). This description affirms that South Asian Americanization narratives are stories that speak to U.S. citizenship more broadly, meaning not only important policies and laws of belonging but idea(l)s that have such significance that they literally overwhelm us and potentially make it impossible to see other realities. However, offering Asian American stories as counterpoint (or counterstroke) meaningfully results in broadening our imaginations to the "fullest" (Adams 416)—meaning that reading ambivalence in the American Dream is a means of making it *more* rather than less relevant to Americans as a whole.

As with the materials described in the next three chapters, which participate in an ongoing dialogue that connects Americans across their differences, empirical studies about South Asians also reflect striking ambivalence toward the American Dream and Americanization. Some recent titles prove this tendency: *Accommodation without Assimilation* by anthropologist Margaret A. Gibson from 1998; *Becoming American, Being Indian* by historian Madhulika S. Khandelwal from 2001; and Sharmila Rudrappa's *Ethnic Routes to Becoming American* from 2004. With each of these titles, the author announces that Americanization is not synonymous with unidirectional assimilation or the negation of ethnic identities. Gibson commences her study with the question "How are [immigrant children] and their families fitting into American society?" (1); she concludes that "pressures to assimilate" combine with "problems of prejudice" in fairly predictable and common patterns in many American high schools. She thus advocates that schools learn to foster opportunities for students "to participate in the mainstream of American society while also, if they so choose, maintaining their separate identities, so that the concept of 'mainstream' itself comprehends multiple cultural identities" (200). In this same vein, Khandelwal mentions that earlier South Asian immigrants seemed to eschew assimilation by constructing ethnic enclaves but that "younger and more progressive leaders" (161), especially women, are operating on models akin to Gibson's notion of multiple identities. Khandelwal's unsupported assumption of teleology toward greater progressiveness notwithstanding, such analyses stress ongoing assimilation negotiations—which I read as active "accommodations" instead of simple absorption into the national culture—being undertaken by South Asians in America.

Denaturalizing both national and ethnic identities implies a certain flexibility in negotiating assimilation processes, but there are of course limits to individual agency in self-reinvention. Even as Khandelwal and

Gibson relay stories of immigrants' asserting affiliations of their choice, because of the often-racist immigration histories that both scholars also document, they affirm how individuals are *acted upon* and *subjected by* institutionalized power. This is a reminder that the process of belonging to any nation-state involves subjectification as well as the opportunity to pursue happiness. In the appropriately titled *Negotiating Ethnicity,* Purkayastha maintains that, for South Asian Americans, "the underlying social relationships ensure that they are not as free to exercise their ethnic options like their white-ethnic peers. Their cultural tools are often ascribed negative meanings by outsiders, so that being ethnic negatively affects their ability to be American," and "supposedly deep-seated cultural characteristics of Asian Americans . . . make them foreign or less American" (7, 10). These explanations help to limn the boundaries of immigrant reinvention and performativity, an important caveat to any presumption that individuals are able to refashion themselves at will. Countering simplified equations of individualism with American identity, contemporary cultural criticism such as this maps a more nuanced relationship between personal will and hegemonic power, suggesting new strategies for enactments of actual agency.

Indeed, interrogating the American Dream as a metaphor for Americanization requires constantly retheorizing power and how different immigrants are interpellated into preexisting nationalisms. Whether immigrants are privileged or disempowered in their relative positionality influences the degree to which they conform to versions of nationalism or choose other means to Americanization. In an analysis of South Asians which tracks institutional pressures that constrain immigrant reinvention, Rudrappa describes her ethnographic research at two Chicago-based organizations, the women's shelter Apna Ghar and the Indo American Center. What she deduces from a year spent working with both groups is that patterns of Americanization as experienced by South Asians today are not so very different from those that overtly and systematically attempted to strip past immigrant generations of their ethnic difference (22); she concludes that, even today,

> incorporation into the American polity is not a benign process where we all exist as separate ingredients in a salad bowl. . . . [It] is still about brute disciplinizing processes where individuals are normalized into becoming a unified citizenry . . . [and] normative American-ness still matters, structuring the way new immigrants get incorporated into the nation's civil body. (193)

As I describe in later chapters, ethnic identities often need to be packaged in limited or even limiting ways in order for immigrants and their children to feel that they have earned the ability to belong in mainstream America. While there is arguably always some degree of control in constructing one's identity, the possibility of most nation-states to contravene such self-naming is hard to dismiss and there is usually a "tension between assignation and assertion" (Koshy, "Category Crisis" 285). Between Gibson's hopefulness that American institutions and citizens may gradually be more able to include immigrants without repeating the egregious exclusions of our national past and Rudrappa's starker conclusions, we can perceive yet another type of ambivalence associated with assimilation. When studies of one group of immigrants sound such different notes, we are forced to ask, What happens if calls for inclusion either preach to the converted or instead fall on deaf ears? What about those who are unable to "become" American? What does it mean, exactly, if an individual or a group does *not* achieve the American Dream?

Many South Asians continue to aspire to the American Dream model of Americanization, despite the "disciplinizing" that immigrants experience as newcomers to an already established national collective. For instance, in a 2005 *New York Times Magazine* piece, fiction writer and journalist Suketu Mehta humanizes members of this community and attempts to establish them as a group of immigrants in the American grain. About the "new new immigrant politics," his article "So the Jains, They Have a Problem with Beef in the School Lunches. Who They Gonna Call?" profiles a sort of Mr. Fix-It for South Asians in New York City, Alex Martins. Mehta claims that, due to the "absence of powerful elected officials" and since "there's not a single South Asian holding a major elected office in New York," South Asians look to people like Martins as alternative "conduits to power" to achieve their immigrant dreams. The development of ethnic networks and resources is common practice for many immigrant communities of appreciable critical mass, but it is a double-edged sword: on the one hand, immigrants may have more success in fulfilling their chosen goals, but, on the other, the process of integration within mainstream America can be hampered. This then has the possibility of merely reinforcing prejudices that these Asian Americans should "Go back to [their] own country!" Despite such slogans exemplifying exclusion, South Asians, like other immigrants, continue to strive for the sometimes-elusive American Dream. Their narratives affirm that newcomers to the United States design their own approaches to assimilation, in both predictable and surprising ways. As each group of immigrants finds its own broad patterns of belonging, then, it seems to develop new strategies of accommodation, its own versions of a dream that has long molded Americanization.

Stories of assimilation are always evolving in Asian American communities, as in any others. Narrative meditations on the nature of assimilation by Asian American authors need not be realist accounts of exploitation and ethnic exclusion in America, accounts which continue to be relevant, but can also imagine "beyond railroad and internment," as Elaine Kim insisted over a decade ago. Just as Asian Americans are a highly heterogeneous panethnic community, so too are their stories varied ones that inform us about identity, nation, and diaspora in multiple ways. Rachel Lee writes about *Through the Arc of the Rainforest* that the author, Karen Tei Yamashita, "challenges the assumption that Asian American cultural texts offer testament to a strictly downtrodden racial-economic subject largely defined by his or her victimization in the West" (118). This has been borne out in my "Asian American Literature" courses, when I sometimes have a difficult time convincing students that Yamashita's (surreal) novel about multiracial characters based in Brazil actually belongs in the course. I teach the text after a historical introduction to Asian American literary studies, in order to expose students to the ways in which disciplinary perspectives have broadened beyond an original concentration on nation-based ethnic identities. Pedagogically and otherwise, this is a way to remind ourselves of the multitude of topics visited in Asian American narrative even as we place the writing within major American traditions, including stories of Americanization.

As stated in the introduction, no one narrative adequately speaks to experiences of belonging in America; ideologically and otherwise, today's newcomers necessarily occupy a different cultural universe than earlier immigrants, even as they, too, must negotiate Americanization processes. Lee writes that it would be misguided to reduce "complex, contradictory, and often ambivalent attitudes towards America to a single unified response" (3). Indeed, different immigration patterns, historical contingencies, individual choices, and economic imperatives—each of these makes "the American experience" impossible to codify. Describing the American Dream, Adams therefore wrote, "In a country as big as America it is as impossible to prophesy as it is to generalize, without being tripped up" (417).

Palimpsestic interactions between nationality, diasporization, ethnicity, gender, and class certainly result in widely varied experiences of assimilation, which may be one process that constitutes a shared heritage in contemporary multicultural/multiethnic countries such as the United

States. Due to the diversity of Americans, we must expect many different stories of America and, thus, Americanization. When we incorporate South Asian American stories about assimilation within a broader framework, we discover insights relevant to other ethnic groups, as well, concerning the way that the national narratives that variously situate Americans are *always* susceptible to rewriting. This confirms that stories of Americanization themselves work to link disparate communities into a hybridized and multivocal national collective. In the next chapter, I look at a very recent contribution to this ongoing (trans)national narrative.

2 / They Came on Buses: "GuyaneseOpportunities" as a Contemporary Americanization Program

I felt proud to be the mayor of a city that continues to make the American dream happen. Schenectady was built and prospered because of immigrants. It only seems natural that we will again grow and prosper with a new generation of immigrants. God bless America.

MAYOR ALBERT P. JURCZYNSKI, "TRIP TO GUYANA BROUGHT HOME THE CONNECTION TO SCHENECTADY"

In Trinidad, "we is watered down Indians—we ain't good grade A Indians. We skin brown, is true, but we doh even think 'bout India unless something happen over dere and it come on de news."

SHANI MOOTOO, "OUT ON MAIN STREET"

In the previous chapter, I laid the foundations for the current and subsequent ones by outlining various layers to the story of South Asian Americanization and diasporization. I pointed out that, contrary to traditional practice, we can make sense of contemporary Americanization processes only by presencing relevant (post)colonial histories as well as more recent migration patterns. In this chapter, I move from cultural, political, and theoretical discourses to a specific contemporary case that proves the necessity of a transnational framework for analyzing national assimilation. This chapter examines assimilation stories among ethnic Indians who emigrated from Guyana to the United States in the late twentieth and early twenty-first centuries.[1] These Guyanese stories—concerning a small American city that actively worked to assimilate a new group of immigrants—emerge from a set of historical experiences that are quite different from those which engendered the South Asian narratives I describe in the next two chapters. Since assimilation history has rarely narrated the voices of immigrant communities targeted by Americanization agendas, this chapter also represents a direct intervention in how perceptions of belonging are shaped.

There are several reasons why, against the backdrop of assumptions about national assimilation, I analyze these stories before the others represented in this book. First, the Indo-Guyanese narratives represented here are responses to an initiative that can be directly compared to historical Americanization programs, illuminating the ways that such efforts continue to reflect particular assimilation ideologies and investments. Also, of the groups described in this book, Indo-Guyanese Americans are the South Asian subdemographic most recently represented in the United States in appreciable numbers. Finally, since I am analyzing self-narrations rather than fictional or filmed stories, I chose to juxtapose these with the "nonfictional" accounts of assimilation in the first chapter. However, as I maintain throughout this book, the "real" and the "imagined" are much more coterminous than might be suggested by interpretations that definitively contrast them. What we imagine to be possible is in some ways only made possible by the imagining and our stories are important vehicles for representing such potential. The overall development of the chapters is therefore a movement from documented histories and ethnographies to individual fictions and, finally, to how the *process* of narrating assimilation—both in national and diasporic terms—functions. In the conclusion of the book, I come full circle in my discussion because the chapters might conceivably have been placed in other orders; in any case, these are inevitably related stories that blur into and inform one another.

Reinforcing the important theme of intertextuality mentioned in the introduction, the first part of the title for this chapter transforms the phrase *They Came in Ships,* which (among other things) is the name of an anthology of Indo-Guyanese writing edited by Joel Benjamin et al. Like the editors of that anthology, one of my aims is to call attention to unprecedented historical journeys that result in dramatic changes, such that a small number of colonial subjects irreversibly linked disparate parts of the globe together. Since academic discussions rarely focus on Guyanese Americans, I am able to fill a noticeable gap, a motivation I share with scholars such as Monisha Das Gupta (*Unruly Immigrants*), Mae M. Ngai (*Impossible Subjects*), and Aihwa Ong (*Flexible Citizenship*), all of whom shift attention from the usual suspects in order to examine transnational experiences which are certainly informative about contemporary geopolitics but are not generally prominent in the public culture. In the case of little-studied Guyanese South Asians, the complexity of identity affiliations will always be a prominent theme because of the various nations, race-ethnicities, cultures, and religions that their historical migrations bind together.

The second part of the chapter title refers to an unusual introduction of Guyanese communities to Schenectady, a small city approximately 160 miles north of New York City. This initiative began when then-mayor Albert P. Jurczynski (quoted in the first epigraph to the chapter) helped to arrange complimentary bus tours of Schenectady for individuals willing to take day trips north from Queens and to consider relocating from primarily working-class urban neighborhoods to a suburban area that actually had a lower cost of living. Jurczynski and other city officials "thought the Guyanese would create a sea change, remaking whole neighborhoods and filling thousands of vacant jobs" (K. Moore A8). Although this goal was never reached, some residents of the area argue that, even if the Guyanese "haven't saved all of the city, . . . they have surely saved the areas they occupied," as reported by Kathleen Moore in Schenectady's *Daily Gazette* in September 2009 (A8). Along with questions about the measurable change effected by Guyanese relocation, the impact and meaning of Schenectady's Americanization initiative remains highly ambiguous and requires careful interpretation. As an official program of assimilation, it is certainly very suggestive about varying investments in narratives of national belonging. It is also a useful phenomenon to juxtapose with historical Americanization programs as another of the means employed in this book for charting narratives of belonging in the United States.

In particular, historical changes to and continuity in the national epic can be mapped by interpreting these unique northern migrations within the framework of Americanization programs. Even if, as one assimilation theorist in the early twentieth century posited, "members of a nationality group have, in the main, identical behavior" and "various nationalities have different behavior in relation to each other" (Speek 246), this reveals a paradox when determining which nationality takes precedence in shaping "identical behavior" among communities whose migrations result in transnational behaviors and identities. The motif of paradoxes is thus one of several that recur in this book, since I maintain that it is through interpreting, although not necessarily resolving, paradoxes that meaning is often produced. This is particularly appropriate for evaluating Americanization projects, which immigrants to the United States have repeatedly described as having "two faces—a generous and welcoming visage, and an anxiety-driven, coercive one," according to historians Otis L. Graham Jr. and Elizabeth Koed (29). The welcome and the coercion commingled in many such historical projects were affirmed in the stories I discuss in this chapter.

Guyanese stories from Schenectady engage topos familiar from broad Americanization histories, but there are a number of reasons why it is worth focusing on these communities specifically in relation to South Asian experiences. Given the "ethnic" group (i.e., "Indian") in which Guyanese Americans were placed in Schenectady, this is the most proximate set of immigrant narratives with which to contextualize their own accounts. We must wait for future comparative analyses to draw connections between Guyanese and other communities who rather recently became American immigrants also through unexpected quirks of and allegiances fostered through history, such as the Hmong.[2] But in light of examinations tending to focus on middle-class, professional South Asians who immigrated between 1965 and the 1980s, we have another important counterpoint for reassessing ideologies of assimilation, just as Asian immigrant history serves as a counterpoint to normative Anglo-European immigration. This broader context emphasizes how Indo-Guyanese Americans understatedly claim multiple affiliations that to others, including South Asians, might seem ill suited or even incompatible. Guyanese Americanization stories confirm cultural critic Kwame Anthony Appiah's argument that "the notion that what has held the United States together historically over its great geographic range is a citizenry centered on a common culture is—to put it politely—not sociologically plausible" (100). Since any group with a hard-to-name identity affirms that there is not a common culture to which all Americans can assimilate, this further forces us to ask, what exactly can or should Americanization represent?

In order to answer such questions, it is useful to pay attention to supposedly "atypical" cases such as those of Guyanese Americans because this methodology confirms the heterogeneity in the United States and *also* in immigrant/ethnic groups. Although South Asians as a broad constituency are gaining somewhat greater visibility since their numbers have increased in the United States, this chapter suggests *why* Indo-Guyanese Americans are often completely overlooked. The lack of familiarity most South Asians—much less most Americans—have with Guyanese American identities can partly be explained by the reality that they are not Indian or Asian, North or South American, or Caribbean but are all of these at the same time. For example, although Guyana is obviously and officially a South American nation, many of its peoples link themselves culturally with the Caribbean. Guyanese of Indian descent share dispersal experiences with other South Asians around the world, but multiple relocations result in versions of diasporization that are uniquely informative about the construction of (trans)national identities. To situate this singular community of immigrants, we might invoke "impossibility," as in Ngai's notion of "a person who cannot be and a problem that cannot be solved" according to standard historiographies (5).[3] Although Ngai's focus on "illegal" immigration (from 1924 to 1965) makes that project notably different from the Guyanese American immigration of the present study, her work similarly points out how some groups of people fall outside the usual parameters within which U.S. immigration and assimilation are analyzed. Unfortunately, it is on the basis of such (limited) analyses that important public policies are frequently formed, based on the "active links . . . between signifying practices and social structure" (Lowe 22).

In a little-known history, the dispersals that resulted in the creation of a new cultural identity (i.e., Indo-Guyanese) began in 1838 with approximately five hundred individuals. One phase of these migrations ended in 1917, by which time close to 240,000 Indian indentured servants had been transported by ship to British Guiana, often under false pretenses about their prospects. The purpose of these displacements, which Devarakshanam Govinden describes as an "'experiment' in social engineering" (57), was to fill a labor shortage following the emancipation of African slaves. Colonial archives list these workers, who were often pejoratively called "coolies," as coming primarily from areas near Madras and Calcutta. In May 1966, Guyana gained its independence from the British, but even today, its residents continue the struggle to create a stable government for the "land of six peoples." In the early twenty-first century, with a poorly developed infrastructure following colonization and chronic political tensions between descendants of former slaves and indentured laborers, Guyanese migrate elsewhere in great numbers. In fact, while the population of Guyana in 2006 was estimated to be approximately seven hundred thousand, nearly two-thirds as many people had relocated abroad since national independence. Depending on one's assumptions about undocumented immigrants, between two and three hundred thousand of these Guyanese currently reside in the United States.

As a result of Guyanese Americans' transnational migrations, their affiliations forestall or complicate categories which work to normatively construct geopolitical associations and distinctions between people, rendering them discursively "impossible." As a case in point, Guyana's role as a host country for diasporic South Asians seemed a relatively forgotten episode in British colonial history for the academics who heard about my preliminary research at the 2002 "International Seminar on

Constructing Identities" in Shillong, India. The difficulty of precisely "naming" Guyanese identity is obviously compounded by the relative lack of international visibility for the tiny South American country. Despite my own training as a scholar concerned with South Asian Americans, it is only in the past few years that I have paid close attention to Indo-Guyanese Americans. My previous research had focused primarily on the experiences of post-1965 immigrants moving directly from India to the United States, as is common to the scholarship more generally.

From the ethnographic and other research I conducted in order to fill in such scholarly gaps, I conclude that, rather than demonstrating the "successful" or "failed" assimilation of Guyanese immigrants, the neo-Americanization project described in this chapter reflected a range of often inconsistent possibilities for belonging. Local government and private initiatives, immigrant choices, and the reaction of Schenectady "natives" to this particular minority community mirrored but also contradicted one another. They collectively reflected political provisionality, cultural mixing, feelings of sameness and difference across ethnic identifications, and exploitations of power as well as cooperative understanding. In all these ways, "GuyaneseOpportunities" is of a kind with prominent Americanization programs from the past, some of which are discussed in this chapter.

Ethnographies[4] of Americanization

Supplementing my other research, the analysis in this chapter was most significantly shaped by the words, ideas, and opinions of Guyanese Americans who described what "coming from India," "being Guyanese," and "becoming American" meant to them after relocation to Schenectady, which is approximately a three-hour drive from Queens, where there is a thriving Guyanese community.[5] Some major aspects of their moves to the upstate Capital District were recorded on a website (now defunct) at the address www.guyaneseopportunities.com, leading to my use of "GuyaneseOpportunities" as a shorthand in this chapter.[6] In addition to reading different types of texts and interviewing other residents of Schenectady, I spoke with Guyanese Americans individually or sometimes in groups in various settings from 2002 to 2004, including at local Guyanese celebrations, at City Hall after a bus tour, in the mayor's office, in the offices of the Schenectady Economic Development Corporation (SEDC),[7] at social events, and over the phone. Each interview began with a personal introduction and a description of my academic, book-length project examining South Asian ethnic and racial identities. During the subsequent conversations, I asked interviewees about their migration histories and their experiences since moving to Schenectady. As we talked, I posed clarifying questions, invited their views on things others had told me or which were part of the public record, and, usually at the end of the interview, shared what I thought about my own identity as an Indian immigrant to the United States.

My conclusions about GuyaneseOpportunities are also based on stories I heard or read in Schenectady about recruiting and assimilating Guyanese immigrants to the area. I followed local forums[8] which devoted time to the question of Guyanese recruitment to Schenectady, conducted a series of interviews with local residents including Mayor Jurczynski, and also took a research trip to the National Archives of Guyana in 2004 for background information. In addition, as part of a service-learning project associated with my course for first-year students in 2003 at Union College, "Designing Utopia," I supervised four groups of students studying the local community. They gathered information about GuyaneseOpportunities by looking at newspaper and online forums, meeting with local officials, identifying problems, and acting as political advocates for recent immigrants.[9] Our collective goal was to assess the viability of a plan that was influenced by the mayor's seemingly utopian belief that his city could "make the American dream happen," as quoted in the epigraph to this chapter. Finally, I posted anonymously to an online forum and asked for people's opinions about the initiative and its racial implications. The efforts of GuyaneseOpportunities lost much of their momentum with the transition to a new local government in 2004 and were subsequently represented largely by the not-for profit SEDC. However, in August 2006, Anne Miller of the *Times Union* (Albany, NY) reported that Schenectady's current mayor, Brian Stratton, was resuming "the previous mayor's push to encourage Guyanese to settle in Schenectady" after a two-year hiatus while Stratton concentrated on the city's finances.[10] Where (if anywhere) the program will go in the future is currently unclear, but an article in September 2009 by Kathleen Moore announced that there was debate about the actual number of Guyanese immigrants in the city, with some residents suggesting that city officials had exaggerated the efficacy of the program. This most recent addendum to the story of Indo-Guyanese assimilation in Schenectady proves as prone to ambivalence and conflict as all that preceded it.

In order to parse this history, in an approach that is not quite like (but is certainly influenced by) previous cultural studies projects, I treated the ethnography as I did the other elements of this study, through an analysis of stories that reflect and create (trans)national realities. This treatment is usefully contextualized by Rey Chow's paradigm of a "new" ethnography in which "we turn our attention to the subjective origins of ethnography as it is practiced by those who were previously ethnographized and who have, in the postcolonial age, taken up the active tasks of ethnographizing their own cultures" (*Primitive Passions* 180). Although it must be acknowledged that naming one's "own" culture often seems quite difficult, Chow's notion of a self-conscious and self-critical ethnographic perspective is a useful one to describe what I attempt in this chapter. To emphasize that this is storytelling rather than supposed "truth" means that I repeatedly asked myself, Who is telling what story? How reliable are different narrators? What is "the plot"? What is the story's main point? Who is the audience, implied or actual? *How* is the story being told? What are the larger implications of the narrative? How am I implicated in the stories I am hearing or how they are told? The direct questions that I posed, in slightly different words, to each interviewee were, How would you describe your identity? In your opinion, have Guyanese in Schenectady assimilated to America? How do you feel about this?

After listening to (and recording) the answers, I was guided in arranging the resulting information by prominent examples of ethnography that have charted a set of related techniques for interpreting cultural meaning. In the introduction, I described the goal of approaching a "thick" description, following a methodology outlined by anthropologist Clifford Geertz in the early 1970s and subsequently highly praised as well as modified through critique. What remains quite powerful in Geertz's classic book is the manner in which Geertz explains "*what doing ethnography is*"—namely, it is an elaborate venture in navigating "piled-up structures of inference and implication" (*The Interpretation of Culture* 5–7). Accordingly, in conducting the research presented in this chapter, I approached ethnography as an enterprise "like that of the literary critic," since I was "trying to read a manuscript" which was "written in transient examples of shaped behavior" (9–10). One of the most well-known precedents for such ethnography focused on Asian American communities is of course historian Ronald Takaki's groundbreaking work. There are other projects that have also importantly broadened understandings of national narratives[11] and I have been particularly influenced by a number of ethnographic studies, often with a feminist focus, about South Asians in diaspora.[12]

To interpret the assimilation stories I collected, I applied familiar tools of literary analysis such as textual exegesis, formal examination, and critical theorizing. As anthropologist Tejaswini Niranjana acknowledges, "literary processes influence not only the writing but also the reading of ethnographies" (81). I was accordingly especially attuned to how reading cultural "texts" in this manner can be an important strategy for attending to diversity by hybridizing our scholarly approaches.[13] To do justice to my interviewees, while I treat their stories collectively in this chapter, I would never suggest that their feelings or ideas should be simplified to what I am reading "textually." Among ethnographers who suggest good practice, I was most guided by Harry F. Wolcott, who lists some of the ethnographer's responsibilities (82–84), and Henrietta Moore, who advocates for a "new ethics of engagement for the analysis of cross-cultural material" that is attuned to different levels of analysis (6, 134).

My overall approach in collecting narratives of belonging was to identify and to try to make sense of repeated themes that illuminated specific discourses. This method, like most ethnographies, resulted in an "incomplete" story. This can be attributed to the ambiguity and ambivalence associated with Americanization processes, but it is also reflective of the version of ethnographic cultural studies in which I am engaged. My examination in this chapter obviously cannot stand as the "whole picture" of Guyanese assimilation in Schenectady but is instead intended to be suggestive of how a number of discrete personal narratives are highly informative about more general patterns of human cultural experience. It "zeroes in on *particular* settings" (Wolcott 102) for South Asian American stories in order to offer an entry point for expanded thinking about the intertwined communities represented in the study as a whole. It is a story that did not *exist* for me to find but came into being as I constructed the narrative from the various pieces at my disposal, including those that I purposely sought out. It seems probable that Wolcott's assertion is on the mark, that ethnography as an approach is most "salutary *for the researcher*," but this does not invalidate the way in which a cultural dialogue is set in motion with an examination that contributes to "discerning and describing the problems as defined and dealt with by any human group—some shared in common with all humanity, others unique to smaller subsets" (Wolcott 88).

It is important, therefore, to be academically precise and honest in acknowledging that *no* intellectual endeavor will ever speak to "everything" (Wolcott 88), rather than hiding behind a master narrative which cannot have adequate explanatory power across countless differences between people. Historically, one of the most severe limitations of anthropology and ethnography has been a tendency to base academic studies on (usually unexamined) ideologies reflecting relentless ethnocentrism. In 1978, in *Orientalism,* which many scholars (including some detractors) mark as the genesis of postcolonial studies, Edward Said outlined a version of this tendency as "Europocentrism" (98).[14] More recently but in a similar vein, Niranjana critiques "naturalizing, dehistoricizing" anthropological methods in which "the transparency of the knowledge [produced] and its univocity serve to mask the inequalities between cultures and languages that the knowledge has actually helped create" (78, 71). Thus, strategically focusing on ambivalence, multivocality, and indeterminacy are purposeful tactics in this chapter for dodging such pitfalls of ethnographic research.

Also, by adding stories of "other" South Asians to academic discussions, one can more thoroughly interrogate their collective narratives of belonging and the unique cultural/ethnic/racial mixing endemic to Guyanese identities. Gender was a latent aspect of many of the stories told by Guyanese Americans but was rarely made the focus (even when I asked specifically about it), so I do not emphasize this axis of identity in the present chapter,[15] although it is central to my analysis in chapter 3. Sexuality was a topic that no one raised, except insofar as there were many implicitly heteronormative assumptions. Concerns about socioeconomic status and class positionality were repeated elements in Guyanese assimilation stories, which is why I pay so much attention to this particular subject. Gayatri Spivak's discussion of the "new subaltern" and class formation is informative in relation to these identities and also gestures to contemporary debates about how to interpret globalization. She writes,

> Although the terrain of the colonial subaltern cannot be explained by capital logic alone, this cannot mean jettisoning the concept of class formation as a descriptive and analytical category. The new subaltern is produced by the logic of global capital that forms classes only instrumentally, in a separate urban sphere, because commercial and finance capital cannot function without an industrial component. ("The New Subaltern" 330)

While "class" will never be the only way to attend to the subaltern histories of the majority of the world (i.e., nonelites), it is important to recognize that the very globalization that some people celebrate for transcending local differences seems to be reinforcing class hierarchies rather than mitigating them. Stories about Guyanese assimilation in Schenectady are telling not only about the experiences of a small group of immigrants, therefore, but are suggestive about other ways in which "racial economics"[16] operate more broadly. They verify the observation made by Jana Evans Braziel and Anita Mannur in the introduction to *Theorizing Diaspora* that the "boundaries of local/global, like those of nation/diaspora, are no longer so clearly distinguishable" ("Nation, Migration, Globalization" 11), and immigration processes affect all of these sites simultaneously.

American/Guyanese/Indian:[17] "Mixed" Metaphors

The politics of race and ethnicity in Guyana must be taken into account when trying to understand the actual multiplicity of identities represented by Guyanese Americans in Schenectady. The six groups that are officially recognized in Guyana are East Indian, African, Chinese, Portuguese, Amerindian, and (officially) "Mixed." These six "races" may seem like an unlikely lineup, but as Kampta Karran writes, demographics as well as other categorizations in Guyana are "influenced by, though not necessarily totally dependent on, the dominant 19th century Western idea that subscribed to the belief in the existence of discrete races" (Introduction 7). Even if "race" was inconsistently ascribed, the names have stuck. In the collection of essays Karran introduces, *Race and Ethnicity in Guyana,* contemporary thinkers address, deconstruct, and reassemble racial categories, all with reference to their influence on "the public life of Guyana" (10). The contexts for these examinations are quite varied, including the "mini-states" of the Caribbean, the perceived and real differences between Afro- and Indo-Guyanese, racial integration and racial justice, language use, and underrepresented Amerindians.

Taken collectively as an analysis of related processes of identity formation for various groups in Guyana, *Race and Ethnicity in Guyana* is highly informative about the ways in which cultural heterogeneity can be ubiquitous without necessarily resulting in *multi*cultural practices. For example, Iris Sukdeo contends that, while interracial conflicts and tensions affiliated with political parties often replicate plantation culture, "Guyanese of all races work side by side practically with little skin-colour consciousness wherever they are found together." Off-setting this optimistic reading, Sukdeo further writes that "this does not mean, however, that prejudice among the races does not exist in a subtle form"

(Karran 40). Ravi Dev explains such seeming inconsistencies when he talks about the ways in which Indians and Africans invented group identities in Guyana: "because they were oppressed as groups based on their origins and culture" (Karran 104), they used narratives of origins and culture as political strategies for overcoming that oppression. Racial pride and racial difference are therefore crucial dynamics in the relationships between different Guyanese communities in South America.

These historical experiences will obviously bear upon Americanization, in sometimes unpredictable ways, to shape shifting ethnic and (trans) national identities. Guyanese in Schenectady associated themselves with cultural categories created in Guyana, but several mentioned that Indo- and Afro-Guyanese racial tensions did not travel with immigrants to the United States. What most of my interviewees repeated was that interracial conflict in Guyana was primarily a matter of political competition for resources rather than ethnic prejudice. One person compared institutional racism in Guyana, the nation of her birth, to that in the nation of her immigration, since advancement in Guyana "was very difficult because of racial motivation and, you know, the prejudice; it is very difficult to get equal access to jobs—very similar to U.S. segregation." When these Guyanese could escape these racial constraints, many considered themselves to have "flexibility to interact" that made them feel able to move between groups and cultures with ease. Correspondingly, interviewees described their identities with reference to music and language from the Caribbean, food and a pidgin language that was Guyanese-specific from African, Indian, and other elements, and religious rituals that were Indian, usually Hindu but with Muslim and Christian influences.

When "they came on buses" to Schenectady, Guyanese immigrants therefore represented three diasporas which implied different things according to American racial economics, but it was the Indian designation that most strongly shaped their assimilation experiences in Schenectady. As one woman explained her own sense of being Indian, Caribbean, and Guyanese, she concluded, "The culture has come with us." In Schenectady, however, the primary culture that was assumed to come with them was that which was associated with other Indian immigrants, albeit usually those migrating from South Asia directly. Guyanese immigrants' notions of their culture might seem to affirm essentialist attitudes toward ethnic identity, but at the same time, it is true that their identities do *not* quite conform to *any other* group of Indians, Caribbeaners, or Guyanese—thus, all these other categories take on different meanings than for other groups and individuals.

When I struggled to appropriately historicize and describe Indo-Guyanese American identities, I came to feel a sense of cultural déjà vu because I realized that people who were involved with GuyaneseOpportunities in Schenectady were interpellating Indians almost *too* similarly to how administrators regarded "coolies" in British Guiana. Starting in the 1830s, British representatives predicted that the colony would benefit from the allegedly superior work ethic of newly introduced Indians after the dissolution of the African slave trade. Documents from the Empire make it clear that Africans came off the worse in comparisons of the two groups of exploited "workers." Reading correspondence associated with John Gladstone, a powerful and wealthy plantation owner in the West Indies, Madhavi Kale notes the motives for transporting indentured Indians to certain colonies: "Indian workers were to be the medium through which sugar planters would reassert their control over Afro-Caribbean workers . . . to alarm, but also to 'educate' and inspire" the former slaves" (76–77). As the editors to *They Came in Ships* summarize about Guyana in the introduction to the first part of their book, colonial discourse "justified indenture as a benevolent system of free labour in which Indians were docile, industrious, thrifty, and sturdily independent, which as a subtext belaboured the Afro-Guyanese for their fecklessness" (11). Other stereotypes of the Indians painted them as both dependent and deceitful, Benjamin et al. remark, but the contradictions were immaterial in the context of a common motif, that there was a "need for the harshly penal system of labour control" (11) to manage workers, whatever the ethnic symbolism. Colonial "estates" or plantations with names such as "Providence" and "Le Bonne Intention" could not disguise the reality that indentured Indian servants lived in conditions nearly identical to those of the former African slaves, but the ethnic characteristics the British associated with either group were nonetheless rigidly dichotomous.

There is a great deal of evidence confirming the degree to which certain American model-minority myths that shaped GuyaneseOpportunities correspond with centuries-old colonial racial apparatuses. Vijay Prashad traces some of the theoretical and cultural background in his section on coolies in *Everybody Was Kung Fu Fighting.* Similarly, in *Coolitude,* the coauthors (historian Marina Carter and linguist/poet Khal Torabully) review how British officials perceived Indians in the chapter "Thrice Victimized: Casting the Coolie." This is the historical backdrop for Torabully's elaboration of "coolitude," which he compares to Aimé Césaire's notion of *négritude* in terms of "the need to redress the state of oblivion and neglect attached to the condition of the Negro, and to that of the Coolie" (143). Torabully purposely alludes to that famous coinage—and to a dialogue between himself and Césaire—in order to "foster a larger community of vision" for peoples of Indian and African descent in former colonies (143), rather than reifying administrative discourses which polarized the groups. Since "the coolie's life-history, albeit in somewhat modified historical circumstances, resembled, in many aspects, that of the slave" (144), Torabully intends the concept of coolitude to remind us of the histories of similarity, rather than accepting imperialistic assumptions about essential differences. Torabully's notion of coolitude works, then, to demystify the racialized ideologies associated with certain British colonies.

During my visit to the National Archives of Guyana, I was able (its unfortunately neglected condition notwithstanding) to read British administrative documents[18] that confirm the need to deconstruct limiting binaries of "Indo" versus "Afro," which also implicitly pervaded the assumptions of GuyaneseOpportunities. For example, in the 1914 *Report to the Secretary to the Government of India on the Condition of Indian Immigrants in Trinidad, British Guiana or Demerara, Fiji, Surinam/Dutch Guiana,* Indian professionals were praised for "commanding respect by their integrity as well as by their authority" (71). According to the report, these role models within the Indian community reinforced the values learned in the colony through hard work and exposure to Christianity, such that "the system makes men of" the Indians. In stark contrast, one observer remarked that "the black labourer is jealous of the Indian who is taking root in the land" (73). Although there was enormous expense involved in importing Indian laborers to British Guiana, in 1893 Surgeon Major D. W. D. Comins had argued in *Notes on Immigration from India to British Guiana, Jamaica, St. Lucia, Trinidad, and on Return Passages* that these were necessary expenses. He believed this was due to the "astonishing laziness, apathy and improvidence which have grown on the negroes since they have been freed," and he concluded that "the tendency of the majority since they have been able to do as they like is rather downward" (5). Comins characterized his own and other similar accounts of Africans in the colony as being based on "general opinion," with no "prejudice based on the account of colour," and deemed them "fair" and even "disinterested" (6–8).

Implicit in such "disinterested" comparisons between Indians and Africans, which were common in colonial discourses, is the assumption that British patronage brought out the best in one group and the worst in the other. Indeed, Comins and overseers who worked to institutionalize the Indians seemed convinced that "doing as they like" was not beneficial for either group. What contributed to strikingly different British attitudes toward this second group of exploited "natives" is the degree to which the administrators felt they had succeeded in assimilating Indians as useful colonial workers. As a case in point, in the 1914 report to India, the authors had admitted that high-caste laborers were "troublesome as workers and as residents"; the solution that managers devised was to separate these workers from one another, which had the added benefit of rendering moot their complaints that there was not enough recognition offered to caste distinctions. Although the original arrangements seemed to include keeping friends together on the plantations, this had to be abrogated in the case of certain groups of Indians "in the interest both of discipline and of peace among immigrants" (74).

Leaving little to chance lest Indians turn out to be workers who were as unsatisfactory as the emancipated slaves, British agents instead contrived to systematically assimilate Indians to the colony by relieving them of seemingly intractable ethnic, linguistic, and religious loyalties. Casting these as efforts to civilize the Indians, Comins described the difference he noticed between "the cooly in India and his children born in the colony" (8). He allowed that the cause could be a range of things, including "change of climate, better food, *easy times*, more responsible duties or position, the influence of travel, or freedom from the narrowness of class prejudice" (8, emphasis added). Unsurprisingly, afforded these types of "freedom," few Guyanese today speak an Indian language, recognize historical castes, or can retrace their origins in India.

Such nineteenth-century British projects to assimilate a new labor pool may be considered analogous to the twenty-first-century GuyaneseOpportunities efforts, especially with regard to valuing certain "ethnic" tendencies that seemed beneficial to the powers that be and eliding other historical realities. The results of coerced assimilation in Guyana are apparent for those of Indian descent who today have little inherited knowledge of or official records bespeaking their specific ancestries. The interviewee who spoke frankly of a mixed racial heritage sadly recounted,

> There are lots of problems with British colonies and problems with Guyana, and one of them is the fact that they did not allow people to speak their language after colonization, and we lost the ability to be a union, as far as the Indian community and the African community, too. They were not speaking the African languages because of that part of the colonization process. . . . We lost the Indian language after the first generation.

There are many different ways in which this loss can be framed: among immigrant experiences around the globe, in the history of Indians relocated to colonies throughout the British Empire, in relation to Caribbean Indo/Afro encounters, or as part of national dialogues in American public culture about bilingualism and multiculturalism. Each of these areas of investigation is very important. I hope to see future discussions that include the Guyanese and augment the current study of a localized site of national assimilation.

Americanization Programs and Their Discontents

With the transnational context firmly in mind, one is better situated to unpack GuyaneseOpportunities in the U.S. context. Varying interpretations of "assimilation," as described in chapter 1, have historically led to Americanization programs which worked to incorporate newcomers to the nation but which diverged widely in their motivations and goals. Program assumptions have ranged from pluralistic interpretations of cultural integration in the United States to implicit ideologies of racial-ethnic discrimination and coercive expectations of normativity.[19] For parts of the nineteenth and twentieth centuries, assimilation was not uncommonly associated with optimistic goals for bettering the lives of immigrants and assisting in their adjustment. Narratives about emancipation in the New World informed these assimilationist hopes; historian Gary Gerstle concludes that Americans seemed united in their "desire to throw off inherited customs and beliefs and to begin anew; a fresh start would put individual and social perfection within human grasp" (557). Varied interests such as women's groups, employers, educators, the military, and state governments therefore worked, on their own as well as collectively, to institute programs whereby immigrants could benefit from assimilation while also contributing to their new nation's culture, economy, or defense. For certain immigrant groups, these projects seemed to meet with a degree of success. In a survey of "the Americanization movement" or the chief agencies interested in assimilating immigrants through to the first two decades of the twentieth century, leading educator Howard C. Hill asserted that "down to 1880 or 1885, foreign immigration presented few obstacles to successful Americanization" because the majority of immigrants were from western Europe and possessed "ideals, customs, standards of living, modes of thought, and religion of the same general tenor" as earlier settlers. This similarity meant that "there was little tendency among the incomers to settle in racial groups," and assimilation to mainstream America was a seemingly positive and viable goal after immigration (610).

As Hill acknowledges and as was made explicit with legislation such as the Chinese Exclusion Act, waves of immigration beginning in the late nineteenth century included groups who were perceived by Americans of the time to be so different as to be practically unassimilable, no matter what program might be developed. In truth, individuals who emigrated due to economic necessity, without an expectation of cultural similarity to others already in America, may well have considered themselves sojourners whose goals did not include assimilation. At particular times, questions of whether and how to assimilate such "aliens" seemed urgent, based on fears of divided allegiances or military threats. For example, some proponents of the Americanization movement worried about the implications of immigrants not getting the "American point of view" (Hill 618). Historian George J. Sanchez clarifies the motives behind such concerns: "as World War I heightened anxieties concerning immigrants, nativist sentiment began to affect Americanization efforts through the '100 Per Cent American' movement, which wanted to ensure the loyalty of the immigrant to the United States" (288). At such times of international crisis, those with a strong desire to Americanize immigrants felt challenged by ethnic groups who did not seem to share the "same general tenor" as those who had come before them.

In the same way as the American Dream and historical developments have meant varied possibilities for assimilation, no stable consensus was ever reached in assimilation programs about how to *define* Americanization exactly. Different individuals and organizations have been inconstant in how they measure national assimilation, basing it on everything from religion to dietary habits. It may be that this is so for all modern nations, or it may be especially germane to "the youngest of all nationalities," as Peter Speek described the United States in 1926 (238). Speek defined nationality[20] in terms that we may associate with stories of American exceptionalism or the nation's "successes greater than any yet know in the history of mankind" (239). In specifying what "American" represents, Speek characteristically cited individualism, a unique willingness to work hard, and voluntary cooperation in industry. In a similar analysis, meanwhile, Hill decided that Americanization could be most associated with "intelligence, co-operation, self-sacrifice" and good citizenship including "public welfare" even when "co-operation may mean personal discomfort and loss" (631). Despite these commonly cited aspects of American identity, diverse traits seemed more or less decisive depending on the interpreter, including military loyalty, common uplift, American foods, giving up all other languages, antidiscrimination, world brotherhood, democracy, standards of American living, religious persuasion, and even nobility (Hill 630–31).

Adding to this variability, certain groups were treated as if they needed particular assistance in being transformed into good citizens because those involved with Americanization programs often based their methods on ethnic stereotypes. For instance, Sanchez notes that instilling reform in diet, hygiene, and work ethic were some of the key aims of concerned Americans working to assimilate Mexican immigrants from 1915 to 1929. This proves that ethnic chauvinism as much as careful research guided Americanization efforts. Analogously, fears of "the yellow peril" shaped national responses to East Asian immigrants in the early part of the twentieth century; by the end of the century, meanwhile, young men calling themselves "Dotbusters" actively expressed their opposition to displays of Hinduism in New Jersey by attacking women who appeared to be ethnically Indian.[21] There are many more examples than these of attitudes toward immigrant groups that have been codified in racialized behavior or language. When unpacked, these race-specific practices reveal Americans' worries about new immigrants because of economic, cultural, religious, sexual, and ethnic difference. Historically, Americanization programs were arguably more influenced by such unexamined ideologies than by other concerns.

Programs for Americanization that developed from particular ideologies of difference are particularly revealing in relation to economics and race in the United States. Racial ideologies consistently played a part in defining what tactics to take with which group, with "race" meaning ethnicity or culture, sometimes interchangeably. Meanwhile, the economic visions associated with the New World have continued to signify incomparable possibilities for upward mobility, supposedly confirmed by the contemporary status of the United States as a capitalist superpower. However, the roles of race and economics in assimilation continue to be debated and are worth analyzing carefully. We may well ask, Is America truly a meritocracy in which any immigrant can succeed, if only he or she works hard enough? Are nonwhite immigrants still less likely to partake in the economic promise of the American Dream? Or is American "classlessness" resilient enough to make institutionalized racism irrelevant? How do culture, religion, gender, and other axes of differences, in relation to economic and race-based identities, influence assimilation outcomes?

As evidence of certain economics of assimilation, Americanization projects have often been undertaken by industrial organizations and have been implicated in politics of capital, labor, and power. Particular economic sectors or industries requiring workers have affiliated themselves with assimilation programs, especially when new immigrants might be induced to accept lower wages than current employees. Since there has never been a national, government-sponsored Americanization program, employers filled a social and economic need. At the same time, since racial assumptions and economic interests often drove attitudes about assimilation, these programs were potentially inimical to immigrant uplift or integration. On the effects of early twentieth-century programs focused on Mexican immigrant women, Sanchez reports that "what was achieved turned out to be little more than second-class citizenship. The most progressive assumptions behind Americanization programs were never fully shared by the government or business interests involved, and thus they could never be fully implemented" (294). Sanchez raises the possibility that sympathy between reformers and business people might well have weakened the forcefulness of the former in advocating for immigrants. Similarly, while many people may have become involved in assimilation initiatives for altruistic reasons, Robert A. Carlson argues that, usually, programs tended "to become directed toward the establishment of conformity to middle-class standards and the maintenance of the status quo in American society" (459). This reinforces the extent to which political ideologies and economic incentives, for immigrants as well as for other Americans, have always had a central part to play in shaping assimilation.

Governmental and private business interests involved in Americanization programs from the first half of the twentieth century were often kindly but were usually quite stern about expectations that assimilation included mandatory conversion, including work habits, languages, cultural practices, religion, and even food. The implicit reward for adopting a mainstream standard was the right to achieve the American Dream. A prominent example of such an Americanization project was the Ford Motor Company's English School, which had "one of the most extensive and best organized efforts" to assimilate immigrants to both America and to work (Hill 633). The company's paternalistic and vaguely threatening attitude toward assimilating immigrants is reflected in the following statement, contained in a publication directed at them: "TO EVERY NON-ENGLISH SPEAKING EMPLOYEE. You must learn to read, write, and speak English. This School was established for your benefit, and you should be glad of this opportunity. . . . There is no excuse for your remaining away from school. . . . COME TODAY" (quoted in Hill 638). Similarly, as Carlson points out about Hull House social settlement workers who had "a humanizing influence in the Americanization drive," there were "subtle, even unintentional, forms of compulsion" including trading in on so-called favors to immigrants. Furthermore, this approach—"so characteristic of the smugness of American life at the time—tended to condescension which elicited only confusion or rebuff from the immigrant" (Carlson 444–45). According to historians such as Carlson, Americanization proponents seemed to believe implicitly in a cultural superiority to which immigrants needed to aspire, even if they were never expected actually to achieve it due to their racial-ethnic limitations.

Assimilation economics were defined through such hierarchies of race and culture, which is why, from the Progressive-era Americanization movement through to contemporary phenomena, disagreements about the import of race-ethnicity partly account for polarized attitudes toward "assimilationism." There have always been prominent American thinkers and leaders who have insisted that assimilation cannot be interpreted as racial homogeneity, as in the case of John Dewey, who maintained,

> No matter how loudly any one proclaims his Americanism, if he assumes that one racial strain, any one component culture, no matter how early settled it was in our territory, or how effective it has proved in its own land, is to furnish a pattern to which all other strains and cultures are to conform, he is a traitor to American nationalism. (204)

Dewey here and others in the 1910s to 1920s criticized Americanization ideologies that seemed to be shaping American culture for the worse rather than the better. Indeed, Gerstle believes that "race constrained invention" such that "the efforts to free American national identity from its affiliation with whiteness have failed." For him, it is unfortunately true that "race, even more than class and gender, still limits the options of those who seek to become American" (553–54). Despite memorable exhortations to welcome and value racial diversity as part of what Dewey imagined as "Americanism," there have historically also been significant obstacles to racial minority groups being fully integrated into the national culture. Although overt legal barriers may no longer exist for racial integration in America, struggles persist with regard to defining the race, ethnicity, and culture of the nation-state.

Culture, race, ethnicity, nationality—each of these is, on the one hand, quite "real" in organizing social systems but, on the other, an intangible collection of inherited truths by which people define themselves. Accordingly, Sandhya Shukla argues, in her study *India Abroad,* for "the idea that Indianness is internally contradictory and fissured" but must concede that "Indianness, or India, is nowhere close to being transcended, even while those categories might be differently inhabited or understood, or even when they might give rise to other possibilities" (251). As Shukla affirms, "Indianness" or related labels for race-ethnicity or culture must be read in relation to other discourses, in stories we choose to repeat, and through acts of imagination. Although European race scientists in the nineteenth and twentieth centuries worked assiduously to provide a racial taxonomy that would catalogue distinctions (and often justify hierarchies), there has been no definitive evidence proving that "race" is measurable or even exists independently of social construction. This leads influential thinkers to propose alternative models to "ethno-racial" identity, the hallmark of American multiculturalism of the 1980s and 1990s; for example, historian David A. Hollinger characterizes contemporary identities as "postethnic" or "acquired largely through affiliation, however prescribed or chosen" (7). For Hollinger, the concepts of affiliation and the "postethnic" imply multiple identities, flexibility, and performativity. These are characteristics quite common to postcolonial and postmodernist theories, yet common sense for most Americans, as for most people, is that identity "simply is" (7). This means that Americans need to heed the ways in which we are all to some degree postethnic, as well as the constraints—in public policy, social practices, languages—against moving somehow *beyond* race and ethnicity as socially meaningful categories.

In particular, the racial economics of Americanization continue to mean that projects for ethno-cultural belonging become embroiled with calculations of assimilation in terms of losses and gains, resulting in a thoroughly "political economy" (Butler, "Merely Cultural" 273). For instance, one common way to describe the value of newcomers to the United States has been to speak of "immigrant gifts," as John Higham did in the 1950s in his seminal work *Strangers in the Land.* As Higham makes clear, the optimistic view, that "each immigrant group had a tangible contribution to make to the building of American culture," which was pervasive among immigration reformers after 1900, was transformed within decades to the more conservative ideology of "100 Per Cent Americanism" that "belligerently demanded universal conformity organized through total national loyalty" as imagined in the "existing social pattern" of the American middle class (121, 205). Higham's analysis, as well as others which have followed it, point to the influence of ethnocentrism in Americanization efforts, highlighting how interpretations of the nation's benefiting from or suffering due to immigration converge through racial ideologies.

Their convergence has at times seemed to justify a chauvinistic conviction that the best way to Americanize, especially nonwhite individuals, is to train immigrants to serve particular labor needs that entail constant supervision. In the early twentieth century, for example, Hill acknowledged how important it was to Americanize nonnaturalized persons and provide literacy training because "war industries are largely dependent on alien labor" (612). It seemed only logical to many people at that time that Americanization programs would encourage immigrants "to promote the welfare of America" while training newcomers to contribute in very specific ways, such as through low-income labor, to that welfare (Hill 614). Promoting the *immigrants'* welfare seemed to be an assumed side effect of these training efforts, since Americanization leaders considered different ethnic groups to be well suited to particular service sectors. Whether or not assimilation in the future will maintain this pattern of racial economics is something that is still being hashed out every day in the United States, in Congress, newspapers, blogs, chat rooms, and talk shows.

In my ethnographic research in Schenectady, I encountered a contemporary Americanization plan that similarly replicated ethnic essentialism and national chauvinism, leavened with strong, continuing investment in the American Dream. What was most striking, within the framework of South Asian Americanization, was the way that Guyanese immigrants matter-of-factly manipulated their various identities depending on the context, while nonetheless they spoke of ethnicity (or culture) as though it "simply is." At the same time, multiple accounts of Guyanese assimilation in Schenectady that were available in the public culture suggest that even simplistic or poorly understood global histories can result in unpredicted possibilities for integrating newcomers into a particular nation. For instance, being Indo-Guyanese afforded former "coolies" of the British Empire an opportunity to benefit from the Asian model-minority stereotype in America, while those categorized as Afro-Guyanese (or Afro-Caribbean) would undoubtedly have been placed in other sorts of racial pigeonholes. Why and how some Guyanese Americans were able to make use of inconsistencies in notions of race-ethnicity is at the heart of understanding Americanization efforts that brought many of them to Schenectady.

Guyanese Opportunities in America

GuyaneseOpportunities represented a series of linked Americanization efforts in upstate New York in the first decade of the twenty-first century, initiatives which were posted on the website described earlier. The quasi-public initiatives associated with GuyaneseOpportunities raised various possibilities for the assimilation of new immigrants to the United States. These efforts were reminiscent of earlier Americanization projects in being a complicated combination of changeable racial ideologies, American utopianism, and certainly economic incentives, built on a foundation of underlying normative assumptions. Although many small American towns and cities today are struggling to integrate (or exclude) newer immigrants,[22] especially in "rust belt" northeastern locations, few seem to be choosing techniques similar to those represented by GuyaneseOpportunities. Part of the reason that this program gained national attention—beginning with a full-page, rather tongue-in-cheek article in the *New York Times* in 2002—was that it bucked the trend of closing doors on or putting up fences to new immigration. In "For Schenectady, a Guyanese Strategy," Sarah Kershaw described the unusual series of events through which almost five thousand Guyanese immigrants from Queens immigrated to a small city further to the north in New York, an "obscure and hard-to-pronounce place called Schenectady" (B4).

One of the strongest motivations for this contemporary Americanization plan—its own racial economics—was that Schenectady was "very much looking for a new ethnic group." These words, quoted in Kershaw's article, were spoken by George Robertson of the SEDC, in an address to potential recruits. It is important to recognize the implications of being "in the market for a new ethnic group," as Kershaw puts it (B1), or basically of "shopping" for ethnicity. In a way, it makes sense that ethnicity itself can be a commodity in a nation abounding in narratives of material prosperity, endless consumption, and laissez-faire economics. As Marilyn Halter argues in her examination of the relationship between ethnic affiliations and consumer culture, "The demassification of American cultural identity during the last three decades has been reflected, even paralleled, in the ways that the business world has reshaped its own marketing tactics. The salience of ideas about diversity and differentiation pertains whether applied to people or products" (6). Confirming the prevalence of such ideologies, one person wrote in an online posting about the effect of GuyaneseOpportunities on Schenectady that the "buying" can go both ways: "To all immigrating here I say two things, carpe diem and caveat emptor" (maxconfus). Other online posters, expressing a great deal of suspicion toward locally elected officials, agreed that Guyanese should be careful consumers themselves. The questions raised by this Americanization plan included, What, exactly, organized the market? What was for sale? What was its value? And who, finally, was buying what?

Regarding the cultural work represented by GuyaneseOpportunities, it meant that South Asian diasporans contributed to shaping the meaning of "Americanness" in Schenectady, just as they did in predominantly Guyanese and Trinidadian neighborhoods in Queens over the past decades. On a local level, these communities are interacting with their new host country in a manner that historically had profound repercussions for Guyana, as well. As Ian McDonald writes in the afterword to *They Came in Ships*, "What would Guyana be without Indian customs, Indian religion and its age-old practices and philosophy, Indian festivals and holy days . . . ? Without this myriad of legacies, contributed out of a great culture, it would simply not be Guyana at all" (273). GuyaneseOpportunities represented hopes for a similarly dramatic effect in contemporary Schenectady, if not nationally. According to Mayor Jurczynski, GuyaneseOpportunities aimed to replace a population lost in the 1980s to white flight and the movement of General Electric industries "south." Thus, some people involved in the initiatives projected that as many as thirty thousand immigrants might relocate from Queens to Schenectady, adding to the existing population of about sixty thousand. (The Guyanese population in Schenectady never grew to that extent and it remains unlikely that it will do so in the future.) As part of GuyaneseOpportunities, local business interests and city government officials actively worked together to recruit immigrants to the area, journeys which were symbolized not by ships but, more prosaically, by summer bus trips from Queens to Schenectady. As reported by the *New York Times* and in regional papers such as the Capital District's *Times Union* and the *Post-Standard* in Syracuse, the bus trips around Schenectady which were led by "Mayor Al" (as he liked to be called) included neighborhood tours, identification of available real estate, introductions to potential employers in the area, meals in city buildings or with the mayor's family, and warm invitations to relocate. When I attended one of the lunches at City Hall in early August 2003, I found the event unprecedented in the institutional commitments being made to a contemporary group of immigrants and yet very familiar in relation to assimilation narratives and historical Americanization plans, particularly those of the Progressive era of the early twentieth century. It seemed to me that GuyaneseOpportunities represented the best and brightest hopes of democratic idealism, as well as the opportunism of the capitalist individualism[23] that is nearly a national religion. Reiterating what every generation of immigrants seems to share, visitors on that bus trip in 2003 wished for an improved quality of life and uplift for the next generation, while also worrying about their abilities to preserve a strong sense of cultural uniqueness. For those who were doing the recruiting, these ambitions were clearly recognized and appreciated, if arguably in reductive terms.

When Guyanese immigrants "came on buses" to Schenectady, they helped to expose contradictions in Americanization ideologies reflected in a variety of narratives (explicit and latent) concerning family, nationality, religion, culture, economics, and, most noticeably, race-ethnicity. Interestingly—even surprisingly, given the usual prominence of religion in narratives of conversion and assimilation—even as Guyanese immigrants came to the notice of the city because of their interest in building a Hindu temple, the question of religion was never really subsequently raised in the public discourse concerning their assimilation to the city. Instead, as the mayor frankly admitted, Schenectady had seen some hard times, and he eagerly anticipated the infusion of new capital, a reinvigorated work ethic, and an immigrant appreciation for the possibilities of relocation. This sentiment was represented by the optimistic words on photocopied packets provided to visitors on bus tours, next to an official seal of Incorporation for the City of Schenectady and below a picture of Mayor Jurczynski: "The word will continue to be spread that if you are willing to work hard, if you are committed to family values, if you are looking for a great new home, then the City of Schenectady is the place for you." Public declarations such as this conspicuously invoke elements of American Dreams: for example, we might hear echoes of narratives about Americans as allegedly a "chosen" people (e.g., the quasi-religious "word" that will spread), as well as America representing increased possibilities of achieving belonging (or "a great new home," which were also literally for sale, although most were old *and* in poor repair) in a classless meritocracy. Thus, GuyaneseOpportunities announced that Schenectady, as a symbol of America, was a place of opportunity for any individual prepared to pull him- or herself up by the bootstraps.

The association made with good citizenship to "family values" and "home" is also a common national theme. Sanchez advises that early twentieth-century assimilation programs often validated traditional family structures—as compared to official and other perceptions that families were obstacles to assimilation (because they would preserve immigrant culture and produce similarly "ethnic" future generations), as in the case for workers such as Chinese immigrant bachelor communities in the late nineteenth century. Indeed, Progressive-era "programs depended on the cohesion of the Mexican family to achieve their goal of assimilation" and as a means of transmitting American values (Sanchez 290–91). However, this rhetoric implies as much inclusion as exclusion. Whose family values? we must ask. And does a "commitment" to family values imply a legal arrangement? If so, does the language welcoming a community of industrious immigrants into the fold implicitly reject those who, because of national or state legislation, cannot legally "commit" to family, such as gay and lesbian Americans? And if this message is one of the ways in which GuyaneseOpportunities signaled the version of America to which newcomers were expected to assimilate, what might the consequences be for anyone who failed to conform?

Schenectady's mayor, as the person who was most associated with GuyaneseOpportunities, is a useful source of information about its intentions. In fact, many people felt that the initiative was the mayor's personal hobbyhorse. As one reporter put it in Albany's *Business Review,* "If you asked outgoing Schenectady Mayor Al Jurczynski what he is most proud of during his time as mayor, he would say unequivocally that it was his role in attracting Guyanese immigrants to the city" (McFadden). Mayor Jurczynski seems to have been "carrying on Americanization work," a phrase used to describe historical programs for integrating immigrants (Hill 625). By fall 2002, in the five months that Schenectady had been actively recruiting Indo-Guyanese, one thousand more had joined a similar number already residing in the vicinity. Later, the mayor made more news by undertaking a "diplomatic" trip to Guyana in 2003 to meet with President Bharrat Jagdeo, at which time Jurczynski floated the possibility of promoting immigration directly from Guyana's capital city of Georgetown to Schenectady.[24]

For all of these efforts at expanding GuyaneseOpportunities, Schenectady's mayor gained a great deal of public attention himself. For example, shortly before I spoke with the mayor, he was featured on the NPR program *This American Life,* as part of an episode called "Middlemen." Broadcast in October 2002, the segment concerning Mayor Jurczynski began with quite a lofty comparison. The narrator intoned,

> Moses was this great leader who brought the Israelis out of Egypt. . . .
> This is the story of someone who is something like that. Most of the people [Al Jurczynski] has convinced to move from the Bronx and Queens are people who emigrated there from the South American country of Guyana. These are people whose ancestors mostly came from India and Africa. (Dorr)

According to Dorr, the radio program's producer, "for a while, Al Jurczynski had this idea to lure Hasidic Jews to Schenectady. He wanted to repopulate certain problem neighborhoods with a group that was self reliant, family oriented and tightly knit. That idea went nowhere. But then, last year some Guyanese people came to him for help, getting an abandoned church for religious services." Dorr's invocation of a type of spiritual exodus for Guyanese immigrants certainly conformed to certain repeated themes that Jurczynski associated with the GuyaneseOpportunities plans. It also interestingly paired Orthodox Jews and a group of Asians, who have sometimes been stereotyped as the "new" Jews because of their purported ability to assimilate and succeed, especially economically.

In championing the Guyanese, Mayor Al saw himself as a leader with an expansive vision trying to engineer a better future for his community; he compared himself not to Moses but to iconic American emancipators. When I asked him about some negative responses to the recruitment of Guyanese immigrants to Schenectady, he responded,

> You know what? I am going to recite something Abraham Lincoln once said: he once said, "If I were to try to read, much less answer, all of the attacks made on me, the shop might as well be closed for any other business. I do the very best I know how with the very best I can, and I need to keep doing so until the end. If the end brings me out all right, what is said against me will not amount to anything, but if the end brings me out wrong, ten angels swearing I was right would make no difference." Now, I feel very, very strongly that the time I spent with the Guyanese is the right thing to do in Schenectady's best interest.

Jurczynski certainly worked very hard on his plans for improving Schenectady and assisting the Guyanese: people remarked with some wonder that he was inviting people to call him on his personal cell phone to learn more about his city. He made multiple announcements on a radio program hosted in Queens by Herman Singh, who was an active participant in GuyaneseOpportunities initiatives. Part of Jurczynski's motivation, he told me, was to help "Schenectady to become the Guyanese capital of North America." Jurczynski connected contemporary assimilation processes with what "happened with [his] grandparents when they came to this country," but what he felt was "cutting edge" was the tremendous effort he was putting in as a public official welcoming newer immigrants (personal interview, 9 July 2003).

It was through a series of pragmatic encounters that Mayor Jurczynski developed such a public association with Indo-Guyanese and became an unexpected ally for a group of people from a nation with which he was initially completely unfamiliar. Before being approached by a local resident about the possibility of having a Hindu temple in the city, Jurczynski admits, "I did not know whether it was Guyanese or Guinean—British Guyana, Dutch Guyana, French Guyana. I did not know how it was pronounced, did not even know where it was, could not have even picked it out on a map if somebody asked." Like many Americans probably do, Jurczynski associated Guyana primarily with the Jonestown massacre in the late 1970s. Eventually, though, the mayor came to feel that the Indo-Guyanese were immigrants in a mold very familiar to him, from his own Polish and his wife's Italian immigrant backgrounds. Jurczynski shared with me,

> It was a very good chemistry. [Guyanese who came to see me] set me straight within the first ten minutes and said, "We do not believe in public assistance. We feel that is a conflict if someone is on public assistance unless they really deserve it, you know." And I said, "Gee, you are singing my tune." . . . Of course, it was a Hindu Temple. Who the hell would have ever thought that there would ever be a Hindu temple in Schenectady?

Despite the mayor's initial surprise at the notion of a Hindu temple in the Albany Capital District, he came to feel ever happier about Guyanese immigration to his city, repeatedly returning to their self-sufficiency as an American value. The main reasons he reported for feeling such "chemistry" included a Guyanese commitment to self-improvement, a sense of traditionalism, and a feeling of family. He expressed amazement at similarities between his experiences and the Guyanese, with both having "very strong, strong family ties and bonds." He went on to say briefly that it was also "macho stuff, you know, and their appreciation of females, . . . so much like Italian households" (personal interview, 24 October 2002).

Reflecting the personal, hands-on approach he took in the assimilation of immigrants who he clearly felt were in the American grain, Jurczynski spent his Saturdays over several summers working to recruit the Guyanese to Schenectady via the infamous bus tours. A typical Saturday, as he described it, began at about 10:30 a.m., when buses pulled up in front of City Hall, then "we have people from the Chamber of Commerce, the hospitals, the school district, the economic-development offices, the small-business people, and we all give our little pitch for Schenectady, and they answer any questions they have, and then after that we break for lunch" (personal interview, 9 July 2003). Some of the services that Schenectady officials and private interests advertised to potential recruits included résumé assistance, legal advice about naturalization procedures, literacy and language training, and access to education. There were Guyanese Americans already living in the area who also participated in the events, such as Elcid Ramotar (of the SEDC), who offered help in dealing with landlords or developing interview skills, and Hemwatie Ramasami (from the mayor's office), who discussed building permits, zoning issues, or the possibility of starting small businesses. After lunch, Jurczynski narrated a four- to five-hour bus tour of Schenectady, which included rides through neighborhoods with abandoned houses in need of industrious new owners. In those cases in which such houses were eventually sold, although at very low prices, it saved the city the cost of demolishing properties that had sometimes been severely neglected by absentee landlords.

Friendly and earnest in the desire to live in a diverse American city that was also economically prosperous, Jurczynski, when discussing GuyaneseOpportunities, consistently alluded to familiar narratives of American exceptionalism and industriousness. During our second interview, he emphasized his belief that "this is a great county, the best country in the world, and anybody can make it." In many different venues when discussing the Guyanese, Jurczynski focused on self-reliance, economic success, and the immigrant work ethic. In particular, he compared this new immigrant community to his ancestors in America and his siblings who "own their own homes as part of the American Dream." In his self-selected role as mentor and adviser to newer immigrants, which earned him a great deal of respect and positive regard within the Schenectady Guyanese community, Jurczynski was convinced that they would be able "to realize the American dream," although certainly "not without working for it." In response to concerns that he was not serving his constituency as a whole but instead "favoring" Guyanese immigrants, the mayor declared that not all people in Schenectady were as willing to work as hard as the Guyanese and that this was what motivated others to resentment. Jurczynski elaborated on this point in an interview with Kim Martineau, staff writer for the *Times Union,* when he said, "Too many people, I think, jump on the band wagon on racial discrimination when they never took up the opportunity to finish high school" (B1). Almost exactly a year later, he clarified for me: "I get sick over that because, in my mind, it goes against everything that is American. American is not about government taking care of you [if you are able-bodied]" (personal interview, 9 July 2003). Like Robertson, who declared that his city was very much in need of a new ethnic group, Jurczynski too expressed a sense of frustration with current Schenectady demographics and seemed convinced that the influx of a new group could only be a boon to the area.

The Racial Economics of Assimilation

It was no secret that, along with Mayor Jurczynski's sense of immigrant similarity, the feelings of "family" and familiarity that he expressed for Indo-Guyanese were bolstered by unabashedly economic motivations. The men (and they almost all seem to have been men) associated with the initiative maintained two intertwined assumptions. Primarily, people involved with various GuyaneseOpportunities efforts envisioned a revitalized local economy. They were also invested in strengthening the city's flagging tax base or earning a profit for themselves as individual investors, real estate brokers, employers, and so on. As Jurczynski tells it, the initiative was particularly promoted by a Guyanese American businessman, whose "motivation is to make money. And also he is a guy with a big heart. . . . But he is a very, very shrewd businessman, good businessman. I am the mayor; he is a businessman from New York City. . . . He is doing it for a profit," Jurczynski concluded, confirming that the guy with "a big heart" sought personal, monetary compensation for acting as the middleman between his own ethnic community and the mayor of a small upstate city looking forward to better times (personal interview, 24 October 2002).

The second major assumption of GuyaneseOpportunities was based on specific readings of "Indian" identity as a cultural model for successful assimilation and as including particular immigrant "gifts." Describing another location where an ethnic Indian community has been highly visible, S. Mitra Kalita writes in *Suburban Sahibs* that, in Edison, New Jersey, "Asian immigrants, the so-called model minority, were lauded for the success they had achieved professionally and academically in a short amount of time" (109). As Indian immigrants have done in that part of central New Jersey (with both positive and negative reactions from others), there was initially a great deal of optimism in Schenectady that new Guyanese residents would start businesses, open restaurants, and buy more properties to expand their community, all without seeking any welfare funds. These projections, which have not been borne out, were based on the supposition that Indo-Guyanese would be hardworking, compliant immigrants (like those who dominate American mythology) who would do anything to fit in. As Sharmila Rudrappa recognizes has been historically true, "adopting American national identity entailed the development of a particular kind of work culture" (151). Unsurprisingly, then, nearly every interview with, article about, and speech by Mayor Jurczynski mentioned the Guyanese work ethic and their refusal to burden the nearly empty coffers of a city like Schenectady. Jurczynski felt an affiliation for this type of "ethnic" identity in America and, according to him, the Indo-Guyanese "cannot believe that a Caucasian mayor is welcoming them to this city, . . . but I tell them there are two kinds of white men: there are full bloods, and there are ethnics. And I tell them I am an ethnic, and I say the funny thing is that I look at Guyanese and I view them as ethnics" (personal interview, 9 July 2003).

There were particular types of racial economics that rendered the Indo-Guyanese familiar "ethnics" to an American mayor several generations removed from European ancestry. All of the relevant parties presumed complicated matrices of racial-ethnic relations; their understandings of certain identities often matched, but there were also dramatic inconsistencies that became apparent in opinions aired in the public culture. In *Callaloo Nation*, anthropologist Aisha Khan relates such varied types of classifications among South Asian Caribbeaners (in Trinidad) to the "capacity of the concept of racial difference to take on a variety of discursive modes" and "to represent other forms of difference" (31). As one example of this phenomenon, the mayor distinguished "ethnics" such as himself and the Indo-Guyanese from other American "minorities." He explained, "I could say that the Guyanese are minorities, and by the true sense of the word they are. But they don't fit in my mind as the typical stereotype of what a minority is in this country." Acknowledging that there were always exceptions, Jurczynski felt that a general distinction could be made:

> You think of an Indian, you think of an Afro-American. You know? There is a different perception for each one. . . . The people in Schenectady called them Guyanese, but I look at

> Guyanese and they basically share all of my values. . . . They are family oriented, they disdain public assistance, they like to own, they don't like to rent. There is a bond or kinship, and I think that that is a model for ethnics in this country. (Personal interview, 9 July 2003)

When asked if this were not a repetition of the "model-minority myth," he responded, "I am glad you asked that because this has been very interesting. White people have a tremendous guilt about how they relate to minorities, because they are always being reminded that they are racist. And you never really have a chance to really test yourself" (personal interview, 9 July 2003). As he participated in assimilation efforts associated with GuyaneseOpportunities, Jurczynski seemed highly conscious of opportunities to define "Americanness" across ethnic differences and to test himself as a particular type of person—perhaps to expiate the white "guilt" to which he alluded?

In the context of such racial economics, GuyaneseOpportunities was consistently informed by perceptions concerning the racial-ethnic identity of the new immigrant group, as well as ideas about America's racial majority and other ethnic minority groups. Nor was it only public officials who participated in the dialogue, although many Schenectady residents did object to the lack of systematic communication about developments in the city. The owner of a shop in Schenectady's downtown area seemed to be well informed about GuyaneseOpportunities and his interpretation is fairly consistent with others I encountered:

> There was a huge Guyanese community, like the Amish, that had reached the maximum expansion capability where they were and were looking to move further out. And [Jurczynski] said, "Come up to Schenectady. We have tons of these impoverished properties. We have a lot of stuff that we own that we can give you incentives to buy and rehab." The first, I think, ripple from that that I heard was people starting to scream, "Why weren't we offered the same deal?" And the city's position was, "Well, the deal was already there—we just never made it obvious to you." (Personal interview, 24 October 2002)

To liken the Guyanese to the Amish is to invoke traditionalism and conservatism. As a contrast, those doing the "screaming" (implying excessively loud complaining, one assumes) were mostly African American. However, other Schenectady residents also objected to incentives that seemed to be focusing on a particular minority group and almost purposefully excluding others.

In response to such concerns about racial discrimination, many Schenectady residents rallied behind initiatives to recruit Indo-Guyanese immigrants, because they agreed with the mayor's reasoning that the group would bring positive change to the city. These views became part of the public culture as multiple types of texts, such as local opinion pieces, postings to online forums, speeches made during city meetings, and even in casual social conversation. An optimistic attitude toward GuyaneseOpportunities was also reiterated in public discussions outside of Schenectady, as evidenced by a *New York Daily News* headline that read, "Immigrants Flocking to an Upstate Haven," for an article by staff writer Warren Woodberry. An editorial in Syracuse's *Post-Standard* matched the tone of this headline, noting that Guyanese "have brought a new vibrancy to the city with a formula others can emulate" ("Consider This"). Similar views within the city included a letter to the editor of Schenectady's *Daily Gazette* in August 2003, in which Robert J. Serotta (a county legislator) described the "hard-working" character of Guyanese families and the "positive contribution to the neighborhood" they had made. Serotta hoped that their "pride and confidence can be contagious." One poster to an online forum declared, "Everyone is welcome here" (PatZ), and other Schenectady residents agreed that racial issues would not preclude Guyanese immigrants from assimilating to Schenectady. Another poster went so far as to say "thank you" to "Guyanese people, for coming here and causing such a stir. . . . We're already made up of every ethnic and religious group I can think of, so the Guyanese should fit right in" (Pat).

However, there was another side to the story of these bright visions of GuyaneseOpportunities, an aspect that touched on some of the most persistent disagreements about Americanization, which many people in Schenectady confronted in ambivalent ways. In the congratulatory editorial from the *Post-Standard,* the writer pointed out the ambivalence when cautioning that Jurczynski's "good example"

> must be applied to Schenectady's other ethnic groups of blacks, Hispanics and Asians to fully build on the wealth of the city's diversity. The mayor has been criticized by some of the city's black residents for not working as hard with other ethnic groups and implying that other, long-time residents don't have as strong a work ethic as the Guyanese do. That must be addressed. ("Consider This")

Eric J. Edwards went a degree further in an op-ed in Albany's *Times Union* when he asked, "How can any city official favor one group of people and not discriminate against others?" There were many people who expressed similar concerns about the racial economics of GuyaneseOpportunities and who were less than sanguine about how Schenectady was going to be transformed or who really belonged in this "upstate haven."

When such concerns represented what Jurczynski called "the race card" (personal interview, 9 July 2003), the racialized narratives that inspired GuyaneseOpportunities were again deployed to deflect allegations of discrimination or favoritism. This became clear in a lengthy essay by a local pundit, Carl Strock, in his column for the *Daily Gazette*. Strock's piece, from the same month when many of the glowing reviews were being published elsewhere, posed the provocative question, "Who heads the nativist block in Schenectady?" The answer he gave was surprising: Strock named two "bloc heads," Schenectady city councilmen, one of them described as a racial minority and the other as an advocate for the rights of veterans and the disabled. Apparently, both councilmen had asked questions about the fairness of GuyaneseOpportunities, similar to those which had been raised repeatedly in Schenectady since word of the bus trips spread. However, Strock expected the connections to minority status or causes to silence their doubts. He found it "beyond imagining" that one of the councilmen, "since he's African-American," was not sympathetic to the Guyanese. Strock hazarded, "You might think he'd be a little more sensitive to group generalizations." Along with refuting the implication that "the newcomers somehow have a leg up" on others in Schenectady, Strock also concluded that the irony of this situation was that no one objected to the "many affirmative action programs I've seen" in Schenectady. In the case of Guyanese immigrants, Strock complained, some "elected officials frown *darkly* and wonder what 'those people' are up to" (emphasis added).

The phrase "those people" is a politically loaded one that was used in the public discourse in Schenectady to ascribe racist motivations to certain interpretations of GuyaneseOpportunities. Just as critiques of GuyaneseOpportunities were usually based on concerns about racial discrimination, so too was Strock convinced that individuals opposed to or questioning of GuyaneseOpportunities must be guilty of prejudice and bigotry—albeit toward a different minority group. To accuse Schenectady residents of fearing "those people" taps into a historical concern about the ethnic "hordes" who might transform America for the worse. Speek, for example, noted the dangers posed by ethnic enclaves, in which "colonies" of immigrants might agitate for rights but refuse the hail to assimilate. He asserted that "immigrants came here and were allowed to land and settle with the understanding that they would become Americanized—become Americans—not that they would perpetuate their nationality by forming compact and self-sufficient" groups (Speek 249). Rejecting this fear, Jurczynski joked about the possibility of Schenectady's being "overrun" by Guyanese immigrants. He claimed, "If I am the only white guy left in Schenectady, I would be totally happy. . . . Schenectady will be a better city because of it." For Jurczynski, this was "a very American story": "and it goes back to me being an ethnic. . . . That is probably why I can relate to it: it's because I have heard the Polack [*sic*] jokes, and I heard the stories from my grandparents when they came here" (personal interview, 9 July 2003). With this dismissal of a certain kind of racial fear, Jurczynski supported his reading of GuyaneseOpportunities as a process that would ameliorate rather than worsen the cultural and economic situation in Schenectady.

Like Mayor Jurczynski, many people in Schenectady were persuaded of a positive outcome to GuyaneseOpportunities, going so far as to impute "dark" motives to people who did not share their views. In fact, certain people in Schenectady seemed almost gleeful at being authorized to chastise racial minorities and lower-income residents whom they claimed simply could not be as hardworking or likable as the Guyanese—or they surely would have *already* made the most of opportunities available to them. Strock made his own attitude explicit with his "honest evaluation" in the conclusion to his column:

> These new Guyanese-American immigrants are showing up the long-established self-pitiers of Schenectady, both black and white.
>
> It looks bad for these locals who complain they can't get ahead without government help if a new group moves in enthusiastically and does just fine without government help, and especially if the newcomers are brown-skinned, as the Guyanese are. That undercuts the racism argument and it prompts resentment.

Obviously agreeing with Strock's point of view, one Schenectady resident characterized people at a city council meeting who were complaining about GuyaneseOpportunities as unfairly criticizing an admirable group of immigrants (Observant). This writer described detractors to GuyaneseOpportunities as "gimme gimme" people and cited a woman who "axed" the mayor for a property like the ones he was giving "those people." Both this Schenectady resident and Strock seemed either to be unaware or to ignore that the local government, through the office of the mayor, was very directly "giving" something to Guyanese immigrants (arguably only the intangible "help" of support and welcome, although these often lead to other types of assistance) in a way that was inconsistent with the status quo of the city. This misunderstanding allowed such critics to stage racialized attacks on communities such as African Americans who have historically been oppressed as a group, rather than being "thanked" for their presence in Schenectady or in America.

Paying close attention to the subtexts, one becomes aware that GuyaneseOpportunities was at least partially an expression of deep-rooted frustrations with so-called problem minorities.[25] This was publicly signaled by the assumption that the "new" (read: model) minority community would be an improvement over the existing ethnic groups in Schenectady. The thinly veiled language about needing a new ethnic group served to summarily dismiss and disparage historically disprivileged and too often stereotyped groups, most notably African Americans. As summarized earlier, local forums in Schenectady both directly and indirectly touched on this sensitive subject, but Jurczynski soundly refuted the criticism that the Guyanese were being treated preferentially. During our first interview, he maintained that he did not care what color a person's skin was but lauded the Guyanese:

> [They] are just wonderful people: dedicated and, you know, [they] do not goof off. And I do not want to say that other minorities as a general rule goof off. You evaluate everybody for who they are and what they are—you know something, if somebody is no account and lazy, I do not want to be around them. I do not want to be around losers. . . . My son, . . . who is eleven years old, his best friend is . . . black, you know. [He] is a good kid. (Personal interview, 24 October 2002)

Either by deflecting the topic of race or by adopting a strategy of "color blindness,"[26] many people (including officials like the mayor, current and new residents of Schenectady, Guyanese and non-Guyanese) refused to confront how influential racial economics were in projects for assimilating a unique group of immigrants to America.

No matter the prevalence of certain racial hierarchies that presume otherwise, Guyanese immigrants cannot simply be categorized within the "Indian" model minority, not without ignoring specific historical and cultural elements of their identities. It is particularly ironic that GuyaneseOpportunities was based on fundamental distinctions between types of "ethnics" or "minorities," since the community does not conform to certain pervasive distinctions. People designing GuyaneseOpportunities initiatives seemed to presume that Guyanese immigrants were good bets for contemporary Americanization based on racial hierarchies that privilege Asian Americans over African Americans. However, by common racial designations, Guyanese are *usually* African and Asian as well as Caribbean Americans. The U.S. Census does not differentiate between people of Indian and African ancestry, but only about two-thirds of this demographic are likely to be ethnically Indian. And this is still not the whole story: many Guyanese today may well be a mixture of both Indian ancestry and African ancestry. For example, Schenectady resident Hemwatie Ramasami calls herself racially "mixed,"[27] but she believes many other Guyanese refuse to admit this about themselves openly. Similarly, Khan reports in her academic study that "much of the scholarly literature on Trinidad has commented on the minimal intermarriage between Indo- and Afro-Trinidadians. Many have surmised that these two populations carry their aversion to the point of boundaries on sexual intimacy. . . . The number of 'douglas' (offspring of Indo and Afro), however, belies this assumption" (9). Affirming this same point, in *The Caribbean Postcolonial,* Shalini Puri links the word *dougla* (meaning "illegitimate") to a methodology for trying to understand the mixed peoples in the Caribbean, suggesting that a "dougla poetics" offers a nuanced discourse of hybridity precisely because of the complicated and often unacknowledged histories the concept represents.

Nearly a century after Progressivism gave rise to a concentration of Americanization plans that operated on many flawed assumptions, GuyaneseOpportunities initiatives also relied on some questionable premises about what assimilation to national and other cultures signifies. As most of the people centrally involved with GuyaneseOpportunities acknowledged, both insiders and outsiders to the Indo-Guyanese community hoped to reap economic benefits (either individually or for the city of Schenectady) from the relocation of an immigrant population stereotypically identified as having a good "work ethic." Given that the stereotype was actually developed around a historically distinct demographic within the same diasporic community (i.e., post-1965, primarily middle-class South Asians relocating from the subcontinent to the United States), and even if it was borne out by individual Indo-Guyanese Americans, this assumption compounded rather than clarified other inconsistencies.

Development strategies for Schenectady relied on what appeared to be sincere admiration for and encouragement of Indo-Guyanese "cultural differences" as practiced in their homes, temples, or churches and on "Guyana Day" at Schenectady's Central Park. However, because there are "two kinds of cultural differences—those that threaten and those that do not" (Rudrappa 188), these hardworking, family-centered national subjects were expected to prove nonthreatening by assimilating to specific racial economics. The public expectations created some tensions for those Guyanese immigrants who maintained a suspicion of bureaucracy, resulting from the legacy of British imperialism, corruption scandals in postindependence Guyana, and fears common to American immigrants who may perceive their legal status to be precarious. This calls to mind a type of subtle coercion that can be described as a "white in public, ethnic at home" paradigm (Rudrappa 22), one of many contradictory, even racist, phenomena which undermine contemporary multicultural activities such as those so often represented in GuyaneseOpportunities.

Guyanese Americans in Schenectady: "How the Story Was Told to Us"

In this section, the focus is on how the story of Guyanese immigrants accommodating to Schenectady was told to me. To find out how members of the targeted immigrant group responded to the complicated ideologies associated with GuyaneseOpportunities, I asked them directly. Along with information gathered from sources listed earlier, I spoke with many self-identified Indians from Guyana who resided in Schenectady, some who had been there decades and others under a year, as well as with other residents of the area, local officials, and business owners. I also came to understand more about mixed identities in Guyana during a research trip there. In this way, in addition to asking how others hoped to Americanize them, I learned about assimilation, nationality, and ethnicity from the immigrant group in question, which has not consistently, or even often, been accomplished in historicizing Americanization projects.

One of my interviewees narrated, in her words, "how the story was told to us," recounting that her great-grandparents had been "fooled into getting aboard a British ship, and they were brought to Guyana"[28]—but coming to America was "a totally different issue from getting migrated to Guyana": "The only reason we came here was for betterment." When speaking with Guyanese Americans in Schenectady, I heard many similar stories. Collectively, they recounted a willingness to accommodate many local and national expectations in exchange for betterment, but they frequently expressed a degree of ambivalence about being "just" American. They spoke instead about their sense of having multiple identities. And while some aspects of these identities were highlighted during GuyaneseOpportunities campaigns (e.g., the model minority, Indian work ethic), others were ignored or downplayed (e.g., the African and Caribbean influences that are stereotyped differently according to American racial ideologies). This raises the theoretical question of whether Guyanese immigrants were expected to "achieve"[29] a proscribed type of American identity that was meant to pull a veil over other consciousnesses.

As contemporary texts representing South Asian identities in America, ethnographic accounts from Schenectady represented unique ethnic, national, and diasporic positionalities typified by Indo-Guyanese communities. The disciplinizing efforts to assimilate "coolies" in British Guiana resulted in a collective ethnic-national designation—Indo-Guyanese—for a group which might well have been segregated according to castes and languages inherited from India, if not for (self-interested) British interventions. The "Indianness" of the Guyanese became something new and different removed from the location of the subcontinent, as happens throughout the diaspora. Unlike some other locations of resettlement, however, those who came in ships to Guyana mostly stayed there, in contrast to those who went to Kenya, for example, from which journeys back to South Asia were more viable.[30] The adherence to certain traditional South Asian categories tended to wane in Guyana, while they remained more central to affiliations in some other parts of the diaspora.

In contrast to how others in Schenectady or in America generally perceived the Guyanese immigrants or to what may usually be implicit assumptions of (un)official Americanization projects, the Guyanese routinely claimed "kind of a mixed culture." In conversation, they shifted between national, ethnic, and panethnic names for their own identities. As Khan suggested in response to my first draft of this chapter presented at the "Annual Conference on South Asia" in Madison, Wisconsin, in 2005, interpretations of Indian identity associated with Guyanese immigrants in Schenectady are familiar from other ethno-cultural narratives in the Caribbean milieu. Khan elaborates that "mixing" is "a literal and metaphorical expression for all forms of experience where biogenetic, social, or cultural boundaries are challenged or transgressed." She further explains, "'Mixing' is among the most persevering of cultural themes in most Caribbean and Latin American countries, coming in a variety of forms" (2), representing both hope and threat. And Schenectady's Guyanese residents did name themselves simultaneously as Indian via custom or religion, Guyanese due to birth or origins, East Indian *and* West Indian, culturally pan-Caribbean, and American[31] in lifestyle. (One clearly shared attitude was a strong dissociation from the British, who were considered previous rulers and oppressors but not usually cultural influences, as compared to some elite South Asians on the subcontinent.)

These intersecting identities suggest that there may *not* be a way to definitively name such historically layered (trans)national affiliations according to current nomenclatures. As Carter and Torabully write in the introduction to their book, to emphasize cultural plurality in this manner is to recognize "complexity—and not clarity" (9), which can seem counterintuitive when one aims to "identify" an individual or a culture. Teasing out this complexity, appropriations of historically pejorative concepts such as coolitude, *mestizo*, mixed, and *négritude* have resulted in reexaminations of earlier epistemologies of group identities. Based on different geographies and histories, analyses of these phenomena by famous thinkers such as Gloria Anzaldúa, Aimé Césaire, Édouard Glissant, and others in dialogue and debate have resulted in helpful paradigms for appreciating identities that exceed ethnic and national boundaries. And these metaphors have suggested how extranational identifications operate for all contemporary subjects, even those without obviously mixed genealogies. Khan provides a useful gloss on these processes when she writes that, in Trinidad,

> *callaloo* symbolizes that felicitous and mutually transforming combination of cultural, racial, and religious diversity. Literally, *callaloo* is the name of a national dish, not surprisingly, a stew with many ingredients. As metaphors, both *callaloo* and *mixed* refer to a heterogeneity that connotes democratic (equal) political representation, a cosmopolitan worldview, and therefore consummate modernity in a global context. (8)

There is a great deal of variation in how one might interpret, positively or more suspiciously, the type of identity "stew" Khan theorizes here, since "people have multiple, and sometimes contradictory, reasons for being invested in particular identities" (Khan 3). Validating this reading, Guyanese immigrants in Schenectady spoke broadly and in matter-of-fact ways about being culturally mixed, but they also invoked different identities in different moments.

In addition to considering themselves simultaneously Guyanese and American, for example, interviewees narrated "Indian" affiliations in sometimes unanticipated and certainly contextually shifting ways.[32] A sense of needing to explain "what happened to our culture" was repeated several times, especially in the context of how ethnicities had been read in Schenectady via an expected Hinduism that has actually metamorphosed dramatically since migration from India to Guyana in the nineteenth century. Such stories of South Asian interpellation through religion have played out elsewhere in the United States; for instance, sociologist Prema Kurien concludes about two Indian groups in Los Angeles that they "made the transition from sojourners to citizens by developing a Hindu American community and identity" or "becoming American by becoming Hindu" (37). Kurien reads such group identities as a *re*-invention of Hinduism and suggests that categorization as an ethno-*religious* community can serve to skirt racial tensions. She thus argues that such a story of Americanization may result in material advantages as well as empowerment for the immigrants in their "symbolic" rather than (somehow) "real" ethnicity. Such innovative diasporic patterns of integration within particular national narratives were corroborated by the ways in which Schenectady Guyanese named "traditional channels," as one interviewee interpreted them, through which religious practices, Hindu names, and Bollywood popular culture circulated. Most of those with whom I spoke in Schenectady did claim Indian culture or religion in terms we might call broadly diasporic, although none had been to India and they did not recall other Guyanese in recent generations making that reverse-diasporic trip. Further reflecting the "distance" from the geographical location of the subcontinent as well as other localized definitions of Indian culture, interviewees identified themselves as "East Indian," which was the common racial designation in Guyana, as well as "West Indian," Christopher Columbus's geographic misnaming to signify people in the Caribbean.

When asked about "Asian" identity in relation to the Guyanese, however, one interviewee answered, "Anything with Asian, I would probably think of India or China or in that direction. I would not associate it with the Caribbean. . . . I would hate to check off 'Asian' because that is not following directly to the East Indian." As Rudrappa makes plain, "Just because South Asian Americans come from a particular geographical region does not automatically constitute them into a natural community" (25). To emphasize that *no* community is "natural," the same interviewee told me that, in Guyana, she would have checked off "East

Indian" or "other" (if offered a choice among such categories as "Caucasian," "black," and "other"). However, in the United States, "Indian" and "Caribbean" were the most significant categories for her.

For the Guyanese immigrants with whom I spoke, the Caribbean connections were undeniable, whereas there seemed to be more precarious (if no less significant) claims to Indian identity. This may be because India was so often an abstraction to represent why they did some of the things they did, whereas the Caribbean was so immediately present in geography and culture. Expressing both types of affiliation simultaneously, ethnic Indians throughout the Caribbean historically developed strong cultural networks, not least through intermarriages. Although they do not share nationality, they share pan-Caribbean histories. This, plus the perceived commonality of Indian ethnicity, made for welcome marital matches, according to some of my interlocutors. Also, the prevalence of such marriages may be explained by such emotional motivations as when one interviewee poignantly expressed a "great yearning for Indian culture." Although many of the Guyanese immigrants professed extremely limited knowledge about India's historical or contemporary politics (as is also depicted in Shani Mootoo's short story with an Indo-Caribbean narrator, from which the second epigraph to this chapter comes), those who had children expressed a strong preference for them to marry other ethnic Indians from any part of the world. Although this at first struck me as potentially contradictory to the other identities claimed by Guyanese immigrants, it proved helpful to remember Caribbean conjunctures in order to interpret this focused affinity for Indians. There is explanatory power to Stuart Hall's theory about how (African) culture has functioned in the construction of some Caribbean identities, such that it is "a way of imposing an imaginary coherence on the experience of dispersal and fragmentation, which is the history of all enforced diasporas" ("Cultural Identity and Diaspora" 235). As he puts it, it is the very "presence/absence" of the cultural space—which is India in the case of Schenectady Guyanese—that makes it the "privileged signifier of new conceptions of Caribbean identity" (241).

Also, in America, Guyanese immigrants invoke Indian ethnicity as an implicit way of leveraging certain racial economics. In the Indo-Trinidadian case, Khan argues that, when claiming ethnic Indian identities, individuals place "new kinds of emphases on the 'high culture' of their civilization, great traditions, and authentic heritage" (58–59). According to Khan, Indo-Caribbean communities interpret religion through race, and race through religion, to construct identities shaped by and in response to colonial discourses. Even more tellingly, they mobilize this claim of ethnic inheritance in the context of social uplift, such that Indo-Caribbeaners might access "forms of assimilation that could empower them through fortifying identities as distinct, nationally recognized, racial-cultural constituencies, recognized on the basis of certain key emblems" (Khan 63). Thus, for descendants of Indian laborers in the Caribbean, a particular type of ethnic affiliation potentially affords them cultural capital that they might not otherwise be able to claim. More broadly, as Peter van der Veer writes, "Those who do not think of themselves as Indians before migration become Indians in diaspora" ("Introduction" 7); although he is speaking of migration from the subcontinent elsewhere, his remarks are perhaps even more significant for Indo-Caribbean communities who encounter the varying salience of Indian ethnicity through multiple migrations. Additionally, this identity that might usually be named "ethnic" or "cultural" is often shaped around presumptions of religion as well. Sucheta Mazumdar contends (in a critique of Hindu nationalisms) that Hinduism in America "serves as a bridge to link the immigrants of Indian origin from Fiji, Guyana, Britain, and Africa," allowing "upwardly mobile immigrants not from the subcontinent cultural linkages that distinguish them from the Afro-Caribbean and African legacies" (249–50).

Due to these conflated identities often associated with the concept of "Indian," Guyanese Americans in Schenectady earned metaphorical, and sometimes social, mobility by being associated with a model minority group. Similar to the colonial stereotype of the "enterprising" Indian laborers, what became possible through GuyaneseOpportunities initiatives was the potential for Guyanese immigrants to benefit from a situation that was explicitly constructed to profit the city of Schenectady or certain of its power brokers. The claim to a type of cultural "Indianness," whether or not it is officially recorded on the U.S. Census, allowed some Guyanese to accommodate themselves to the United States without becoming victims of a contemporary, possibly coercive Americanization scheme. As such, they became another group of immigrants who "attempted to bend and twist Americanism to fit their needs and aspirations" (Gerstle 546). This ability to "bend and twist" has limits, of course; several of my interviewees deferred the question of broader political representation to the future, as something that would eventually have to be systematically addressed by Guyanese Americans. This reminds us that transforming symbolic belonging into measurable citizenship rights is not an inevitable process and certainly cannot be taken for granted.

In narrating their identities, Guyanese immigrants in Schenectady co-opted many mixed metaphors of "Americanness," in addition to claiming multiple, intertwined cultures. Interviewees seemed to glory in narratives of the New World, without abandoning the desire to remain culturally distinct. As one person put it, "Coming to the U.S., we continue to do what we did in Guyana"—but she nonetheless followed up by saying, "I love America." Guyanese immigrants consistently mentioned the "the land of opportunity" and the ability for immigrants to achieve the American Dream if they were willing to work hard. Their self-narrations were reminiscent of John T. Adams's description of a dream "realized more fully in actual life" ("though very imperfectly") in America, of a classless society in which anyone could succeed "regardless of the fortuitous circumstances of birth or position" (415–16). For my interviewees, this dream was linked to the notion of community uplift, or to "make ourselves better than what our parents were, or what we were in Guyana." Their interpretations of assimilation in Schenectady, where many of the Guyanese moved to escape perceived negative aspects of an urban environment, affirm what Kalita writes about "the explosion in central New Jersey's Indian population," that "it is the suburb—with all its promise—that lures" (162). One person linked a desire for a better quality of life for his family in the suburbs to the discourse of immigrant gifts: "I present myself from a standpoint of doing something for them and in return open up the doors not just for me but for many other people like myself." Several interviewees similarly viewed immigrants as "going above and beyond what they are supposed to do."

Interestingly, during these conversations, Guyanese immigrants often differentiated between the implications of "becoming" versus "being" American. A successful businessman insisted, "It is the greatest country [my children] can want to live [in]," but he simultaneously opined, "For the average American, culture—I think it's boring." When asked, he defined culture as "how people live, from a standpoint, how they do things." This interviewee continued by saying, "I look at myself through many of my peers, and sometimes I look them in the eyes and think, 'I am more American than you are because I think your sense of value is a lot less than mine; you take more for granted.'" Other interviewees shared his conviction that newer immigrants have a greater ability than "average" Americans to appreciate what the nation truly represents. Another interviewee reasoned that immigrants are less likely to take for granted that "American culture is freedom"; in general, he felt, "people tend to abuse freedom."

The paradox was a striking one: immigrants wanted to assimilate to certain "cultural" traits of the nation—but they simultaneously implied that successful integration would mean an inability to value any longer what they currently identified as the nation's defining character. Jurczynski suggested something similar when explaining his commitment to Guyanese immigration to Schenectady. What "culture" meant varied from speaker to speaker, but many in Schenectady defined Americanization as an ability to recognize and take advantage of immigration as an opportunity for an improved quality of life. We might wonder: do most or many Americans interpret assimilation to mean that "success" somehow prevents later generations from actively striving for the American Dream? Srikanth's conclusion that, "perhaps, to be a better American means to challenge the nation to live up to its ideals," rather than taking those ideals as a given, may offer a possible answer (65)—and may also usefully anticipate readings of Bharati Mukherjee's controversial fiction, which I discuss in chapter 3.

Bracketing these thought-provoking contradictions for the moment, it is important to note that all of my interviewees focused on their belonging "in America now." They did not generally express the sojourner's sensibility about returning elsewhere, partly because the lack of economic and educational opportunities in Guyana seemed to discourage the development of a homeland mythology and also because India is quite remote, both in distance and in their direct experience. One common sentiment was, "I don't want to live [in Guyana], but I want to go back to see where I came from." Guyanese Americans described "loving our country" in reference to both Guyana and America, rather than defining their putative nationality based solely on the current place of residence. This claiming of two countries seems to reflect the inability of some groups to assimilate fully, since one interviewee noted that, for his son, "it's hard for him to say, 'I'm an American,' and then he looks like me." Another resignedly acknowledged, "I will not say I am accepted as an American," even after living in the United States for twenty years, especially after 9/11 aroused suspicion in some Americans about brown-skinned men. Despite feelings of exclusion such as this, Guyanese immigrants did not suggest that belonging was an unattainable goal for them. It helped that there were clear invitations to inclusion in Schenectady, represented so dramatically by GuyaneseOpportunities projects.

Describing experiences of belonging as well as alienation, interviewees represented assimilation not as a fully accomplished outcome but rather as an ongoing process of deciding how to narrate "kind of a mixed culture," or as a series of accommodations to sociopolitical imperatives. When Mayor Jurczynski stepped down from his position in 2004 in order to act as deputy chief of the Governor's Office of Small Cities (GOSC), some observers believed this to be an undeserved sinecure for an official under whose watch the city of Schenectady basically went bankrupt over eight years.[33] More certainly, Jurczynski's departure meant that there was no longer an official base of support for the continued Americanization of local Guyanese through such processes as legal advising, employment fairs, and the aid that can be provided by influential men in local politics. This leaves open the question of what was accomplished before the mayor left office.

Narrative and Other Implications of GuyaneseOpportunities

Over time, Indo-Guyanese immigration to Schenectady met with inconsistent, sometimes hotly debated, reactions. The dialogue surrounding GuyaneseOpportunities initiatives reminds us of the ways in which American narratives are constantly shifting in relation to new immigrants, whether to their benefit or not. The cultural texts associated with Guyanese Americans suggest noticeable continuities with the experiences of immigrant groups over the course of the twentieth century. For example, despite a commonly held belief that Americanization is a more fluid and diversity-friendly process today than in earlier periods, it may unfortunately demonstrate a greater resemblance to problematic assimilation projects of a century ago than Americans would generally like to admit.

More specifically, the potentially problematic racial economics of GuyaneseOpportunities projects bear out that a less than systematically acknowledged aspect of immigration to the United States has been the degree to which *trans*national developments unpredictably influence immigration and Americanization. As a case in point, in early 2006, Celia W. Dugger reported for the *New York Times* that a shortage of American-trained nurses might lead to policy opening up immigration from certain parts of the world. Dugger noted that a Senate provision to immigration legislation, "which removes the limit on the number of nurses who can immigrate," was "*largely overlooked* in the emotional debate over illegal immigration" (emphasis added). Even while certain nativist sentiments are again or continue running strongly against immigrants, whether "legal" or not, this Senate provision repeats a pattern of inviting and even attracting select Asian professionals to the United

States, a pattern that also existed in 1965, after the passage of the Hart-Cellar Act increased immigration quotas.

When we try to read immigrant experiences and integration within the American national imaginary, we must actively recognize that emigration to the United States owes to more than merely American issues and is often a reflection of cyclic economic trends on a global scale. For example, previously prevented from immigrating in large numbers, after 1965, South Asians gained preference through revised immigration policy and they are also likely to be impacted by the new legislation, since one of the targeted English-speaking but "poor nations" is India, where thousands of nurses a year already migrate due to the higher pay and benefits of American employment. If one solution to a shortage of certain types of trained personnel in the United States is to encourage immigration by foreign-trained individuals, then it must be acknowledged that the nation is as materially indebted to its immigrants as those immigrants may be said to be to their new government. The "magnetic pull" Dugger attributes to the United States is itself worth fuller elaboration, since another location likely to be influenced by this legislation is the Philippines, a former U.S. territory. E. San Juan Jr. argues that the contemporary "diaspora exhibits a peculiar configuration" because there is no "Filipino nation that they can identify with" (379), pointing to the neoimperialism which thoroughly informs certain histories of migration.

To forget historical, (trans)national circumstances when looking at particular immigrant communities—for example, when we try to make sense of and participate in current debates over immigration—results in dangerous binaristic ideologies which pit groups against one another, such as us versus them, American versus immigrant, and illegal versus legitimate. Who gets to be an American, indeed: the Philippines was once American in name, but its immigrants today are often figured as unwanted "aliens," and San Juan documents that "Filipino Americans as a whole have not made it" into the model minority (379). Such paradoxes of history, identity, and power are inevitably reproduced when transformative policy is enacted through what Dugger calls a "little-known provision" to a bill in the Senate. Invitations from the government or private industries have repeatedly recruited immigrants to the United States, but these are not necessarily acknowledged when times are tough. As in the case of Chinese workers who contributed at the turn of the twentieth century to the construction of the transcontinental railroad, invited immigrants are quickly transformed into undesirable outsiders when their labor is not as much in demand and racial economics work against particular groups. When we start to ask what the conditions were that resulted in the Chinese choosing or being forced to emigrate to begin with and historicize the high degree of internal strife as well as the poverty of displaced farmers in the middle to late 1800s in China, we start to get a fuller sense of the realities that shape immigrant communities for multiple generations after immigration.

In order to avoid too-narrow national analyses, it is important to locate communities such as South Asian Americans within a diasporic framework, which means presencing global influences as they have affected present-day Americans, if in primarily symbolic terms. It seems obvious to point out that the multiethnic United States, a nation of immigrants, owes much to the diverse cultures, religions, languages, and foods which were imported along with the many different groups who have relocated here. Yet the current wrangles over the proper treatment of undocumented immigrants often overlook such significant histories, and, unfortunately, African and Chicana/o Americans are among groups who continue to be considered "problems" for the nation. Even token attention to the history of complicated disputes over land between the United States and Mexico teaches us that the border has been an unstable and argued-over artifact for hundreds of years, that "Mexican" and "American" are not as neatly distinguished as many people would like. How to go forward after tangled and emotionally fraught past relations between these two contemporary nations is not obvious, nor will it be easy, but it might be a more efficient and certainly a more just proposition if the particularity of the past were not so often forgotten, with regard to both international political relations and minority-group histories. A physical fence seems an unlikely way to resolve these conflicts resulting from shifting boundaries and layered identities.

Theoretically, at least, searching for mechanisms to incorporate transnationalism into our visions of American identity might lead to more holistic, pragmatic, and egalitarian processes for assimilation projects. For example, challenging narratives of American exceptionalism, which equate good citizenship with a narrow range of ethnic and ideological parameters, may lead to a worldview that more appropriately represents the many nations from which immigrants arrive to America. As Rajini Srikanth argues, "If we think of the United States as always entwined with the experiences of other countries, then perhaps it will be easier for us to conceive of the nation as part of a global network of policies, aware that our actions have repercussions on the lives of peoples elsewhere"

(31). Americanization programs will always reveal the investments of people working on integrating new immigrants and these investments need to be viewed in explicitly transnational terms. As a case in point, labor efforts geared toward national defense were central priorities during World War I but have not been at other historical conjunctures. In other times and locations, shortages in certain types of skilled work or service-sector jobs determine how newcomers are perceived. This is perhaps commonly acknowledged, but what needs more focused attention are the ways in which global trends dramatically change the meaning of immigration, labor, and identity in the United States, as well. To pay greater attention to the way the world has been reshaped by diasporization means recognizing what Hall calls the "Third, 'New World' presence," which he imagines as "not so much power, as ground, place, territory . . . where the creolizations and assimilations and syncretisms were negotiated" ("Cultural Identity and Diaspora" 243). Such aspects of displacements and dislocations must be taken into account when understanding or judging how communities may become "Americanized."

Disrupting Assimilation Teleologies

The foregoing analysis of assimilation, economics, ideology, and (trans)national identities represents *my* story about what GuyaneseOpportunities signifies or, as Geertz would have it, my "own constructions of other peoples' constructions of what they and their compatriots are up to" ("Thick Description" 9). It is certainly an attempt to trace the "curve of social discourse" and fix "it into an inspectable form" for my reader (19). Through my interview choices, my selection of relevant passages to read closely, and the juxtaposition of different texts, I have created a narrative that is my best effort to represent how the story was told to me.

My interviews with local residents were personally fascinating for many reasons. At times, I was disappointed when I had almost anticipated active rejection of what sounded like essentialist narratives of "Indian" cultural identity. At other moments, I found myself, for perhaps the first time in my life, feeling "authentically" Indian because I was born in India, immigrated to the United States at a very young age, regularly travel back to the subcontinent to visit family, and speak Hindi fairly fluently. However, it is only in the contrast with these other members of my diasporic community—for whom what Meena Alexander calls the "fault lines" of identity seem even more dramatic than in my case—that this unfamiliar sense of belonging occurred. The conversations I had with

Guyanese Americans therefore helped to remind me that I have as often troubled over my sense of "Indianness" as I have over the implications of Americanization for South Asian communities.

In broader terms, I heard that cultural belonging could, without obvious tension, signify so many different things simultaneously. Many interviewees spoke about the significance of Indian traditions in their lives as an important ancestral connection, but, unlike the myth of a return to "homeland" so common to traditional diasporic stories, it was a place they did not expect to visit and for which they did not actively feel nostalgic. The ease with which individuals narrated borrowing from multiple faiths—in daily religious practices and foundational belief systems—without focusing on personal conflict *or* community disapproval was, frankly, unparalleled in my personal experience with various South Asian American communities. This was another aspect of affiliation in which pan-Caribbean cultural practices prominently defined Indo-Guyanese American identities. It must be said that, rather than having disentangled "mixed" meanings, I left most interviews with new questions about Americanization, South Asian diasporization, and national public culture, which are beyond the scope of this chapter.

What I can attest to is that, while a logical "test" of any Americanization program might be measuring the degree to which the immigrants in question have become assimilated to mainstream America (and demographic information can certainly be gathered), this is a nearly impossible measurement to make in more metaphorical and metaphysical terms. There *are*, however, ways to theorize about better or worse mechanisms for engaging immigrant populations in public culture. For instance, in response to a request for an overview of assimilation policy, Otis Graham Jr. and Elizabeth Koed concluded that the guided mediation provided by Americanization projects might be useful *if* undertaken systematically and after prolonged, open discussion. What is especially noteworthy about Graham and Koed's study is that it reveals the degree to which we collectively seem no more prepared to define or assess Americanization in the early twenty-first century than we were throughout the past century. With the end of World War I, Progressive-era-type programs became less prominent and eventually faded away. From that time until today, there remain many unanswered questions about what difference Americanization programs have made or can make. Robert Carlson summarizes that, for "100 percent" Americanism efforts of the 1920s, the results seemed negligible, there were ethical issues that remained unaddressed, racial differences continued to elicit conflict, and one of the central goals (i.e., increased literacy) was not achieved (454).

This lack of clarity in measuring assimilation shows that it is unfeasible to try to judge the "success" of Americanization, partly because the standards for assessment can be so varied or, rather disastrously, can go unexamined. Furthermore, the very act of trying to measure assimilation to an American identity presumes an ability to define what has historically been a contested ideal for an insistently heterogeneous population. Attempts to assess assimilation may also lead to a denial of the dynamic nature of cultural evolution that is evident in the shifting priorities of American generations, resulting from ongoing immigration, international developments, financial incentives, and many other factors. As George Sanchez writes, programs for intentional and guided Americanization can thus only offer "idealized versions of American values" (294). In the case of many immigrant groups, whether or not they assimilated to America was not unduly influenced by opportunities provided by assimilation programs under Progressivism or in more recent decades. Sanchez argues that this is because of a tendency to institute a "limited, inconsistent scheme which could not handle the demographic realities" of the group in question (293). Similarly, along with the challenges of measuring whether or not Guyanese Americans have truly been "assimilated" in Schenectady, the narrow group focus of GuyaneseOpportunities plans and ambivalent responses to them may help to explain the short-lived nature of the initiative. However, the project of one of my interviewees, to create a television program about his culture "targeted to the American audience . . . to really break down that stereotyping of people," if he sees it through, may encourage more systematic attention to the distinctive experiences of this community.

Meanwhile, the continued difficulty of assessing Americanization confirms my argument throughout this study that assimilation to the nation, as well as to ethnically defined identities within the nation or other affiliations associated with transnational communities, are ongoing and unstable processes. Thus, Americans return again and again to related questions about what it *really* means to belong, how we *should* define good citizenship, and to what extent we can be similar in our differences. This uncertainty is likely why Americanization cannot be measured more absolutely than it is here. This indeterminacy was also represented in earlier analyses of assimilation; as Carlson understated in 1970, "A clear-cut evaluation of Americanization is, at best, difficult" (458). Early twentieth-century proponents of Americanization programs such as Hill and Speek may have been correct in arguing that only a centralized, federally funded project will result in widespread and "successful" assimilation of immigrants into a cohesive (and homogeneous?) national culture. In the absence of any such program, Americans continue to share stories about struggling for a sense of community that is defined nationally but in so many other ways, as well.

Refusing to fix on one definition of what "Americanization" meant to them, Guyanese immigrants in Schenectady—like every other group of Americans—told unique, revealing stories about their ethnic identities and their imagined communities. Their accounts of assimilation and accommodation augment the changing national narrative, by repeating familiar themes of managing differences and maximizing individual happiness, while "translating" those themes for themselves in the process. And, as the American Dream continues to symbolize, Guyanese Americans expressed hope for a future that is better than the past, although even in this limited context "better" continues to have many different meanings. Even though Speek sneered at "cosmopolitanists" who "deny the existence of nationality" and even "that there are Americans," he was not far off when he argued that even "these people, theoretically denying the existence of Americans as a distinct nationality, recognize the American nationality as a very tangible and indisputable fact in their daily intercourse" (238). Many decades ago, Speek rather nicely summed up the continuing ambivalence of Americanization: there is certainty about what it means to "be American" despite consistently incomplete efforts at finding a way to name it once and for all.

Rather than attempting to do so myself, in the next two chapters, I focus on South Asian fiction and film as creative texts that represent the continuing search for ways to narrate belonging in America. Imaginative possibilities within the bildungsroman literary genre and those connected to independent cinema lend themselves to distinct types of analysis. In the final chapter, I also have an opportunity to examine intergenerational relationships that influence South Asians' experiences. As Sanchez notes, one major effect of Americanization programs was to accentuate differences between generations born in America and their immigrant parents. Whether this will be true of Guyanese Americans remains to be seen, although it is suggestive that several interviewees predicted that their children are unlikely to think of themselves as "coming from India." As richer background for my preliminary account of how Guyanese Americans are experiencing assimilation in Schenectady, New York, much more in-depth research is certainly necessary on this and other topics. In the meantime, in chapter 3, I closely read metaphors of assimilation and immigration deployed by authors representing other types of contemporary South Asian American experiences.

3 / "Stretched over Dark Femaleness": Three South Asian Novels of Americanization

The first chapter of this book laid the foundation for analyzing distinct sets of South Asian stories and the second chapter moved from the theoretical to the empirical, highlighting how narratives of assimilation are always in dialogue with one another across local and global contexts. This third chapter complements "official," socio-historical, and ethnographic accounts of diasporization and Americanization by concentrating on published fictions—Meena Alexander's *Manhattan Music*, Bharati Mukherjee's *Wife* and *Jasmine*, and Bapsi Sidhwa's *An American Brat*[1]—which are centrally concerned with contradictory imperatives and choices surrounding assimilation. By treating varied representations of Americanization as related texts, I continue to emphasize that imaginative and lived experiences are *equally* important for shaping what Arjun Appadurai has called "ethnoscapes" (48), which can be understood as possibilities for community belonging which contemporary (trans)national individuals must navigate. The published fictions also offer opportunities for examining issues that might have been more muted or less relevant in the other cases, while also reminding us—in the contrast with the other sets of stories—what these novels leave out. For instance, although the influence of gender was not directly or conspicuously emphasized in my chapter about Indo-Guyanese Americans in Schenectady, it is integral to the narratives discussed in this chapter. Conversely, questions of economic uplift that were so pervasive in GuyaneseOpportunities were relatively deprioritized in these novels. These related sets of stories from ethnography and literature are truly complementary in understanding Americanization as a multifarious, unpredictable process reflecting universal themes with infinite iterations—as with any good story.

As part of my overall strategy of adopting a methodology that is responsive to the texts in question rather than rigidly formulaic, the narratives in this chapter are analyzed in separate sections rather than being discussed collectively and arranged by topic, as in other chapters. There are several reasons for this, including each author's distinctive oeuvre, which has resulted in a body of texts that are useful for framing the particular novel(s) by an author which I discuss in this chapter. This organization allows me to contextualize each Americanization narrative within a history of the author's literary engagements and critical responses to the writing. Also, these texts are overtly bounded since they are published as books, which is not true of the ethnographies I collected or of the visual medium of film, which leads me to offer more precisely demarcated analyses in this chapter. Finally, my discussion in each chapter has been uniquely shaped based on what I consider to be the most informative discourses of belonging for illuminating that set of texts. In this case, after offering a reading of gendered and hybridized bodies, which are major shared tropes in the novels, I then discuss the authors' very different projects concerning South Asian American women's assimilation.

Indeed, the selected novels represent some of the most focused literary examinations of South Asian assimilation at the turn of the twenty-first century, although scholars have not tended to read them in relation to one another as creative depictions of tropes of Americanization.[2] In these particular novels that are part of the bildungsroman tradition in English, the narrative focus is an individual's interpretation of her relationship to her current nation *and* to processes of diasporization. Although the bildungsroman was initially associated with German national identity, scholars have traced subsequent traditions in other European, British, American, and postcolonial[3] literatures. Some critics in the United States argue for the continued relevance of a genre that other postmodern critiques relegate to a bygone age in which selfhood was understood in more static, Enlightenment terms. The bildungsroman pattern of narrating the education of national citizens currently seems to be reflected most often in writing by women and multiethnic Americans.[4] With a focus on Asian American literature, Patricia P. Chu explains that novels such as these share the central focus of the traditional bildungsroman, "which socializes readers by inviting them to identify with protagonists as they strive to become good citizens of their nation" (12). Mukherjee, Sidhwa, and Alexander take their place in this tradition through their narratives of "becoming American." They expose how immigration can result in the disruption of familiar metanarratives of multiple nations, implicating family, community, ethnicity, and gendered identities. For the conventions of a classical genre to have such contemporary significance affirms the importance of reading South Asian narratives as unique contributions to evolving ideologies of Americanization.

For instance, the image of Americanness becoming "stretched" when it is required to cover "dark femaleness"[5] comes from Alexander's *Manhattan Music* (1997), in a passage that alludes to several important aspects of South Asian Americanization. The protagonist, Sandhya, in comparing her troubled and fractured sense of trying to belong in contemporary America to that of her husband[6] and his family,

> felt that there was no way she could draw on his experience to help her live her life. Bred in the late sixties, Stephen's liberal vision offered him a sense of equality that buckled under the weight of his wife's life. She should take America head on, he felt. Her difficulties in the street would surely ease. By his light, Jewish immigration had laid out the groundwork and now Sandhya Rosenblum could benefit. But often his resolution wavered, and the truths he had discovered for himself wore thin when stretched over his wife's dark femaleness. (39)

In this passage, Alexander's imagery—of a woman trying and miserably failing to fit in another's skin and be at "ease" in America—forces readers to acknowledge that women experience particularly ambivalent relationships with dominant national narratives.[7] Sandhya's tone in this passage is despairing and almost defeated, which is also true of other moments in the novel when she reflects on her life after immigration. She implies that, although South Asians may "benefit" or learn from earlier examples of seemingly successful assimilation—and South Asians do often compare their stories to those of Jewish Americans[8]—these experiences cannot be read as identical without gross simplification of layered affiliations, which would then be stretched "thin." There is also an implicit criticism in this passage of Stephen's ahistorical "liberal vision," since the alleged "truths" he had discovered cannot actually sustain her. Her "difficulties," which is an understatement in describing perpetual alienation and sometimes threatening encounters, represent the weight of her lived experiences under which his assumptions cannot stand.

Finally, the stretching of "resolution" to the point of uselessness uncovers the paradox of accommodating oneself to a country in which one's very body—racialized and/or gendered—has been read as monstrously misshapen[9] because it is so different from the norm. Jim Cullen also uses imagery of stretching in his history of the American Dream to describe a shared American activity of working to belong; he writes, "The American dream continues to be stretched, not always comfortably by those from elsewhere—which, in the final analysis, is where every American, even those Native Americans who crossed the Bering Strait thousands of years ago, is from" (188).

"Darkness," meanwhile, also accomplishes specific cultural work, including an allusion to race-ethnicity as it inescapably influences Americanization outcomes, which is discussed in detail later in this chapter. Also, literary metaphors of darkness have often implied the unknown, threatening, mysterious, and/or impure; in the United States, such metaphors have been used in conjunction with deployments of the notion of "blackness," usually but not solely in relation to African American histories and identities. In more global terms, British author Joseph Conrad's examination of the "heart" of darkness in his famous novella is a narrative engagement with histories and myths of how colonial natives, especially in Africa, acted as sources of both fascination and fear for Europeans participating in the scramble to claim the continent. Figurative language of darkness shaped and was shaped by responses to differences in appearance between groups of people, with ideologies of racial and cultural superiority that privileged lighter (whiter) skin becoming naturalized over time. In another site of colonial racialization, under the Raj, historical prejudices against dark skin in India were heightened such that, for Indians as well as the British, darkness was something to be avoided if one wished to signal elite status and a disaffiliation with subaltern natives. This tendency has proved a lasting legacy in South Asia, as well as in other parts of the world, with important implications for discourses surrounding arranged marriage, beauty, and behavior (such as avoiding the sun). For instance, in contemporary as well as earlier, twentieth-century marriage advertisements, skin color is frequently noted, and there is greater value attached to lighter than to darker skin tones, particularly for the marriageability of women. These layered histories make "dark femaleness" a particularly apt paradigm within which to examine South Asian American women's narratives about Americanization.

Indeed, in each of the works discussed in this chapter, the authors confirm that "dark femaleness" uncomfortably stretches what it means to assimilate to the quintessential nation of immigrants, despite long-term belief in the largesse of that American dream—the "dream of a land in which life should be better and richer and fuller for every man, with opportunity for each according to his ability or achievement" (Adams 415). Just as this particular citation from James T. Adams early in the twentieth century presumed universality implicitly based on (white) male patterns of assimilation,[10] so too do contemporary assumptions about multicultural America and "the free world" continue to disguise actual experiences of impossible, stalled, or disastrous Americanization. Protagonists in these South Asian fictions therefore both desire and mistrust the American Dream. This narrative ambivalence reflects how Asian/American belonging represents "the persistent deferral of the status of 'American,'" as David Palumbo-Liu's puts it (1). While the economic aspects of successful assimilation have traditionally been among the most prominent, as is reinforced by the racial economics of GuyaneseOpportunities in Schenectady which are described in the previous chapter, the literary texts discussed here tend to associate other, nonmaterial achievements with the notion of a "richer and fuller" life. And in each case in which the protagonist feels herself able to accommodate to her new nation, she develops what she considers an alternative paradigm to those presupposed by either American or South Asian normative scripts.

The image of "dark femaleness" in *Manhattan Music* therefore gestures to what is similar in otherwise very different novels: each of them corroborates that assimilation is an inevitably ambivalent process because South Asian female immigrants, metaphorically and physically, do not "fit" conventional stories. In a study of postcolonial women's texts as expressions of representation and resistance, Jaspal Kaur Singh has similarly pointed out that "many women writers reinscribe themselves to disrupt the dominant narratives through painful and maddening inscriptions" (27), concluding that "it may be only in maddening or contradictory spaces that re-articulation and revision of a changing consciousness seeking empowerment can take place" (199). Confronting an ill-fitting narrative therefore often forces a rewriting of the familiar scripts. This common characteristic in the novels I discuss proves that dominant (trans)national narratives influence gender no less than they do class and racial-ethnic[11] identities, although the gender of Americanization has often gone unexamined in assimilation studies. As immigrant women's stories from other communities have done, these novels fill a narrative absence by depicting the major obstacles to assimilation faced by those who are not part of what Audre Lorde called "the mythical norm" (189). In this case, national exclusion operates by virtue of race-ethnicity (not white) and/or gender (not male), to name two major categories by which hegemonic states organize citizens. My analyses in this chapter are therefore structured by closely reading "dark femaleness" as it produces certain fictional American identities, which are furthermore consistently informed by other axes of identity, including social status as defined by education or other types of cultural privilege.[12]

Neither race-ethnicity nor gender serves as *the* explanation for national and (trans)national hierarchies of power, but one can usefully employ each to illuminate other categories of identification and so to locate a starting place for an analysis that can range more broadly. It is not simply a matter of adding disprivileges to calculate degrees of oppression but, rather, developing models about the relationship between self and nation that are suitably nuanced and historically informed. As Rachel C. Lee writes, "gender opposition, gender difference, and gender hierarchy become convenient ways for understanding, enacting, and reinforcing opposition, difference, and hierarchy more generally and in an array of social relationships criss-crossed by racial, class-based, regional, and national differences" (4). At the same time, she appropriately cautions against allowing a transnational focus in Asian American studies to force gender issues to take a secondary place to "debates over whether diaspora, exile, postcoloniality, or transnationalism shall replace the nation as an alternative identity formation" (10). Structures of power governing race, gender, or class do not operate in identical ways, and we must trace the effects of each carefully, in terms which are both local and global; each type of identification offers a particular opportunity for certain stories. When we analyze the intersections, furthermore, we learn how they harmonize with or contradict each other, forcing a negotiated process of belonging for every national subject.

Without sacrificing this type of intersectional analysis,[13] therefore, one can hone in on how processes of assimilation are *always* gendered and how gender thus becomes a defining (if usually assumed rather than questioned) element in any national narrative. Through convention, religion, and law, nation-building processes across the world have placed women in the position of minorities whatever their numbers in a country. Anne McClintock puts it succinctly: "All nationalisms are gendered" (89). Historically, not only has nation been "typically identified with the frustrations and aspirations of men, but the representation of male *national* power depends on the prior construction of *gender* difference"

(90). As McClintock's examination of power and difference emphasizes, national belonging has often been imagined through discrepancies as much as through a consistent narrative. Women may be accorded roles within narratives of a national family—for example, being revered as "mothers" of the nation or being associated with honored traditions—without equal participation in the workings of the nation-state. Although there have of course been notable instances around the globe of women collectively and individually resisting such status, the general condition of women in reference to nation has been one of simultaneous symbolic importance and relative political invisibility. This paradox requires careful unpacking for the ways in which women's relationships to nations are conflated with family genealogies or mediated through men rather than being understood as women acting as autonomous subjects within nationalist, antinationalist, and/or postnationalist movements.

For immigrant communities such as South Asian Americans, this paradox is compounded when women are expected to be, at one and the same time, bearers of an alleged "ancestral culture" in a new host country *and* representatives of their model minority group. On this topic, Uma Narayan deconstructs the "perils" of authenticity (about which I say much more in the next chapter) in relation to Third World "insider" expectations, whereby someone is "the *only* person" authorized to speak for or about his community (143), meaning that a self-willed essentialism is deployed. Such conflicting sets of demands reflect coercive assimilationist expectations of immigrant "gifts" to the host country and *also* to the idealized homeland. Arguing against this kind of disturbing conflation, mother-daughter writers Shamita Das Dasgupta and Sayantani DasGupta have analyzed how gendered relationships to nation may constrain immigrant and second-generation Indian women's activism because it is interpreted as a betrayal of their ethnic communities. Disguising sexism as ethnic solidarity, some members of a community may deride feminisms as a consequence of assimilation instead of considering them to be meaningful attempts at empowerment within a new national matrix. Purvi Shah further suggests how certain versions of nationalism are used to substantiate the immigrant bourgeoisie's similarity to the white middle-class majority in the United States. This unfortunately comes at the expense of South Asian women or others within the community who challenge such hegemonies.

Each narrative discussed in this chapter touches on these phenomena concerning the composition of the national body, but each does so in a unique style and using diverse metaphors, thus staking out very different ground in the field of possible accounts of Americanization. After first suggesting some of their commonalities, I address the various novels in separate discussions in order to contextualize them in relation to each author's body of writing and her place in American literary history. Briefly put, Alexander develops metaphors of fragmentation and rebirth to portray Americanization through transformation and activism. In *Jasmine,* meanwhile, Mukherjee's protagonist exploits the fluidity of diasporic immigrant identity to reconceptualize the (national) family and represent American "maximalists."[14] In Sidhwa's novel, her protagonist's Parsee identity is imagined as an expanded, multidimensional worldview that allows her to analyze the implications of being "free" in America, as both a material and symbolic prospect. In each of the novels, except for Mukherjee's *Wife,* which narrates a different outcome, a sense of accommodation to the nation at the story's close is determinedly not associated with a sense of finality. Instead, there is possibility and hope, as well as constraint and despair, in the lessons the protagonists learn through immigration. Most important, in their lack of narrative closure—which affirms that the "process of subjectification, of becoming a subject, is never a finished one or a closed one" (H. Moore 41)—these novels collectively also imply that the story of *America* is not somehow "finished."

Narratives of the Hybrid National "Body"

As became apparent in stories about Guyanese Americans (chapter 2), "mixing" can be a useful metaphor for the ambivalences, contradictions, and inconsistencies that are particularly relevant to South Asian Americanization. In the published fictions, related imagery which links the stories to each other—and to those in the other chapters—also works to suggest why "dark femaleness" poses such a problem for some Americanization ideologies. If most national narratives have either taken for granted or insisted on recognizably shared characteristics on which to base a political collectivity, then "dark" and "female" (as characteristics of physical bodies which tend to be visually quite evident) describe two very concrete ways in which commonality is made impossible.

Race-ethnicity have been prominent elements of discourses concerning Americanization, but gender has been a more muted theme; to pay simultaneous attention to these factors as they disrupt national narratives of purity and sameness suggests why "hybridity" has become a preferred descriptor for contemporary national and diasporic subjectivities. In theoretical studies attuned to such interpretations, from Lisa Lowe's well-known concept of "heterogeneity, hybridity, and multiplicity" to Homi Bhabha's oft-discussed descriptions of "third space," it is possible to read the investments of particular thinkers in positing that (trans) national identities are mixed and fluid rather than homogeneous and static. Without engaging all of the recent discussions of hybridity, it is still possible to sketch the outlines of some major issues associated with the resulting dialogue. For instance, in a useful overview of why the concept of hybridity has been so influential, in the introduction to *Theorizing Diaspora,* Jana Evans Braziel and Anita Mannur argue that hybridity "offers a way to theorize nationhood and belonging as a process always in change and always mediated by issues of class, ethnicity, gender, and sexuality" (14). Similarly, most analyses of hybridity focus on theoretically opposing how national narratives have historically developed by eliding such significant aspects of difference.

By the early twenty-first century, there were many versions of hybridity talk, which narrate some of the same ambivalences as the novels discussed in this chapter. Postcolonialist, Asian Americanist, and feminist theorists have developed different, sometimes overlapping, methodologies based on privileging mixing, performativity, and processes of identity formation, as contrasted with the assumption of an essential Self. And, as with theories of diaspora, cosmopolitanism, and globalization, there was an explosion of interest and countless spin-offs when contemporary theorizing about hybridity dramatically affected many thinkers at once. Broad engagement with the concept was followed by increasingly critical reassessments when "hybridity" came to be treated as if it had almost endless explanatory power.[15] Lowe's critique of interpretations of hybridization as "'free' oscillation between or among identities" points to ways in which hybridity talk is always liable to being appropriated and commodified as well as representing resistance (82). With the proliferation of readings of hybridity, these possibilities are sometimes lost, with negative consequences for attending to the material implications of cultures.

What various hybridity theories do usefully share is a preoccupation with understanding the metaphorical implications of "crossing," "composites," and "speciation."[16] Because such language, from biology and genetics, for example, stresses material transformations as well as long-term and potentially metaphysical implications, *cultural* hybridity has come to be viewed by many scholars as a set of powerful tools for analyzing what can also be described as "pluralism,"[17] which comes up for its fair share of critique, as well. There is a great deal of common ground covered by varied discussions attending to the possibilities of cultural amalgamation. Ella Shohat and Robert Stam argue that these variations gesture to incessant, intertwining areas of analysis because "syncretism has always pervaded history and the arts" (43). Although the concerns evinced in recent hybridity theories are therefore not new, theoretical discussions have evolved to include insights gained through interdisciplinary critiques of many sociopolitical projects for policing "purity." These academic developments often reflect a self-conscious commitment not only to noting and understanding cultural hybridity as it relates to processes of "grafting" but also to exposing and challenging asymmetrical power hierarchies.

Contemporary readings of hybridity often focus on how being attuned to nonnormative and unpredictable cultural developments better approximates lived experiences, as well as undermining a fixation on ideal "types" which might be said to cohere to national narratives. What thus distinguishes earlier notions of pluralism from prominent hybridity theories developed in the 1980s and 1990s (as well as from the debates or ennui currently evoked by hybridity studies) is the *degree* to which academics propose that hybridity can be a tool for counterhegemonic practices. Hybridity has come to be particularly associated with certain sets of progressive politics, such as antiracism and decentering privilege. Geographer Katharyne Mitchell therefore writes that contemporary theories that are based on models of cultural hybridity and devoted to interrogating the very construction of the nation space seem to "enable[] the alteration of its hegemonic narration" (190). One example is what Shohat and Stam describe as "unthinking Eurocentrism" because, "as an ideological substratum common to colonialist, imperialist, and racist discourse, Eurocentrism is a form of vestigial thinking which permeates and structures *contemporary* practices and representations even after the formal end of colonialism" (2). As an antidote, positing hybridity may denaturalize those processes that make Eurocentrism seem like "common sense" (Shohat and Stam 1). No wonder, then, that "hybridity talk" has developed into a set of liberatory ideologies mapping how minorities or other Others literally do and theoretically might deconstruct overdetermined cultural and sociopolitical hierarchies.

Furthermore, if "hybridity" is interpreted spatially/physically as well as temporally in terms of transformations in the present which alter the imaginable future, ontologies and epistemologies may shift to foreground continual (re)negotiations between self and society, in active minority resistance to those Enlightenment discourses of universality and Selfhood which buttressed systems of extreme inequalities. Bhabha has been particularly notorious for developing theories of hybridity concerning these aspects of cultural and discursive hybridization, with arguably too little articulation of how such theories are reflected in diverse lived experiences. With respect to what have been generative implications, Bhabha has joined other scholars in delineating how wielding the concept of process (for example, to examine the construction of native and imperialist subjectivities) can destabilize the very ground on which traditional relationships of power are constructed. He argues that hybridity allows for "a contestation of the given symbols of authority . . . in the time lag of sign/symbol, which is a space in-between the rules of engagement" (*The Location of Culture* 192). Whether or not he overemphasizes the revolutionary nature of theorized hybridity, Bhabha has been a prominent interlocutor in postcolonial dialogues on the subject particularly because of his emphasis on (post)colonial identities as ongoing performances rather than fixed, and therefore unchanging and inevitable, subject(ed) positions.

Even if Bhabha's theories of hybridity did not offer what many readers sought in terms of praxis, in the "in-between" space he helped to chart is where new possibilities for agency have often been located. For instance, in an anthology focused on antiracism, *Debating Cultural Hybridity,* anthropologist Pnina Werbner writes in the introduction about the ways in which "process" has figured in the "current fascination with hybridity" (1). Since viewing identities as "products" of contemporary global capitalism both dehumanizes individuals and reifies binaries between different groups (such as the marginalized and the dominant), Werbner argues that the "challenge, then, is to develop processual models of hybridity" (22) to replace limiting readings of identity as static or homogeneous. In another essay in *Debating Cultural Hybridity,* sociologist Alberto Melucci elaborates that master narratives, or what he calls "traditional coordinates of personal identity (family, church, party, race, class)," cannot account for the "multiplication of our social memberships, the constant surge of possibilities and messages, that floods the field of our experience" (61). As contrasted with many national narratives, discussions such as these two and others represented in that anthology theorize ways to accommodate hybrid identities and processes, rather than considering them as problems to be fixed. These theoretical essays are therefore politically motivated to posit expanded opportunities for recognizing multiple narratives of belonging. With varied responses such as these, "hybridity talk" has evolved from earlier instantiations, with intellectual debates clarifying political agendas as well as theory's limits.

In addition to considerations of hybrid processes reflecting ethnic minoritization and subalternity, there have been many efforts to understand what Bhabha's calls the "rules of engagement" as they affect gender dynamics. For instance, combining literary criticism with psychoanalysis into a uniquely hybrid voice, Julia Kristeva posited that one should "view the subject in language as decentering the transcendental ego, cutting through it, and opening it up to a dialectic in which its syntactic and categorical understanding is merely the liminary moment of the process" (61). Although she has not always provided as careful a decentering of the language of race as one might hope, Kristeva's work has been seminal in demonstrating how subjectivity is not innate but instead a naming process in language that is continuously reimagined in various dialogues that an individual has within herself and with the outside world. With more explicit political attention to negotiating various systems of oppression, theorist Judith Butler demonstrates that identity is a constant performance constructing and reconstructing fictions of sex and gender; for example, she analyzes how "*woman* itself is a term in process, a becoming, a constructing that cannot rightfully be said to originate or end. As an ongoing discursive practice, it is open to intervention and resignification" (*Gender Trouble* 33). Like Bhabha and other contemporary thinkers building on long academic traditions devoted to understanding subjectivity, Kristeva and Butler emphasize invention, narrative, and process as integral aspects of identity formation and, thus, nation. Although this may be commonplace for many academics today (if not "on the ground"), it is important to remember what cultural interventions these thinkers were attempting, in offering alternatives to certain hegemonies through interpretations of subjectivity as unpredictable, changeable, and emphatically *not* natural fact. Depending on one's perspective, such cultural work suggests liberating models highlighting choices people make about their identities or, alternatively, destroys cohesive narratives of belonging and is thus meaningless or threatening.

The dialogue that results from these contradictory responses is very telling about priorities and ideologies at play in (trans)national narratives, but, as I pointed out about diaspora in chapter 1, there are limits to what *solely* discursive and metaphorical concepts can accomplish.[18] As Peter Hitchcock cautions, it is important not to posit hybridity as a general condition but, instead, to be conscious of "particular forms of this articulation rather than, willy-nilly, its quotidian pervasiveness" (7). Shohat and Stam reinforce this attitude when they write that "a celebration of syncretism and hybridity *per se,* if not articulated with questions of historical hegemonies, risks sanctifying the *fait accompli* of colonial violence" and that hybridity as "a descriptive catch-all term . . . fails to discriminate between the diverse modalities of hybridity" (43). There are many other scholars who support such criticisms of overabstracted theories of hybridity. What these responses to the explosion of "hybridity talk" strongly assert is the need to remember that narratives affect actuality, and vice versa, but this does not mean that hybridity or any other metaphor is the panacea of all ills related to local and global politics of inequality.

With this caveat in mind, readers can more fully appreciate hybridity imagery in the novels of South Asian Americanization presented in this chapter. In order to pay due attention to these literary motifs without overstating the case for the empowering political effects of hybridization, it is useful to maintain the interpretation of hybridity as the marker of a contested site of cultural debate. John Tomlinson observes that "the idea of hybridization is a useful way of describing a substantive aspect of the process of deterritorialization. Some term is clearly needed to capture the general phenomenon of cultural mixing that is unquestionably increasing with the advance of globalization" and producing "new cultural identifications" (147). With the dramatic turns in cultural interpretation in the late twentieth century accompanying such related paradigms as poststructuralism, postmodernism, and postcolonialism, it is clear that ways of understanding the world around us and our identities are up for debate. Geographical changes in the construction of bounded communities and the ways in which the Internet links up distant parts of the globe—these and many other symptoms of globalization require new language for representing seeming breaks from certain norms of the past. In academic discussions, hybridity (along with diasporization and cosmopolitanism) has become one way to mark alternatives among attitudes toward global structures and patterns.

In fictional manifestations of such theories, the novels discussed in this chapter invoke varieties of hybridity through distinctive metaphors. Meena Alexander's *Manhattan Music* presents readers with motifs of syncretism, métissage, and bricolage through the author's original imagery (also used in her other literary texts) of "multiple anchorages," identity "bits and pieces" making immigrants like Frankenstein's monster (154), and "hybrid syllables" (102). The protagonist of *Manhattan Music* confronts incessant cultural mixture in the United States and eventually learns to accommodate it in order to construct an acceptable narrative for herself. In this way, the novel reveals how personal heterogeneity can be mapped onto one's nation of belonging, which is one way to create a sense of belonging without having to seamlessly fit any one narrative. Fragmentation in this story is suggested in relation to physical bodies as well as more abstract desires to belong; these themes are yet again reinforced by the consonance between the form of and content in the novel.

Although Bharati Mukherjee's *Jasmine* tells a very different story, it too foregrounds immigrant and national hybridity.[19] Displacements of cultural meaning from India to the United States, particularly religious narratives and rituals, are portrayed in a way that emphasizes how migration demands new names for oneself and new scripts which one can self-consciously shape by selecting various influences, rather than being victimized by imposed narratives. This vision of assimilation as self-directed is depicted most prominently in relation to one immigrant character whose assertive choices help the protagonist decide what her own nontraditional pattern of Americanization will be. This is the story of Jasmine's adopted son, Du, a Vietnamese refugee whom she admires for his skills in perfecting "recombinant" practices (139). Jasmine interprets his activities to mean that Du is actively constructing a working model for himself so that he can accommodate the nation without succumbing to the many "humiliations" he faces as a poor, nonwhite foreigner in the United States. As Jasmine herself learns to do, Du has discovered how to scavenge things from his surroundings and transform odds and ends into what he needs, creating innovative new hybrids from leftover bits and pieces. Gail Ching-Liang Low notes that, as compared to other depictions of hybridity in literature, Du's "strategy of hybridization" (12) is imagined as necessary for literal survival rather than being an option or a luxury.

Meanwhile, Bapsi Sidhwa's *An American Brat* reflects hybridity through its portrayal of minoritization as simultaneously experienced in relation to multiple types of belonging. In the novel, the protagonist's immigration and assimilation experiences show that national, regional, and diasporic identities cannot meaningfully be separated for a woman who is a racial minority, the ethnic Other to dominant American symbology, Pakistani (often subsumed in North American scholarship under the rubric of South Asia but not actually represented), and Parsee. The Parsee diaspora is a rather unusual minority community wherever they reside who have no discrete homeland to which they can return. Feroza Jussawalla has written, "The Parsis of India have always seen themselves as attainers of hybridity par excellence" ("Navjote Ceremonies" 82). The numerous narratives of belonging symbolized by Sidhwa's fictional

Parsee American character are therefore telling example of palimpsestic identities which are so often prominent in South Asian Americanization more broadly.

Meena Alexander: Americanization and Activism

In considering why there may be more fictions of Americanization published about South Asian immigrant women than men, writing by Meena Alexander provides a good starting point. Both in her novels and in her life as a public intellectual, Alexander focuses on communities of activist women theorizing about how race-ethnicity and gender intersect in shaping American experiences. As Rajini Srikanth summarizes, Alexander's "is the globalism of outrage, of moral indignation, of social justice, of compassion for those others like us who are also a part of this world" (88). Alexander is a critically acclaimed novelist, poet, and essayist, as well as a teacher and activist engaged in progressive politics in New York City, which is also the setting of her novel of Americanization, *Manhattan Music.* A diasporan par excellence, she was born in Allahabad, India, in 1951 but divided her childhood between southwest India and northeastern Africa, eventually pursuing her Ph.D. in Romantic literature in England and subsequently relocating permanently to the United States in 1980. Alexander has published multiple collections of poetry, including *River and Bridge, Illiterate Heart, Raw Silk,* and *Quickly Changing River*; three autobiographical works, *Fault Lines: A Memoir, The Shock of Arrival: Reflections on Postcolonial Experience,* and *Poetics of Dislocation*; and two novels, *Nampally Road* and *Manhattan Music.*

Alexander is best known for her insights into the paradoxical nature of migration, which represents both the possibility of an individual making herself anew and the trauma of dislocation. Her memoirs, for example, testify to her own experiences of multiple migrations as well as the "postcolonial consciousness" she shares with other diasporic women and men: "a life reworked through the seams of a language that is mine and not mine, clothing, forms of life that all retain the bite of old oppressions as well as the pungency of newness" (*The Shock of Arrival* 142). In this quotation, Alexander envisions diasporization as reinvention in terms of active "work" because of one's uncertainty about what to claim or not. She also foregrounds the physicality of belonging, with the penetrating words "bite" and "pungent," which suggest active discomfort in their intensity. As a writer, this is one of her great gifts, of being able to yoke together the "real" and the imagined in memorable ways. Within

South Asian and Asian American studies, the growing body of criticism on Meena Alexander has therefore tended to focus on the ways in which, "for Alexander, art is 'always political,'" to quote Ketu Katrak ("South Asian American Literature" 208).

Creating a character who is an immigrant diasporan in *Manhattan Music,* Alexander tells the story of the fictional Sandhya Rosenblum. The novel commences with the protagonist living in New York, having emigrated from India with her husband, Stephen, three years earlier. The novel relates their meeting while on vacation in India and their marriage a month later. As the story unfolds, it becomes clear that Sandhya married partly as an attempt to overcome the death of her lover, Gautam, a student activist who was imprisoned and tortured. After several years in Manhattan, Sandhya confronts her need to identify her own place in America, especially once her responsibilities as a mother are transformed. As she undertakes this quest, Sandhya is portrayed both in her daily life in New York and during visits to her family home in Tiruvella in south India. Other significant characters in the novel include her friend Draupadi, her cousin Jay, her childhood friend Sakhi, and her lover Rashid. All of these characters are activists of different kinds and although Sandhya does not have a definitive sense of her role in progressive politics, by the end of the novel she is poised to identify her own type of activism through her interactions with these other characters. In this novel, as in most of her writing, Alexander proposes "pluralism as a means of reconciling an individual to a community," as Shilpa Davé describes one of the writer's most often repeated themes ("The Doors to Home and History" 111).

In this contemporary bildungsroman, Sandhya's self-construction parallels her revisioning of the American nation, which is represented in the text by the diversity and cosmopolitanism often associated with Manhattan. The narrative unfolds in a nonlinear, impressionistic, and lyrical fashion, formally deconstructing a straightforward Americanization plot. Instead, the novel portrays assimilation as self-conscious accommodation, meaning an active political agenda for transformation instead of a passive willingness to be absorbed into the fabric of the nation, as Americanization is often perceived. *Manhattan Music* emphasizes that the protagonist's self-definition develops through belonging to multiple communities and fashioning them to be politically more progressive. By its conclusion, the narrative offers us a vision of America as a country founded on the very concept of difference and well imagined as music that is "fragrant, subtle as flesh, countless voices singing" (221). This metaphor of "Manhattan music" challenges perceptions of this nation as one that is or should be monotonal or, by analogy, monochromatic.

In a text that instead emphasizes multivocality, musical metaphors and forms link processes of assimilation to hybridizing cultural influences. *Manhattan Music* portrays the process by which the protagonist comes to consider herself as belonging to America by remembering—in place of excising or renouncing—her past, which Alexander elsewhere symbolizes as "a stringed instrument I must play, inventing what I need" (*The Shock of Arrival* 126). In narrating the invention of immigrant identity, the novel is meanwhile constructed through the juxtaposition of various chords making up a musical whole, which formally results in a mixing of harmonious and clashing pieces. The novel opens with an overture that raises the themes subsequently recombined in and augmented by different segments of the narrative. Long chapters about Sandhya's story are broken up by brief interludes or counterpoints devoted to other characters in which the perspectives alternate between first- and third-person narration. Near the end of the novel, a series of disjointed passages further function as riffs on the central narrative. Finally, there is a coda of poems to *Manhattan Music* that teases out some of the repeated patterns in Sandhya's development.

This genre mixing and fragmentation suitably reflect the multiple valences of Alexander's fiction of Americanization, since it is through instantiations of hybridity and in punctuated moments of insight that Sandhya comes to productively negotiate the ambivalence of arrival in her new nation. One of the most important foil characters in the narrative is Draupadi Dinkins, a part Indian, part African, part Asian American performance artist. Draupadi is one of the best drawn figures in the book; her first name invokes Hindu mythology,[20] her last name is the less exotic "Dinkins," and she uses her cultural inheritances to assert various cultural affiliations through often-confrontational performance art. Draupadi chooses to act as a mentor for Sandhya and provides one of the central metaphors of Americanization in the novel—self-recognition in place of external definitions—when she asks, "Who would hold up a lamp so that [Sandhya's] eyes, darting like twin fish, could see themselves seeing?" (4). The novel closes with a scene that recalls such imagery as Sandhya stares into a lake in Central Park and catches "sight of two eyes staring back at her" and realizes, "those are my own eyes staring back at me" (227). Finally able to recognize herself as a moving target, emphasizing different "bits and pieces" of herself at particular moments, Sandhya realizes that it is not her fault that her husband Stephen's "truths" cannot stand for her, nor can his American Dream be transferred to her.

Processes of self-recognition and Americanization proceed through the same fragmentary and unpredictable pattern suggested by the metaphor of "Manhattan music." Even as the protagonist achieves greater insight about herself and the independent role she will play in her new nation, such as when she declares, "I have to find my own way" (222), the narrative implies that such processes are ongoing and inevitably uneven in their development, because human experiences defy scripted pacing. And Sandhya's Americanization is a fraught quotidian process in the face of negative attitudes toward her "dark femaleness" expressed through popular opinion and local acts of intolerance, if not official exclusion. As a novel of national accommodation, *Manhattan Music* might conclude with imagery of rebirth and newness, of a dragonfly "struggling out of its translucent pupae, the large eye coverings left behind in the crumpling skin, the new body gleaming with moisture" (227), but it undermines any sense of a true resolution. Instead, it leaves readers with a much less final declaration by its protagonist, even in the moment of making some peace with herself and with America: "Perhaps in a few months, a few years, it would all splinter again and she would be seized by unknown passions welling out of her flesh. But for now, she would be, she would let herself be" (215). Once again connecting the search for an adequate narrative of belonging to one's actual "flesh," Alexander ironically positions her protagonist in Central Park, "nature" *constructed* in a quintessentially urban space. The paradox nicely emphasizes the changeability of readings of her body, thus of her identity. It is only "natural" that Sandhya thinks of herself, not as a somehow finished product or alternately as broken down by her experiences, but instead as painfully "splintered" yet potentially hybrid because the pieces are still attached rather than lost in immigrant forgetting.

The part of this scene I want to stress is its *potentiality*: since Sandhya does not fit certain normative ideals of Americanness, it is painfully clear to her that "neither gestures nor words came out right" (7) until she can define her own possible Americanization. Prior to this, her very person—her dark femaleness—problematizes her belonging to America. Incidents of racism and exclusion that are poignantly related in the narrative force the character, as well as readers, to accept this unfortunate reality. In a passage that emphasizes the degree to which an internal sense of alienation is related to external darkness and femaleness, Sandhya wonders,

> Supposing she were to swallow the green card, ingest that plastic, would it pour though her flesh, a curious alchemy that would make her all right in the new world? She gazed at her two hands, extended now in front of her. What if she could peel off her brown skin, dye her hair blonde, turn her body into a pale, Caucasian thing, would it work better with Stephen? (7)

In this passage, the character's actual flesh poses a problem for her assimilation, and she responds by imagining how she might overcome it by literally trying to ingest "Americanness" while simultaneously shedding anything that marks her as nonwhite. Generalizing this sensibility from one individual to a broader community, *Manhattan Music* also recounts that America is a land where dark-skinned women are usually most noticeable as housemaids and where anti-Asian legislation was once publicly expressed in signs reading "THIS LAND IS NOT YOUR LAND" (37). Thus, even though Sandhya has the privilege of a green card and gains certain "rights," this does not guarantee that others in the country accept her as an American.

Even if Sandhya does not have to struggle to gain citizenship since it is granted to her via marriage, she and other characters in the novel still feel they are denied many of the symbolic aspects of belonging which we might assume accompany official recognition,[21] what Mae M. Ngai describes as "substantive citizenship" (6). It is also informative to think about Sandhya's desire to "swallow" official documentation in relation to Palumbo-Liu's reading of Asian America in terms of body, psyche, and space: actual bodies expose multiple mechanisms by which subjects are acculturated to an "idealized American" type (7). The unpredictable ways in which internal and external markers are related to one another means that actual ingestion will not render Sandhya more assimilable, but since she cannot look otherwise, it seems impossible to prove that she too is the "'face' of the nation" (Palumbo-Liu 81).

Even as characters such as Draupadi model patterns of belonging to America through hybridized self-identification, Sandhya's attempts to construct such a pattern for herself are often faltering and require constant reassessment in a way that is common to the tradition of female bildungsromane. Looking at earlier British and American versions, Joanne S. Frye has argued that fictional women in bildungsromane face a conflict between cultural conformity and "the autonomous urge to self-definition" (9); she concludes that, as compared to male heroes, they often find autonomy difficult to achieve, even when conforming to expectations is not in their best interest. Frye argues that, in novels as diverse as *The Bluest Eye, Lives of Women and Girls,* and *The Stone Angel,* protagonists face "the temptations of traditional plots, of the expected cultural . . . explanations of [women's] lives" (9), which too often depict female protagonists succumbing either to normative sex/gender roles or to self-destruction. Self-destruction is one of the tragic outcomes to ambivalent Americanization that *Manhattan Music* imagines, invoking other female fictions even as it reflects ways in which gender norms changed and sometimes expanded in the late twentieth century. That suicide has been one of the more likely *telos* of female bildungsromane is suggested by the prevalence of narratives in English from the nineteenth and twentieth centuries which end in madness and/or death, a tendency well documented in literary studies such as *The Voyage In,* edited by Elizabeth Abel et al. Such gynocriticisms in the past several decades, following Elaine Showalter's seminal *A Literature of Their Own* in the late 1970s, have often focused on compensating for earlier literary interpretations focused primarily on male narratives. Challenging the universality of literary tropes such as the heroic quest, feminist reconsideration of the most canonical stories in the English tradition have thus paid careful attention to prevailing scripts made available to particular women. American literary classics such as Kate Chopin's *The Awakening* have not been rediscovered to become feminist staples without good cause, for they powerfully convey limited choices that seem to have made suicide a historical and current possibility in the lives of too many women.

This theme is revisited in *Manhattan Music* in a way that represents gendered, as well as racial-ethnic, assimilation processes as challenging opportunities for asserting immigrant agency. In a chapter entitled "Rope Mark," Draupadi returns to her apartment to discover that Sandhya has used a part of Draupadi's latest performance-art installation to hang herself. Earlier, Draupadi had told her friend that she was not sure what use she would make of the knotted rope, one of many odds and ends piled up around the apartment which will eventually have a place in a piece Draupadi is planning for a citywide South Asian celebration of Diwali,[22] or the festival of lights. The piece is as yet but an idea in Draupadi's mind,

> "something to do with Indians and Columbus's misadventures. They have a new stamp now, have you seen it?"
>
> Draupadi extended her palm, a gray-and-white stamp lying flat on it. "Well, take a look. It has a picture of a man. And the caption."

> She read it very slowly. "'The first Americans crossed over from Asia.' I guess we belong here, after all. If the postal service says so." (199)

The word choice and tone in this scene prove Draupadi's willingness to treat hallowed national narratives with irreverence and facetiousness, in order to disrupt their traditional meanings and create a space for her by presencing global migrations. Citing "misadventures" as the path to the supposed New World, Draupadi refocuses attention from famous European journeys to no less significant globe crossings that often go unremarked. Noting the "official" or institutional powers that can name her, she is clearly planning to ironically comment on her ability to belong by enacting American art on a South Asian holiday. Draupadi's attempts at claiming America are therefore based on active and *activist* methods for negotiating Americanization, a process that also implicates individuals who are not literally new to the country. This is a common theme throughout Alexander's writing; Draupadi's interruption of Sandhya's suicide attempt implies that national belonging through self-critique is what makes it possible for one "dark" and female American to rescue another.

The narrative does not end with Sandhya's suicide, which is figured as her capitulation to forces that she feels she cannot overcome even as she is unable to assimilate to their expectations. This "writing beyond the ending" marks it as a literary deviation from earlier female bildungsromane in English. Feminist critic Rachel Blau DuPlessis's concept of such writing is that it continues stories beyond conventional conclusions in order to suggest different outcomes for women's lives than those that traditionally dominated literary representations. Unlike Edna Pontellier in *The Awakening,* Sandhya does not succeed in a suicide that she hopes will "free" her from assimilation demands; instead, she must confront the process any citizen faces in assimilating to social collectives, a process that those who do not look like the official "face" of the national "body" often find especially taxing. Because she survives her suicide attempt thanks to her mentor in Americanization, Sandhya is forced to accommodate herself to her host country. When she decides to do so, she adopts a positionality similar to Draupadi's, although not identical to it, since she knows, "I don't want to play the part she is giving me" (222).[23] Choosing to identify herself as a woman in a community of activists committed to challenging intolerance, Sandhya redefines assimilation and begins to shape a different narrative for the future. Thus, after her recovery, the protagonist anticipates her eventual acceptance of Americanization. In her chosen accommodation to her new nation, there is as much resistance to norms of gender and racial-ethnic belonging as there is a pleasure in the "countless voices" that narrate America.

As depicted in *Manhattan Music,* assimilation through the active rewriting of traditional scripts means that South Asian Americans contribute to the evolving national narrative even as they are Americanized in certain ways. Scholarship about South Asian literature and sociohistorical contexts confirms this. For instance, Rashmi Sharma points out, "'Who am I' through immigrant eyes parallels 'who we want to be' as a society" (12). South Asian immigrant self-shaping includes diasporic and hybrid notions of "Who am I" which significantly inform national identity; as one of the characters in *Manhattan Music* announces, no immigrant should feel as if she is "mortgaging one world for another" through immigration (132). Furthermore, as Maira and Srikanth write in the introduction to *Contours of the Heart,* it is a faulty notion that South Asians or other immigrant communities merely "follow the terrain already charted for us—leading our lives as unobtrusively as possible. . . . We are, instead, clearing new ground and imprinting ourselves on North American landscapes in unmistakable terms" (xix). In these representative moments in the development of South Asian American studies, academics and artists tell related stories in different media, gesturing to the mutual influence of self and society, as well as actual choices which are available to immigrants even if certain aspects of assimilation are not really optional.

Accordingly, much of the "active" development in *Manhattan Music* is internal accommodation to a new nation, punctuated by dramatic moments of activity or enhanced insight, through which the mental landscape of a new immigrant alters such that she feels compelled to change interpretations of America as well. For Sandhya, there are transformations that need to and do occur as part of her Americanization. These signal the inevitability of being changed and choosing differently due to the dislocation of immigration. Sandhya Rosenblum is a dramatically different woman than when she first emigrated from India, in a way that is symbolically highlighted in the novel when she refashions her physical appearance. Coming home one day, the photographer-activist Jay sees someone waiting for him,

> uncurling as mist might, a body dark as stone. . . . It was his cousin Sandhya Rosenblum. Jay stared, hardly believing the change that

> had come over her. Her hair was shorn close to her head and she was dressed in worn-out men's clothing. Perhaps men's clothing was wrong, but except for the silk scarf around her throat there was nothing feminine about her attire. (185–86)

Readers learn that Sandhya has drastically deconstructed the external signs of her femininity, foreshadowing the new self-positioning that is signified by the conclusion of the novel. The image of "uncurling mist" suggests movement and fluidity, which is immediately contrasted with "stone," suggesting hardness and emplacement: these two images therefore work together to reflect transformation as well as that which is heavy and perhaps set. That it is her "body" which seems weighted rather than airy confirms how centrally "dark femaleness" shapes this Americanization narrative. By the novel's end, it is also clear that Sandhya's altered appearance inevitably reflects back on the nation in which such transformations have occurred and on the diaspora to which she still belongs.

This is particularly apparent in a scene in which Sandhya recalls stories of how gender struggles are common to women around the world. She reminds Sakhi about a pregnant girl from their village in south India who had "fallen" into a well. Comforting her friend, Sakhi reminds her that the "poor girl, she jumped in because she thought that was her life, the only thing she could do with the shame they made her feel. But you and I . . ." At this point, Sakhi trails off, because Sandhya too has acted on the presumption that her agency was limited to what others made possible for her. Sandhya, acknowledging that she needs to narrate her own story rather than hoping that "truths" appropriate to Stephen, Draupadi, or anyone else can stand as her own, replies to Sakhi's incomplete thought, "You and I have to fight against that. There's no reason why women should pay this terrible price. A price for having been born, for feeling passion, for bearing life" (210). Sandhya here signals her awareness that she has almost paid with her life for interpreting her gender according to proscription and allowing traditional scripts to circumscribe her. At the same time, she voices a conviction that she must actively resist such narratives. In doing so, Sandhya becomes an American activist who wants to teach other women how to "see themselves seeing."

At the close of *Manhattan Music,* then, Sandhya is certain that "there was a place for her here, though what it might be she could never have spelled out. And she, who had never trusted words very much, knew that she would live out her life in America" (228). These parting sentiments reflect a certainty, on the one hand, about the need to accommodate

America and to find some measures of belonging without, on the other hand, trying to definitively name the ideal citizen. This is what makes Alexander's bildungsroman such a thoughtful, thought-provoking narrative of ambivalence and belonging.

Bharati Mukherjee's Minimalists and "Maximalists"

An author who is fascinated with America's celebratory stories of itself as a country of immigrants, Bharati Mukherjee[24] has been very forthright about her vision of the revitalizing power and the imaginative importance of new arrivals in America. As a result, her stories of Americanization have been highly visible in public culture.[25] Her writing includes two short-story collections, many political essays and interviews, and multiple novels—including *The Tiger's Daughter, Wife, Jasmine, The Holder of the World, Leave It to Me, Desirable Daughters,* and *The Tree Bride.* In this chapter, juxtaposing her novels *Wife* (1975)[26] and *Jasmine* (1989) reveals diametrically opposed responses to assimilation pressures. Both of these works are clearly in the tradition of immigrant-assimilation and coming-of-age narratives and, in their contrasting conclusions, they engage dominant ideologies about immigration, about women, and about community. Thus, *Wife* and *Jasmine* are worth reading together, which other scholars have not usually done,[27] even though there is likely more criticism concerning Mukherjee than any other South Asian American author. Adding to this body of scholarship with a twist, I read these two Mukherjee novels as complementary narratives which broadcast the author's interpretation of Americanization as an "individual search and striving"—which is how John T. Adams popularized the American Dream (423). In Mukherjee's words, this dream of belonging requires immigrants to be "maximalists" ("Immigrant Writing: Give Us Your Maximalists!").

When reading *Wife* and *Jasmine* together while bearing in mind other stories the author has set in North America, it becomes clearer that Mukherjee is at least in part testing different definitions of America and Americanness in her literary texts.[28] Controversial partly because of her provocative rejection of minoritized ethnic identity in America, Mukherjee insists on her status as a (unhyphenated) writer who upholds traditions of newcomers aggressively altering the national and literary landscape. In a fairly typical statement of her stance on Americanization, she therefore claimed,

> Mine is a clear-eyed but definite love of America. I'm aware of the brutalities, the violences here, but in the long run my characters are survivors; they've been helped, as I have, by good strong people of conviction. Like Jasmine, I feel there are people born to be Americans. By American I mean an intensity of spirit and a quality of desire. I feel American in a very fundamental way. (Quoted in Göbel 115)

Here, Mukherjee does not flinch from writing about cultural "violences" associated with Americanization, but she implies that these cannot prevent a character such as Jasmine from using her "intensity of spirit and quality of desire" to become American. Still, academics, especially within ethnic studies, are quite convincing in their criticisms of Mukherjee's tendency through this and other characters to negatively depict India, confirming a simplified story of dystopian "Old World" versus utopian "New World," thus potentially promoting full-scale and grateful assimilation. At the same time, the novel continues to "sell" to popular reading audiences and is often included in American, Asian American, or South Asian literature courses. This paradox combined with Mukherjee's idiosyncratic definitions of America are signs of her alternative—if no less debatable than normative—narratives of Americanization as challenges to those stories shaped by conventional affiliations such as race or ethnicity.[29]

As represented by a famous Modern Language Association panel at which criticisms and defenses were parried, academic and other readers have vehemently disagreed about the value of Mukherjee's writing and especially the eponymous Jasmine, who has been considered an exemplary immigrant or, alternately, a caricaturish stereotype. Reviewing the scholarship about *Jasmine* which emerged starting soon after its publication, in the early 1990s, one can observe that many readers conflate Mukherjee the person, Mukherjee the writer, and Mukherjee's texts because of the prominence the author has gained, which means that too many readers consider her an "authority" on "the" South Asian American experience. Unsurprisingly, critics who have been most committed to dispelling this simplified type of reading usually specialize in South Asian studies and are sometimes themselves Indian or South Asian. In a representative moment, in "Reading and Writing the South Asian Diaspora," Inderpal Grewal contrasts Mukherjee's *Jasmine,* as a novel which participates in problematic nationalist discourses from both North America and South Asia, with Alexander's coalition building;

Grewal also offers a critique of *Jasmine* for its neoliberalism in *Transnational America.* During an event in San Francisco over a decade after the publication of *Jasmine,* at which Mukherjee read from a new novel and I seemed to be one of only two South Asians in a crowd of several dozen, it was quite obvious how bifurcated her audiences are. The many readers present (self-identifying as nonacademics) repeatedly implied that that they could "understand" South Asians by asking Mukherjee's opinion, while I sat silently cringing at the types of essentialism in play (to which the author indeed seemed to be pandering).

In the most recent focused critique of Mukherjee's work, Jaspal Singh persuasively argues that problematic and essentializing racial politics are reinforced throughout Mukherjee's writing. Singh reads "the operation of ideology and the gaps and absences" in South Asian and African women's writing in order to expose how a "paradigm of liberation that focuses only on individual freedom without looking at the larger socio-economic and political conditions in a postcolonial and global world is rather limiting" (25, 27). Because of similar and other simplifications, Singh believes that key gender and class "complexities are not represented in Mukherjee's texts" (62), especially *Jasmine,* in which "Mukherjee seems to suggest that Jasmine can symbolically trash the old traditions and, hence, her traditional identity" (71). Pointing out that the strategies for liberation suggested in *Wife* and *Jasmine* are reductive about issues of autonomy, multiculturalism, and oppression, Singh argues that writers such as Mukherjee are complicit with Eurocentrism and Orientalism[30] because "they inadvertently betray their internalization of dominant mythologies through implicit reinforcement of the binaries, categories and logic of the West" (198). Even though Mukherjee's writing may resonate with women readers, Singh points out that her fictions negatively portray Indian women and shore up colonial ideologies.

Other feminist readers (including Anu Aneja, Shamita Das Dasgupta and Sayantani DasGupta, Susan Koshy, Shirley Geok-lin Lim, Gita Rajan, Sangeeta Ray, and Rajini Srikanth) have also offered informative critiques of Mukherjee's writing in terms of politics of belonging. Many of these critics persuasively point out the ways in which a novel such as *Jasmine* reinforces a simplistic East/West binary; we might therefore interpret the novel as a version of neo-Orientalism. Ray believes that such fiction "prevents this latest migrant minority from challenging the monolithic imaginary presentation of the American nation as the triumphant melting pot" ("The Nation in Performance" 228–29). Meanwhile, Ranee Kaur Banerjee, though not especially critical of Mukherjee's writing, does note a number of inconsistent and antifactual aspects of *Jasmine,* which result in immigrants being "characterized simply with an exaggerated overuse of the present continuous made 'Indian' to America by Peter Sellers" (199–200). There are also readers such as Andrea Dlaska and Kent Bales, who usefully analyze aspects of Mukherjee's writing and also defend or praise the author herself—in explicit contrast to critiques such as those described earlier. The level of animosity can be quite high when critics such as these dismiss others, in the middle of which back-and-forth the fiction may become less a matter of texts under analysis than bones of contention.

Rather than rehearsing the animated debates surrounding this author, which I do elsewhere,[31] it is critical to my arguments to notice how polarized interpretations of Mukherjee's fiction of "maximalism" *substantiate* the ambivalence that characterizes Americanization. Mixed responses are more accurately the history of assimilation narratives rather than extremes such as uncomplicated celebrations of the American Dream or whole-scale rejection of newness via immigration. Mukherjee's model of Americanization is indeed highly problematic in certain instances; nonetheless her writing consistently portrays different immigrant accommodations that directly respond to dominant narratives of the nation. For example, the author—like Meena Alexander—claims literary ancestors in Walt Whitman and other American writers who have attempted to represent the New World as a metaphor and a lived experience. Thus, Mukherjee argues in the introduction to her collection of short stories *Darkness* that she writes in the American grain, not from marginalized immigrant positionality. According to this self-canonization, her fictions of immigration are part of a tradition of constituting America.

In her particular version of this continually evolving story, Mukherjee repeatedly advocates that immigrant maximalists actively grasp all that is available through Americanization without nostalgia for India—but also without nostalgia for *America,* or at least its self-mythologizing. This means forgoing a sense of loss for one's origins by accepting that "whatever we were raised with is in us already. It's in our eyes and ears and in some special categories of our brains" ("Immigrant Writing" 29). Even as Mukherjee's most (in)famous immigrant maximalist, Jasmine, embodies this process of assimilation, she abandons "homesickness" about both her original and host countries; this is akin to the "clear-eyed but definite love" of America which Mukherjee claims for herself. Although Mukherjee may do so in her autobiographical writing, the character Jasmine does not glorify America. Jasmine instead maximizes her potential by choosing what she considers to be alternative narratives of inclusion and exclusion. That these alternatives seem to offer no hope for immigrant maximalism within an ethnic community, but merely for exceptional individuals, points to tensions between self and society that are inherent to assimilation processes in general.

Given this context for Mukherjee's stories about America in general, it is informative to read *Wife* and *Jasmine* as contrasting narratives, which makes it hard to choose one as *the* story of South Asian Americanization. Dimple Basu's experiences in *Wife* imply that Americanization may actually reinforce gender victimization rather than offering an alternative sense of belonging to an immigrant woman. While the main character of that novel is merely introduced as "wife," the protagonist Jasmine has a much higher degree of "en-titlement" and autonomy. Stylistically, *Jasmine* is arguably a more intimate story, with its first-person narrative and fragmented style inviting a reader to identify with the psychological transformations of the protagonist. *Wife,* in contrast, employs a more distant third-person narrative voice delivering a fairly uncomplicated story that matches the lack of depth associated with the main character. The titles match the outcomes, in that the character defined by her relation to institutionally recognized gender roles remains firmly inscribed within them, whereas Jasmine is able to "reposition the stars" (214) and evade her expected fate. Jasmine thus calls to mind Horatio Alder's Ragged Dick, the bootblack who defied the odds, in spite of her numerous differences from that earlier hero. *Wife* and *Jasmine* have dramatically dissimilar ends, but, in narrating these opposing conclusions, each helps to reveal the inconsistent and multivalent nature of experiences of assimilation and accommodation.

The first to be published, *Wife,* is mostly unremarkable in stylistic terms, but it does, at first, bear a resemblance to historical narratives about genteel British women, which is surprising since it is set in the late twentieth century. It particularly calls to mind certain genres of Victorian literature, such as comedies of manners like Jane Austen's *Pride and Prejudice.* R. S. Krishnan is among critics[32] who have commented on this intertextuality, claiming, "The opening lines of the novel signal Mukherjee's intention to reshape the hegemonic conventions, by appropriating and revising Austen's ironic representation of marriage" (90). It is indeed clear from the first ironic sentence of the novel—"Dimple Dasgupta had set her heart on marrying a neurosurgeon, but her father was looking for engineers" (3)—that the protagonist is impatiently waiting for a man with a good fortune to seek her as his wife, mostly so she can escape the tedium of single life in her parents' home in India. In the context of literature in English, Dimple's expectations of the world seem more similar to middle-class (white) women in nineteenth-century British and American bildungsromane than to contemporary mores.

Dimple patterns herself (and finds herself failing) in ways that are reminiscent of the sympathetic and self-sacrificing "angel in the house" so despised by Virginia Woolf. Woolf wrote that "the angel" had to be killed off because she prevented women from being honest and having minds of their own. Following Woolf, many feminists have read this image as the embodiment of cultural lies about gender.[33] Firmly installed in the private world of her family and certain that marriage will be the beginning of "real life" (13), Dimple dismisses education and other potential interests as things a woman such as herself does only to be distracted beforehand, since "reading novels, studying for exams, flipping through film magazines were strategies of waiting" (9). Throughout the novel, Dimple seems to continue "waiting" for a sense of belonging that seems so elusive as to be impossible. After her marriage to Amit Basu is arranged, Dimple goes to live in his family's home in Calcutta and discovers that her married life is really no different than before, except that she now has to conform to the expectations of her husband *and* her mother-in-law. Once Amit decides to move them to the United States, Dimple purposely skips rope on her way to miscarriage, for fear of endangering the new, "freer" life she believes she will have in the United States. Expecting that immigration to America will provide her with glamour and excitement, Dimple instead becomes more and more unhappy, plotting ways to kill herself and acting out against the husband who does not fulfill her ill-defined needs.

Mukherjee's portrayal of Dimple as a character who cannot adequately script a life for herself beyond bourgeois, patriarchal relationships has serious implications for the protagonist's ability to reinvent herself after immigration, much less to accommodate to her new nation. When her fantasies about marriage are shattered one by one in the quotidian tediousness of life with Amit, Dimple discovers that she has little idea about who she is separate from her husband or what she actually wants, being certain only that she always feels that she is somehow at odds with her surroundings; this is one of the few ways in which she is very similar to the character Sandhya in *Manhattan Music.* Outwardly assimilating to others' expectations does not ease her stubborn conviction that she deserves more, like the fictional women who "suffered through the Ping-Pong volley of their fates with courage" on the American soap operas to which she eventually becomes addicted after immigrating (73). Dimple has thoroughly internalized foolish, romanticized fantasies of marriage glorified in women's magazines, stories of the mythical "good wife" Sita,[34] and Hollywood/Bollywood images. Her naive reference to these simplified fictions as models for her own Americanization is presented in the novel without commentary, one of the many instances in which Dimple's self-perception begs to be read satirically.[35] Such sentiments make her a character who indicts the failings of her socialization because she can find no viable way to claim belonging in the cultures within which she lives.

If *Manhattan Music* can be interpreted as a type of "writing beyond the ending," then *Wife* represents a conventional unhappy ending for a rebellious woman in an unforgiving society. Particularly as a counterpoint to *Jasmine,* it may well stand as the American how-*not*-to book of immigration. The novel ends with Dimple finally losing all patience and lashing out at her husband, without having achieved a clear sense of self-defined identity or national belonging. Dimple's inability to feel at "home" after immigration seems most connected to her epiphany that "individual initiative, that's what it came down to, and her life had been devoted only to pleasing others, not herself" (211). Killing off her husband (whether in actuality or just in her imagination) by the end of the novel, Dimple feels that she has failed in her dream of transitioning from a boring Indian housewife to a glamorous American working girl. Her fantasies about how her Americanization might develop take odd, hilarious turns, showing her to be a naive and hapless protagonist, as compared to a "fighter and adapter" such as Jasmine (*Jasmine* 35). For example, Dimple takes a lover, Milt Glass, whom she tries to fit into a familiar script of Indian arranged marriage. Dimple writes a letter to "Miss Problem-Walla" (a columnist who dispenses beauty advice to women in India), asking about Milt's suitability as if seeking a potential husband (202). In scenes such as this, the novel provides an obvious critique of conventional scripts for marriage and for women. It narrates a process that might very well be called "growing down," following Annis Pratt's readings of "archetypal patterns" in women's writing (14).

Dimple, rather than choosing her own accommodation to America, begins to mistake convenience and consumption for empowerment and fulfillment. She chastises herself for poor assimilation to gendered American norms, since "she might have been a better person, a better wife at any rate, if she could have produced more glamorous leftovers" (119). Instead, she is a woman "with no degree and not a single marketable skill"

(40). Dimple's regression is therefore a direct result of her internalization of ideals for a traditional Indian wife combined with the influences of American pop culture at its worst—glorified violence on television and rampant materialism as purported routes to liberation. One such example in the novel is her recourse to the "backs of cereal boxes that promised 'FREE INSIDE!'" (156) whenever she feels panicky or uncertain about her place in the United States. This is also why she is comforted by her husband's buying power, is proud of her "acquisitiveness" (130), and rationalizes at first "how lucky she was to be among . . . appliances, to explore the wonders of modern American living, unencumbered by philosophical questions about happiness" (136). Her minimalist assimilation results, however, in her self-image as "a pitiful immigrant among demanding appliances" (186) who cannot latch onto the happiness that those conveniences were allegedly going to provide her. By the conclusion of the novel, Dimple learns the unsatisfying reality of stereotypic gender roles in Indian and American pop culture, which she mistakenly read as examples of self-determination.

While the dominant narrative in *Wife* exposes Dimple Basu as a type of South Asian American antihero, the latent plot beneath its pervasive irony implies that there can be no successful Americanization when a character merely conforms to normative ideology concerning women's roles. Portraying sexism in both Indian and American manifestations throughout *Wife,* Mukherjee implies that Dimple learns all too well how to be no more than what she is told befits a woman and wife: dependent, overly domestic and bound to the home, and (at least superficially) compliant. Her tendency to confuse American consumerism with feminism also does not stand her in good stead, a tendency for which Grewal offers a trenchant critique when describing neoliberal America as a site in which commercialism is regularly conflated with "choice" (*Transnational America* 3). As both the novel and such theory affirm, movements westward from India to America do not inevitably result in "liberation" from normative pressures, of gender or other types—although they obviously take altered forms when an adulterous lover offers salvation, versus the husband to whom Dimple's marriage was arranged. Postcolonial feminists have postulated that construing female liberation as a "Western" ideal is a common assumption of "the white American women's movement,"[36] and some critics take Mukherjee to task for supporting just such an assumption. However, this does not seem like a convincing reading of *Wife,* since all of the characters in the novel, Indian or American, similarly hold out hobbling gender expectations for Dimple.

In striking contrast to *Wife,* Mukherjee's *Jasmine* is a narrative of the seemingly "successful"[37] Americanization of Jyoti, who becomes Jasmine—as well as Jane, Jazzy, and Jase. Jasmine is first renamed by her husband, Prakash Vijh, and subsequently shape-shifts with seeming ease. The novel begins with her moving from her feudal village in the Punjab in India to the bigger city of Jullundhar after her wedding at the age of fourteen. She is widowed soon after when a Sikh terrorist's bomb kills Prakash.[38] Deciding that she must somehow fulfill her husband's wish to immigrate to the United States to study, Jasmine illegally enters America in order to commit *sati*[39] at the university he would have attended. Raped and provoked into murder when her attacker defiles the items she intended to use in the ritual, Jasmine is subsequently aided by a series of people and manages to thrive in spite of being "undocumented." Living for a brief time with a former professor of Prakash's and his wife in Flushing, New York, Jasmine eventually leaves that immigrant community for a job as an au pair with Taylor, Wylie, and Duff Hayes in Manhattan, where she feels she becomes an American through their example. Unfortunately driven from a happy life with the Hayeses by her paranoid certainty that her husband's murderer has followed her to New York, Jasmine retreats to Baden, Iowa. There, she eventually moves in with Bud Ripplemeyer, is artificially inseminated with his child, and adopts a teenager named Du. At the end of the narrative, she decides to join Taylor and Duff in their westward migration (to California) and abandons the safe haven she seemed to have found in a small midwestern town with Bud. While being personally empowering, her strategies of national accommodation also risk abandoning *any* possibilities for community belonging.

In an alternative fiction of Americanization when contrasted with Dimple's descent into a kind of madness, Jasmine learns to destabilize conventional community-building practices and to reject essentialist expectations of identity. Jasmine glories in the way that she "shuttled between identities" (70) rather than remaining consistent or loyal to one idea of herself and any group to which she may belong. In this way, the protagonist manages to elude constraining gender narratives that entrap Dimple. Regarding this type of shifting between identities, Angelika Bammer describes "the peculiarly postmodern geography of identity: both here *and* there and neither here *nor* there at one and the same time" (xii). In the case of *Jasmine,* the displacement of migration to the United States results in an ethnic-minority immigrant woman identifying herself at the borders between multiple cultures and leveraging this positionality to choose between different instantiations of self. Part of becoming American for her means learning to deftly balance "in-between" (i.e., hybrid) moments of geographical migration (ever westward) and transition (between identities), such that being neither here nor there, part of neither this group nor that, does not prevent her from finding what she deems an acceptable sense of belonging. Ruth Maxey reads this as a "pro-assimilationist stance" by which Mukherjee's character reveals her "eminent capacity for Americanization" ("The Messiness of Rebirth as an Immigrant" 189). Whether this sense of belonging is in any way replicable is matter for another story.

The story of "maximalist" national belonging in *Jasmine* is thus constructed through the protagonist's individualistic efforts to gain personal satisfaction, all the while negotiating inescapable, often oppressive, gendered and ethnic expectations in America. Despite ambivalent responses to the novel, most readers agree about the heroism that the narrative assigns to Jasmine. In contrast to Dimple, Jasmine learns to manipulate her surroundings, refusing the role of victim and shaping her own identity in opposition to normative expectations. When her "dark femaleness" is most salient, Jasmine's response is to exploit so-called exotic qualities that render her an "Indian princess" (192), a very different reaction from Sandhya's in *Manhattan Music.* And even as Jasmine makes a place for herself in America, she refuses to hold sacred the fictions that America is "the land of the free." Jennifer Drake claims that, in Mukherjee's fictions, "hope's transformative violence—a gritty leap toward 'freedom'—dialogues with the false hope offered by an American dream premised on white supremacy and disseminated by global capitalism's exploitations" (61–62). Redefining assimilation as "looting," Drake here reads Mukherjee's narratives of becoming American as acts of reinvigorating the myths of America that many immigrants experience as false promises. It is certainly true that Jasmine does not experience America as a nation full of "generous, hard-working, democratic, lovers of truth and defenders of equal opportunity for all" (61), as Drake describes such myths of America. Instead, Jasmine records encounters with violence, anti-immigrant hatred, hypocrisy, ignorance, and exclusions that do not encourage naive faith in America.

Even as Jasmine thus demystifies the American Dream, she does not reject it entirely, revealing an ambivalent attitude to classic notions of Americanization that serves her well. She reconfigures dominant narratives of assimilation with an ironic awareness of how far short of reality they fall and claims from them whatever empowerment she can. Bonnie

Hoover Braendlin has called such a process "demythification" in ethnic women's bildungsromane (79), asserting that female protagonists who are "disenfranchised Americans, . . . people whose sex or color renders them unacceptable to the dominant society" (75), must create a space for themselves within national narratives. Braendlin interprets such narratives as ones that express a "struggle for individuation and a part in the American dream, which society simultaneously proffers and denies" ethnic women (75). She links this struggle to the overdetermined processes by which a female character may be portrayed as an outsider and even a social pariah because she rejects dominant views of herself.[40]

Whereas Dimple and other immigrants in Mukherjee's fictions maintain a type of expatriate existence based on past allegiances or a diasporic longing for the homeland, Jasmine eschews social determinism of the kind Braendlin describes. Instead, Jasmine is an expert at embracing different potential identities and rejects either of the two courses of action that many people see as the only ones available to immigrants, according to the binaristic logic I discussed in chapter 1: assimilation into the melting pot or ethnic separatism. This is why she refuses to remain a part of a South Asian immigrant community in Flushing, even though it offers her community support. In this immigrant enclave, Jasmine feels unable to explore the new land to which she has come, because of what she considers to be "artificially maintained Indianness" (128). Unlike Dimple, not only does Jasmine refuse the gendered scripts that might limit "maximalism," but she also rejects ethnic expectations, insisting that "dark femaleness" will not bar her from an Americanization of her choosing.

By constructing an alternative family with her former (Anglo-American) employer and his daughter instead of maintaining strictly ethnic loyalties, Jasmine implicitly rejects expectations of women within traditional communities and families. Priscilla Wald historicizes how the family has been a metaphor and medium for Americanization, according to which immigrants were children to the establishment—with clear race and gender hierarchies, one notes. The concept of family as employed in the process of assimilating new Americans, Wald writes, is a reflection of the fear of "race suicide" (254) that will allegedly afflict white America if immigration is unchecked and allowed to challenge "traditional" white, middle-class family expectations. *Jasmine* offers a direct challenge to this conservative version of "family values" (on which many contemporary stories of America and policies of exclusion are based), by showing how the protagonist's alternative family allows a greater possibility than a normative family for an immigrant woman to achieve her dreams.

Closely related to this challenge to tradition is also Mukherjee's destabilizing of the idea of "home" as the site in which conventional family roles are played out, so that disrupting "family" in *Jasmine* also means disrupting genealogical histories and certainties. This in turn denaturalizes associations of the American nation *with* family, specifically an intact, nuclear family conforming to patriarchal ideologies. Jasmine's modified idea of family is, by contrast, a progressive vision of social groups that do not conform to more traditional or mainstream models and, due to their alternative configurations, have the potential to positively empower her. Walter Göbel critiques such families in Mukherjee's fiction as a "shared homelessness within a heteroglot community situated on an island of the mind which is not precisely located or named" (116), which raises another critical debate about metaphorical versus actual, especially forced, (dis)placement that cannot be pursued in this study. Whatever we term it, the American family which the protagonist chooses at the end of *Jasmine* is transitional and willful rather than "natural" or inevitable, which is how many people might regard family and home.

Combining various influences into a new sense of self in "provisionality" (287), *Jasmine* calls attention to ways in which "America," too, is mutable and will repeatedly be reimagined by diasporic immigrants such as her. Co-opting familiar myths of the country as the land of unlimited opportunity, Jasmine puts them to her own uses, not flinching from the antagonisms and unpleasantness that those fairy tales gloss over. She experiences and records dystopian tendencies that demystify a propagandistic equation of America with "THE PERFECT FREEDOM" (75), which is how the U.S. Postal Service advertises the nation. Appropriating such stories and rejecting victimization or "minority" status, Jasmine decides she can achieve the supposed American Dream *despite* other Americans who might deny her, by reminding herself that the country has been actively imagined, thus created, by waves of immigrants. Correspondingly, Mary Dearborn comments that "the central feature of American identity is the experience of migration, that Americans are in fact all descended from immigrants and that American selfhood is based on a seemingly paradoxical sense of shared difference" (3). Mukherjee's protagonist Jasmine reasserts this quality of the nation that might be forgotten when nativism gains ground and newer immigrants are scapegoated for the problems of the country or face coercive assimilation, which is not merely a fictional possibility but also part of the history of assimilation that I traced in chapter 1. Like the other narratives in this study, Mukherjee's second novel of becoming American participates in a project of "constituting" America that is ongoing and full of contradictions. *Jasmine* is therefore a novel that continues in the tradition of writers both rehearsing and unsettling traditional, official stories of America in order to dramatize the in-betweenness of the immigrant (and other Others in the United States) through what Wald calls "revisionary" narratives (298).

As becomes more apparent after juxtaposing *Wife* and *Jasmine*, ambivalence should be an anticipated response to demands on immigrants to accommodate themselves to a new nation. Such ambivalence is linked both to histories elsewhere that cannot be erased, even through purposeful cultural amnesia, as well to inconsistent equality in the "land of the free." Engaging with nationalist rhetoric that "has so many ways of humiliating or disappointing" (*Jasmine* 25) by claiming to include people such as Jasmine and Du but always with a patronizing sense of their Otherness, Mukherjee's "maximalist" responds to such narratives with an audacious refusal to be that Other, to be negatively marked by her "dark femaleness." Learning not to be victim to a nationalism that may disguise itself as the best form of democracy, shored up by icons such as the Statue of Liberty welcoming the world's vulnerable and dispossessed, Jasmine instead acts as if America can still be an open frontier[41] for someone like herself, as long as she openly confronts its contradictions and refuses to participate in false glorifications of the American Dream. At the same time, Jasmine alters official or normative stories of South Asia, as well; for example, she opts for alternatives to gendered icons such as Sita, most notably Kali, the goddess of destruction. She links the Hindu concept of reincarnation[42]—"I am sure that I have been reborn several times" (113)—to her various identities and the promise of America as a place in which many cultures collide with and borrow from each other.

In the contrast with Dimple, Jasmine comes across as a character typifying (admittedly problematic notions of) American exceptionalism, which may explain why Mukherjee's novel has met with praise in American public culture, since this is a very familiar national narrative. Since novels such as *Jasmine* are celebrated while other, related fictions are largely ignored, there have been ongoing debates about authors who have become canonical enough to seem to "speak for" a certain community. Scholarly discussions of Mukherjee and Maxine Hong Kingston are cases in point, since both writers have become representatives of their ethnic subcultures for broad American reading audiences. Obviously, no writer should be expected to play this role. Still, it happens, and some critics fear that minority writers are popular precisely because they indulge the stereotypes of "white" audiences, thus reinforcing hegemonic Orientalisms. Shirley Geok-lin Lim concludes that Mukherjee has been canonized as part of "the popular adoption of selected Asian American texts—illustrating, for example, Western feminist notions of Asian patriarchal modes, or Western literary ideas of the postmodern"—and further believes that this "points to the dispersal of their strangeness, and finally to the Americanization of Asia" (302). Mukherjee has no doubt received mixed reviews because many scholars concur with Lim. Such critiques are usually well founded, but continuing anxieties about the "authentic Indianness" (which is further discussed in chapter 4) portrayed in Mukherjee's writing may be of too limited utility.

More productively, we might address how Jasmine's appropriation of the American Dream seems utopian and/or apolitical, as many critics have argued: these responses are themselves confirmations of the radically contested history of assimilation ideologies in the United States. While some readers interpret the story in *Jasmine* to suggest that anyone can become American like the protagonist, the narrative emphasizes that her "maximalist" assimilation is aided by her so-called unique spirit, by serendipity, and by the (mixed) privilege of fulfilling certain exotic fantasies of the "East" without being considered an ethnic threat. Even more significantly, Jasmine creates unorthodox "families" which are not based on "blood" ties or on identity politics such as race and gender coalitions—meaning that she is willing enough to surrender conventional types of solidarity. As Göbel advises, "For minorities like the African-Americans, who have for centuries been marginalised, Mukherjee's idea of Americanality may well seem a return to the age-old ideology of the melting-pot: that is, of cultural homogenisation through assimilation" (115). What Göbel reminds us here is that the master's tools may never dismantle the master's house, to borrow another concept from Lorde's *Sister Outsider,* and that Mukherjee's vision of Americanization is not a viable model for all marginalized Americans. Such analyses are important correctives for those readers who might cite stories such as *Jasmine* as evidence with which to excoriate minorities for not assimilating more thoroughly to mainstream America.

However, it is important to remember not to read *Jasmine* simply as documentary or ethnography; we might do well to follow Samir Dayal's categorization of the novel as an "identarian fable" of Americanization ("Creating, Preserving, Destroying" 83). In this context, Jasmine can be read as manipulating narratives of the country in order to assimilate without, well, assimilating—a case in which "accommodation" may well be a more suitable description than Americanization. The novel ends with the character embarking on yet another adventure without a sense of certainty about her future, representing a deferral of recognition as American in a way that conforms to David Palumbo-Liu's reading of Asian America—but this deferral is *of her own choosing.* This choice implies that it is the process of continuing to respond to Americanization as Jasmine does, with provisionality, that makes one American, rather than matching a supposed standard which could never fit all Americans across their differences. By reading *Jasmine* in comparison to Bharati Mukherjee's other novel of (not) becoming American, readers can feel a sense of hope in the possibility for immigrant agency in accommodation, as compared to the hopelessness of that unhappy wife and "failed American" Dimple Basu. Calling to mind Bhabha's discussion of "unhomeliness" in *The Location of Culture,* Claudia Egerer describes similar literary themes in works by other minoritized writers in terms of the "homelessness" which is symptomatic of the "(in)betweenness [that] is the result of repeated border crossings, between and across diverse conceptual and cultural boundaries" (50). Mukherjee's "maximalist" Jasmine embraces the fluid possibilities represented by such border crossing, but there is no denying that the risks of not belonging are ridiculously high.

Nonetheless, in that frequently quoted article, "Immigrant Writing: Give Us Your Maximalists!" Mukherjee urges immigrant writers to actively welcome and opportunistically exploit the "messiness of rebirth as an immigrant" (28). Her intention seems to be to undermine tendencies to view immigrants as either passive victims of the alienation of a new society or sojourners nostalgic for their "homelands." This advice reinforces the critique of certain kinds of Americanization that Mukherjee makes through the narrative in *Wife*—and the kinds she promotes in *Jasmine.*

Bapsi Sidhwa: Assimilationists, Inc.

A Pakistani American author, Bapsi Sidhwa is a Parsee,[43] part of a tiny ethno-religious community settled mostly in South Asia but also dispersed to other parts of the world. Her writing includes short stories, essays, and four novels: *The Bride* (released in India as *The Pakistani Bride*), *The Crow Eaters,* and *Cracking India* (originally titled *Ice-Candy-Man* and the basis for Canadian director Deepa Mehta's critically acclaimed film *Earth*). Even as Sidhwa's fourth novel, *An American Brat* (1993), narrates diasporic lessons learned by the Parsees, the author also contributes to discussions about "Who is American?" and "What does America represent?" As in all of the novels discussed in this chapter, the personal maturation of the female protagonist parallels her immigration, and her diasporization supplements her growing feelings of national belonging rather than ultimately proving an obstacle to them. At this time, I am among only a handful of critics who places Sidhwa within American literary histories, but there is certainly more that can be said about the author in this context.

To appreciate the (trans)national complexities informing what may seem to be a fairly straightforward coming-of-age narrative in *An American Brat,* it is necessary to historicize the Parsee diaspora of which the protagonist is a member. In an essay titled "Why Do I Write?" Sidhwa characterizes the Parsees as "a resourceful and accommodating community tucked away in the forgotten crevices of history" (33). The melancholy tone of this description can be attributed to the reality that Parsees have such small numbers in the world that they face a chronic possibility of becoming culturally extinct, a condition that is a backdrop to Sidhwa's novel about America. Ambreen Hai lists some of the other unique qualities that characterize Parsees: "This community is historically diasporic (exiled from Persia since the seventh century),[44] ethnically distinct, and founded upon an ancient religious tradition independent of both Judeo-Christian-Islamic monotheism and Hinduism" (387). Meanwhile, Novy Kapadia documents how the Parsee practice of endogamy has raised questions about whether "Parsee" is a religious label or actually designates something else. He notes that, legally, at least a few judges in South Asia consider "Zoroastrianism" to be the religion of an individual and "Parsee" to indicate a person's nationality or community. Kapadia concludes that "according to the 1906 legal definition, there is no doubt that a Parsi continues to remain a Parsi even after he or she marries a non-Parsi" ("Expatriate Experience" 198), despite orthodox Parsee views to the contrary. The Parsees have been the subjects of a number of studies interested in untangling these various labels that defy categorization by many familiar standards. For example, Parsees lack a consistent or unitary national identification; in contemporary terms, they are neither solely Indian nor Pakistani since their tight-knit diasporic community crosses these subcontinental borders; and they are most famous for their commitment to cultural accommodation without religious conversion.[45]

Oft-noted "Parsee paradoxes" include an ability to thrive despite their minority status in each site of relocation and after historical episodes of persecution and exile. Originally from an area that is now southern Iran, the Parsees were expelled after refusing to convert from Zoroastrianism to Islam when Arabian invaders colonized the area. After their expulsion from Persia, the Parsees settled in coastal areas in South Asia, including Bombay, which is still arguably the hub of the subcontinental Parsee community. There are also large Parsee settlements in two of Pakistan's major cities, Karachi and Lahore. Parsees now constitute less than 1 percent of the total population of India and number just about one hundred thousand on the subcontinent. Despite their small numbers, Kapadia notes that "their feeling of group identity and active participation in the social, cultural, and economic life of both India and Pakistan is immense" ("The Parsi Paradox" 125). Highly noticeable despite their minuscule population, the Parsees are easily identified by their unusual style of dress, their tendency to live in close proximity to other members of the community, their physiognomy which hints at Iranian ancestry, and several distinguishing religious practices, including the disposal of their dead at *dokhmas,* or what the British called Towers of Silence.

Parsee communities make a point of adapting as fully as possible to prevailing cultural and political expectations where they settle, within the limits of their religious practices. Feroza Jussawalla writes that the "case of the Parsis is quintessential hybridism" ("'Hybridity,' Our Ancestral Heritage" 200), reading cultural hybridity here as the indissoluble grafting together of multiple types of affiliation. The famous parable representing this accommodation-without-complete-assimilation has it that, upon being allowed onto the mainland of Gujarat after their expulsion from Iran many centuries ago, the Parsees convinced the reigning rajah to accept them by comparing themselves to the "sugar in the milk" of the existing settlement. In Sidhwa's novel *The Crow Eaters,* a character elaborates that "the refugees would get absorbed into the country. . . . And with their decency and industry sweeten the lives of [the Prince's] subjects" (47).[46] Parsee characters in that text interpret the parable to mean that they are able to blend into the societies of their settlement after dispersal (and often after subsequent migrations) without bitterness or regret, having indelibly altered those societies such that they will never be able to separate them out again entirely. The dominant American narrative of the homogenizing melting pot comes to mind; however, the lingering Parsee "sweetness," which supposedly improves any nation, continues to be contingent on their particularity and their ability to maintain "difference." The overall effect is therefore not of cultural loss, as is often associated with the melting-pot metaphor.

The Parsee history of adaptation without homogenization in India also gestures to another notable characteristic of the diaspora: their general lack of focus on an originating homeland to which they can return. Instead, Parsee communities have experienced continuous hybridization through interaction with other groups. Robin Cohen writes, "Just as [the Parsees] accept that the move from Persia to India in response to Muslim persecution was a necessary survival strategy, so they think of the dispersal from India to the 'new world' (which, includes in this context, Europe), as another stage of 'moving on.' They are not so much a travelling nation then . . . as a travelling religion" (188). A traveling community disconnected from a particular national territory as *the* location of their culture, the Parsees arguably maintain a type of nonaligned status that means they disrupt the automatic association of a racial, ethnic, or religious identity with a particular national body. Their self-positioning therefore potentially presents a serious challenge to conventional understandings of individual and collective identification.[47]

This challenge is evident in how efforts to situate Sidhwa, a Parsee/Pakistani/American writer, can lead to inconsistencies which have not always helped with the marketing of her books. Scholars who are making related arguments to this one do not necessarily conform in how they label her, as seen in the contrast between Ambreen Hai's introduction of "a non-canonical Anglophone Pakistani woman" writer (385) and Sangeeta Ray's classification of Sidhwa as a South Asian and even South Asian American writer. Other critics vary in calling Sidhwa one of the most notable authors from India, which is the country into which she was born; or from Pakistan, which is the country that now claims Lahore, where she grew up; or, more recently, as a writer of the South Asian diaspora and as an American author. As to the material consequences of such discursive variation, Fawzia Afzal-Khan points out that "the David Higham award, given to *The Crow Eaters* for best first novel in 1980, was withheld because Pakistan was no longer part of the British Commonwealth" (271). Such ironies of history and naming are highly informative about the meanings of Sidhwa's fictions.

Sidhwa's only novel set primarily in America, *An American Brat* is a fictional account of how the unique history of the Parsees continues to inform their contemporary relocations. It narrates how a young woman from a minority community in Pakistan migrates to America in the late 1970s. Coming to adolescence in Pakistan just as General Zia overthrows Zulfikar Ali Bhutto and enacts martial law, Feroza Ginwalla has been adversely influenced, according to her mother, Zareen, by the rising tide of fundamentalism and Islamicization of the country. Zareen typically believes that their community of Parsees is more forward looking and cosmopolitan than any others in South Asia, a legacy which she wishes to see continue with her own daughter. Instead, Feroza is awkward, wanting to be like her classmates rather than being identified as a non-Muslim in an increasingly Muslim country, sullen with her parents, and antisocial to boot. Intended to be a visit with her uncle lasting a few months, Feroza's sojourn in the United States instead becomes a permanent immigration through a series of unexpected choices. Eventually, as a young adult woman in America, Feroza comes to understand that she is well equipped to challenge certain (trans)national orthodoxies in a way that she did not recognize as a teenager in Pakistan.

In fact, just as her Parsee ancestors historically dispersed and contributed their distinctiveness to host nations, the protagonist Feroza comes to realize that she, too, will never "fully" assimilate. After immigrating to yet another host country, Feroza maintains cultural habits of her diasporic community, including a sustained engagement with local politics controlled by other communities, an insistent sense of alterity, and a commitment to justice emerging from experiences of marginalization. The centrality of this training is foundational in allowing Feroza to envision playing a part in American national narratives. Adamant that neither her religious affiliation nor her past history in diaspora are expendable, Feroza uses her cultural education in Pakistan among the Parsees as a basis for assessing and potentially transforming America as she comes to know it, both flawed and fulfilling. In the narrative, seemingly hollowed-out concepts such as the melting pot are redeployed and reconceived in light of the endemic conditions of people in diaspora, who are always "compelled to live with and tolerate the 'other'" (313). This diasporic condition, or "accommodating mind" (which I discuss later), allows Feroza to view assimilation as a process of inevitable accommodation *and* transformation of the dominant national myths which affects established communities no less than new arrivals.

Through Feroza's story, *An American Brat* makes clear why multiracial America, with its cultural diversity and its spectrum of socioeconomic privilege, is such an important geopolitical space for deploying common Parsee strategies of adaptation. Citing dominant symbolism of the American nation as the main character tests their meanings, the story raises possibilities for and challenges to social and political equality among heterogeneous communities. Diasporization adds another layer of complexity to the experiences of Americans in minority communities, for all of whom assimilation is a type of belonging that can be both alluring and self-negating when one is dramatically dissimilar to the majority population. As Dayal writes, "For the postcolonial diasporic, there is always the question of whether the impulse toward assimilation is linked to the ambivalent desire to become like those who have historically inculcated the fables of their own superiority to the *darker* races that they colonized" ("Min(d)ing the Gap" 255, emphasis added). This theoretical point seems highly relevant to the ways in which *An American Brat* depicts Feroza's longing for "gleaming white skin" (153); the unusually (for South Asians) light-skinned Parsees inherited complex sets of possibilities and meanings for assimilation from the multiple majority groups under whose reigns they lived as minorities.

In classic bildungsroman fashion, Feroza's maturation is represented in *An American Brat* as a process that is shaped by her efforts to claim belonging within the American nation, but it is also envisioned as a process that members of her community have repeated multiple times, which is an innovative departure from earlier works in the tradition. In other words, the text itself assimilates to, while also transforming, the literary context in which it belongs. With regard to the broader implications of the novel, to continue to be "in diaspora" while being settled in the United States means recognizing that national assimilation, too, represents accommodation, meaning chronic negotiation rather than a finality. The novel implies that, through acts of creative and willful self-positioning, Feroza will continue to balance nation and diaspora in a literary text well worth recognition within traditions of immigrant fiction about America and the American Dream. At the conclusion of *An American Brat,* the narrator says of Feroza, "There would be no going back for her, but she could go back at will" (317), insisting on the diasporic space she creates for herself within the national imaginary of her new country. In this way, Sidhwa's novel confirms Yunte Huang's recent arguments that American literature is a "national literature *rooted* in transnationalism" (5, emphasis added), overturning assumptions of innate or grounded identities in order to note that (trans)nationalism is the shared origin of certain kinds of stories.

Specifically, *An American Brat* narrates how diasporization affects Americanization when the protagonist questions Americans' images of themselves as "free" in their pursuit of happiness. Like the others described in this chapter, Sidhwa's story of immigration is certainly an engagement with that most revered and also most disputed stories of assimilation and success, the American Dream. For example, the sixteen-year-old protagonist of *An American Brat* faces an "induction into the self-sufficient, industrious, and independent way of American life" (119), as her eccentric and often-pompous young uncle, Manek, puts it when he welcomes her to America. In one of a limited number of scholarly analyses focused solely on this text, Geoffrey Kain therefore aptly calls the novel "a very American tale" (245) which develops in "classic/mythic American fashion" (240). In Sidhwa's contribution to traditions of American immigrant fiction, even as the Parsee particularity of the hero uniquely informs her story of immigration, there is noticeable continuity in the protagonist's struggle to understand the contemporary implications of the American Dream. Feroza thus resembles characters in earlier novels who struggled with assimilation processes as members of "new" ethnic groups.

An American Brat documents the constraints on Americanization as "free" self-invention by highlighting that gender, race, and socioeconomic conventions are related structures of exclusion and Othering. Early episodes in the novel focus on the vulnerabilities which "dark femaleness" confers because of patterns of gendered violence. Feroza encounters predatory male sexuality soon after arrival, on a visit to New York. There were the "dark, impersonal face of the man leering at her in the mirror when she looked up from brushing her teeth, the brutal faces of the men who slyly muttered obscenities in the halls, the dangerous, focused stare of the drug dealer who had loomed *whitely* out of the recessed doorway on Forty-second Street" (91, emphasis added). Each of these markers of whiteness or dominant culture in the United States represents dangerous possibilities for the new immigrant, because they are dehumanizing in their "impersonal" and "brutal" regard of her and also suggestive of the physical/sexualized violence anticipated by "leers," "sly" mutterings, and intrusive stares. From the beginning of Feroza's immigration to America, these encounters inform her that her gender has both ideological and material effects on her ability to accommodate herself to her new nation. Despite a tendency for North American and European countries to be associated with feminist activism and thus supposedly to be "more free" from gender inequality than non-Western locations, histories of patriarchy throughout the world have analogous structural effects. The novel suggests that, although these are varied in their particulars, American gender systems are no less significant than South Asian institutions in differentially organizing society for men and women, as Feroza discovers in a terrifying way.

Paradoxical and self-contradictory possibilities for belonging in the nation reveal to the protagonist that the rewards associated with Americanization may be barbed lures for immigrants because they demand denial of such realities and submission to other problematic social hierarchies. Along with her gender identity, her ethnic difference from the majority helps Feroza recognize that many Americanization narratives are not quite the right fit for her "dark femaleness." In college, she

> became aware of her different color and the reaction it appeared to have on strangers like that rude saleswoman, and on some of her classmates. . . . She sensed she was not accepted by them. Dismayed by her own brown skin, the emblem of her foreignness, she felt it was inferior to the gleaming white skin in the washrooms and the roseate faces in the classroom. (152–53)

In this passage and other key textual moments, there is clear emphasis on how "color" provokes a sense of "foreignness" or alienation which thwarts belonging; "brown" is repeatedly juxtaposed against "white" such that darkness becomes something ugly, contrasted with not only rosy but also bright and promising ("roseate") visages. Although being a woman or an ethnic minority does not inevitably result in alienation from the dominant culture or in disempowerment, Feroza's "body proper is alien in America," as Diane S. Allen puts it (78). The protagonist's self-conscious recognition of her "dark femaleness" is therefore centrally informative about her responses to assimilation processes. Through these, she comes to develop an attitude that is more questioning of assimilation to national narratives than she was in her original country of residence, Pakistan. Both too young to have a highly developed sense of the politics of identity and without personal experiences of migration—especially to the "New World"—before immigration, she had not been as cognizant of the ways in which national belonging is always defined through sameness and difference, thus inclusion and exclusion. After she immigrates, her steadily developing awareness throughout the narrative is that the American Dream, although allegedly attainable through hard work, is in fact a mirage.

Feroza calls to mind characters in other American novels who have struggled with assimilation processes that were imbued with exclusionary ideologies—for example, Social Darwinism as well as ethnocentrism and sexism—and therefore undermined the American Dream. In an interesting if unexpected likeness, given Feroza's elite class background, *An American Brat* revisits themes which have been particularly associated with Upton Sinclair's *The Jungle* or the less well-known, recently recovered Asian American "personal history" by Carlos Bulosan, *America Is in the Heart.* These works narrate the tragic outcomes for two male immigrant Americans in the first half of the twentieth century and demystify the association of unchanging poverty with the Old World or easily achieved prosperity with the New World. In Sinclair's canonical immigrant fiction, the main character, Jurgis Rudkus, heart-breakingly realizes that his repeated declaration in the face of adversity—"I will work harder"—is based on an illusory meritocracy, a realization which is echoed in Carlos Bulosan's narration of increasing immigrant disillusionment. In *The Jungle,* Jurgis turns to socialism as a potential solution to the economic inequalities that impede his realization of the American Dream, and Bulosan narrates idealistic plans by labor activists to change the status quo. These are fitting engagements with a dream that was first offered in the context of a socialist critique of laissez-faire economies, as Demetrios J. Lallas documents.

One might well argue that Feroza is an unlikely spokesperson for class critique and that her Americanization is much less difficult than for other immigrants positioned in the working classes or living in poverty, but her narrative nonetheless structurally matches the others in her increasing recognition that American dreams of prosperity do not represent the realities for most, or even many, people in the nation. She becomes highly motivated by her awareness of and deep regret for "the schizophrenia she perceived at the core of America's relationship to its own citizenry and to those in poor countries like hers" (*An American Brat* 172). It seems that diasporization combined with immigration compel Feroza to reassess her own affluence and the social injustices related to capitalist economics. Thus, Feroza in America confronts the reality of stark disparities veiled by the nation's image as "the free world," eventually leading to her pledge to "fight injustice wherever she was" (313). These heroic words strike a melodramatic chord in an often light-hearted and even comedic work. This might be considered a flawed tone in the narrative, but there is clear literary precedent here in canonical works such as *The Jungle, America Is in the Heart,* or Ralph Ellison's *Invisible Man,* a narrative which suggests by its conclusion that the protagonist may any day emerge from his basement darkness to radically threaten the racial status quo.

As in many such fictions about the Other in mainstream America, Feroza is initially quite bedazzled by prosperity and possibilities in America, but she eventually commits herself to a rather idealistic vision of Americanness as a response to actual inequality and intolerance she encounters. Upon arriving in the United States, like Jurgis and the fictional Carlos Bulosan or the invisible man coming to the North, Feroza marvels at the limitless possibilities for ever-upward mobility and material acquisitions seemingly available to any ambitious newcomer. Accordingly, South Asians in *An American Brat* recount to each other and to families back home the marvels of uninterrupted energy, of "convenience" foods and stores, and of other "seductive entitlements of the First World" (313). And Feroza lists "Happy Hour, telephones that worked, the surfeit of food, freezers, electricity, and clean and abundant water, the malls, skyscrapers, and highways" among the many temptations America holds for her (313). Clearly, the technology of the "West" is no small incentive for this diasporic immigrant who perceives that

> she was not alone in her desire for privacy and plenty. A sizable portion of the world was experiencing this phenomenon, on this scale at least, for the first time in human history, and the rest of the jam-packed and impoverished world—no matter how much they might moan about the loss of human contact, privacy, and the dwindling family—also hankered for it. (313)

In passages such as these, *An American Brat* envisions independence and prosperity in a manner that seemingly favors the modern "First World" over allegedly orthodox societies in which technological "impoverishment" is the punishment for traditionalism and communalism. This alludes to a familiar theme in South Asian literature, what Dayal in an article about *Jasmine* describes as the "debate of tradition versus modernity" ("Creating, Preserving, Destroying" 68).

Sidhwa's novel thus reproduces conventional tropes of the land of plenty associated with the American Dream, but it also deconstructs them as Feroza becomes further immersed in her new, "strangely paradoxical nation" (313). This narrative of becoming American does not hesitate to point out that greater physical comfort and routine conveniences are serious inducements offered by the "First World" to a "Third World woman"[48] such as Feroza and even to her mother. No stranger to wealth or her own buying power, Zareen is nonetheless overcome by all the promising glitter of the mall when she travels from Pakistan to rescue her daughter (now labeled an American "brat") from her unexpected relocation. However, the protagonist does not associate these amenities with cultural superiority, which is a danger of unproblematically valorizing Americanization, and she furthermore recognizes the ready evidence against "development." For example, Feroza thinks that the extreme poverty of homelessness at the Port Authority Bus Terminal "personified the callous heart of the rich country that allowed such savage neglect to occur" (81), suggesting indifference but also fierce cruelty through a failure to act as duty might dictate. Poverty unalleviated by the state is also, of course, a chronic condition throughout South Asia that nationalistic rhetorics cannot obscure. *An American Brat* narrates quotidian confrontations with similarly squalid realities in America; the American Dream as a defining narrative otherwise potentially shrouds these other stories, such that mythology of unlimited opportunity often belies actual poverty or leads to blaming the poor for their circumstances.

Instead of being complicit with such assumptions, Feroza forces herself to confront paradoxical realities in the United States—a country teeming with immigrants and thus genuinely diversified yet simultaneously indifferent or harmful to many within its borders who are in extreme need. For her, the contradictions at play in America are

> shaping a New World, the future in microcosm, the melting-pot in which every race and creed was being increasingly represented, compelled to live with and tolerate the "other," and she would play her part, however minuscule it was, in shaping the future. She would leave room for the ideals of generosity and constancy she had grown up with and the attachment to the family and their claim on her. She would manage her life to suit her heart; after all, the pursuit of happiness was enshrined in the constitution of the country she had grown to love, despite her growing knowledge of its faults, and she would pursue her happiness her way. (314)

This epiphanic moment near the close of the novel best represents Feroza's particular accommodation of herself to the nation. The major themes in this passage include dynamic change ("increasingly represented") balanced with certain types of "constancy" and "attachment"; small things being recognized as importantly representative of larger processes, even if they are often dismissed as "minuscule" or "in microcosm"; and the challenges to agency when one is "compelled" by others' "claims" on one. That the passage ends with references to emotions ("her heart," "happiness, "love") suggests how much this accommodation is a matter of the body, mind, and feelings rather than existing in only one register. In "becoming American," then, Feroza has not dismissed the "faults" of America but balances them with its promise of "the pursuit of happiness" that she can undertake with others becoming American all around her. In this language, readers may note echoes of nationalist sentiments developed over the past two centuries that are transformed by "diaspora talk"—because global belonging is equally presenced—into another new narrative of America.

In a text that complicates the dream of assimilation to America, the protagonist embraces dynamic and even paradoxical possibilities that accompany migration and new circumstances. When Feroza's anticipated temporary sojourn to the United States instead becomes a permanent "dislocation" (312), she decides that America offers her the chance to make herself anew, at a distance from familiar community or familial expectations. As Kain writes, "in this dynamic society of mobile individuals, tenuous relationships, changing careers, and variegated and merging cultural groups, ruptures of all kinds have become a source of American continuity and tradition: who *hasn't* experienced some significant dislocation?" (238). This is furthermore a vision of the country that has resonated with immigrants from the very first Europeans to colonize North America and, sadly, also with the indigenous groups displaced by that colonization. Dislocation in newness reveals itself in *An American Brat* superficially through college-context experimentation in Idaho and also through Feroza's more profound life-altering decision to become engaged to a non-Parsee American man, marriage to whom would signify excommunication from her Parsee community.

The ability to think the previously unthinkable in a new country with novel cultural expectations is clearly linked to expanded opportunities and independence, especially for women, but the main character must eventually also decide what she actively wishes to retain. For example, Zareen envies her daughter's ability to work outside the home and realizes that in her own "many more years on earth, she had missed out on something. . . . The money Feroza earned and spent must give her a sense of control over her life, a sense of accomplishment that Zareen had very little experience with" (240). However, even though Feroza does indeed resist certain Parsee orthodoxies while in the United States, she also questions, "was this the price one paid for . . . non-interference and . . . privacy?" when she encounters American family members almost wholly disconnected from one another (212), which reminds her that individuality and community exist in a sometimes fragile balance. She realizes that new visions of belonging are necessary for the type of freedom she values in the United States, rather than an "anything goes" attitude separated from discourses of accountability. Feroza clearly does not read Americanization as an individual contract for entitlement, what

Robert J. Samuelson in another context calls "the American dream of 'getting ahead'" (52), but rather as a series of opportunities for synthesizing immigrant newness and diasporic connectedness.

Although Feroza is charmed by many aspects of American life, she understands the desperate need for fighting injustice in the nation. She believes there is

> enough cause: in the pious platitudes, in the narrow vision of a world seen through the cold prisms of self-interest and self-pity, in this strangely paradoxical nation that dealt in "death," that sold the world's most lethal weapons to impoverished countries and simultaneously absorbed the dispossessed of the chronically dispelling world. (313)

Thus, the girl who traveled to the United States—thrilled to be going to "the land of glossy magazines, of 'Bewitched' and 'Star Trek,' of rock stars and jeans" (27)—becomes a young adult woman capable of holding in the balance the gleaming wonders of America and the sobering underside of nationalist narratives. Many of Feroza's insights about the paradoxical economic might of America contain implicit critiques of other axes of power which create "impoverished" and "dispossessed" minorities in multiple ways. Thus, her questioning stance vis-à-vis Americanization also represents her response to the experiences of gender inequality and racial intolerance in the United States that are narrated in *An American Brat*. As reflected in the passage just quoted, ambivalence is an inevitable response to belonging in a nation in which both wonder and despair are ironically related to America's status as a multicultural nation of immigrants and a simultaneous capitalist superpower selling weapons of mass destruction along with the American Dream.

Rather than striving to be "100 Per Cent" American, then, Feroza ends up resisting what she identifies as "the callous heart" of her new nation, explicitly linking her own choices concerning national accommodation to social justice concerns with which Parsee communities, as perpetual minorities, are well acquainted. For instance, Feroza realizes in Boston with Manek that she "could only guess at how he had been taught American ways, American manners. He must have endured countless humiliations. And his experiences—the positive and the humiliating—had affected him, changed him not on the surface but fundamentally" (102). From fairly early on in the narrative, responding to "humiliations" just as Jasmine in Mukherjee's novel does, Feroza recognizes that assimilating in America is often quite an unpleasant and even coercive process. Her vision of Manek's assimilation therefore recalls the effects of Americanization programs from the post–World War I period, which directly advocated for immigrants to dispense with all previous affiliations but which could never ensure the homogeneity suggested by 100 percent assimilation (Higham 121). After being convinced by Manek to attend college in Twin Falls, Idaho, rather than returning to Pakistan as she initially expected to do, Feroza is forced through mundane interactions to recognize that she can never be totally Americanized because of her diasporization and also because her very color is disconcerting, just as many actual immigrants throughout the world are relegated to social as well as institutional marginalization. In many striking passages, the novel explicitly reveals certain attitudes that newcomers to America may well be unable to overcome: racism, sexism, xenophobia, and ethnocentrism.

In response, even as Feroza strives to accommodate herself to her new nation, she also tries to defend against certain types of intolerance in the United States as well as in her diasporic community. This defiance is usually represented in a humorous tone that avoids turning literature into full-blown polemic. The novel is not a work of radical politics but instead an imaginative linking of the metaphors of American assimilation to those of diasporization and the maintenance of several imagined communities. Unlike activist characters in Alexander's novel, Feroza is hardly likely to march in the streets in order to advertise her political awareness of America's problematic role in global politics or the destitution of many of its residents. Instead, just as the novel shows her becoming American through small, daily acts of learning how to live in a new society with different cultural technologies and normative expectations than she has previously encountered, it also shows Feroza contributing her own hybridity to the nation without much fanfare. For instance, in the last pages of *An American Brat,* the protagonist conducts a private religious ceremony in order to reconnect with her Parsee ancestry and faith, even though patriarchies from her community threaten to exclude her *and* her religion is not commonly practiced in North America. In discussing this aspect of the text, Kapadia concludes, "Sidhwa does not take a rebellious stance against the dominating ideology of her community. However Sidhwa is no conformist. She does not endorse the traditional Parsi code on inter-community marriage. Instead through Zareen and Feroza's reactions she hints at the need for change" ("Expatriate Experience" 195). Sidhwa shows Feroza concentrating on community building in America due to two distinct but overlapping motives: to identify a suitable narrative of belonging for herself but also to make the country more accepting and inclusive of others like her.

Feroza's efforts at reimagining Americanization occur primarily through the ways in which she influences the people and the localities around her, representing one of the most important effects of diasporization that the Parsees can claim. The protagonist maintains both "imagined" and local communities, interestingly revealing that diasporic as well as national identities are as much mythic as empirical. Feroza reshapes American constituencies, for example, by teaching her Anglo-American roommate Jo to approach information in the United States from a diasporic perspective:

> Feroza pointed out that the news about Pakistan and other Third World countries was one-sided. Under Feroza's influence, Jo began watching the news with her on TV, and she began to realize the extent of the bias and how pervasive it was on all the networks. Then she became gratifyingly provoked, involved, and curious, and Feroza was touched. (171)

Shocked at the apathy many Americans feel for political realities of both local and global significance, Feroza uses her experiences before immigration to counter this tendency. For example, she notes, "In Pakistan, politics, with its special brew of martial law and religion, influenced every aspect of day-to-day living" (11). Feroza's influence on others affirms pluralistic visions of Americanization, which have historically focused on the immigrant "gifts" that would benefit the entire nation and continually add a dynamic newness to the "New World," as discussed in chapter 1. Gary Gerstle usefully historicizes this attitude toward assimilation in the following manner: "Rather than the American environment emancipating immigrants from their old ways and making them into a new race of men, immigrants . . . would save America from its slide into anomie and conformity. The immigrant, by *refusing to assimilate completely,* would invigorate the nation's democratic institutions" (534, emphasis added). This type of immigrant "invigoration" is very evident in Feroza's story since she has a positive politicizing effect on her roommate; in a more subtle example from the novel, Feroza's South Asian–style English alters Jo's linguistic register since they need to discover a new "language" in which to communicate across their differences.

Even as Feroza relocates to the United States and commits herself locally to more expansive visions of justice, she remains connected to the global Parsee and national Pakistani communities among whom she previously experienced belonging as well as alienation. This is undeniably true even as she first departs from Lahore, when her

> sense of self, enlarged by the osmosis of identity with her community and with her group of school friends, stayed with her like a permanence. . . . This cushioning stilled her fear of the unknown: an unconscious panic that lay coiled somewhere between her navel and her ribs and was just beginning to manifest itself in a fleeting irregularity of her heartbeat. (52)

In addition to again pairing the bodily and metaphoric challenges of immigration, this passage nicely captures the fear and panic inspired by relocation as well as the rewards of sustaining multiple allegiances in a manner that provides comfort, or "cushioning," and continuity, or "permanence," as one's identity evolves. It is a powerful image of the hybridized (trans)national belonging that often distinguishes Parsee communities. With phrases such as "enlarged . . . osmosis of identity," Sidhwa's novel employs imagery of a literally expanded worldview, thus suggesting that diasporization and assimilation are not processes in inevitable contradiction. Instead, they are mutually influential in ways that are much more reconcilable than one might assume. Furthermore, as Feroza departs from the city of her birth, "all at once it struck her that she was going far from Lahore, from the sights, the sounds, and the fragrances that were dear to her, from the people she loved and had taken for granted. Her vision grew inward and, in a strange dreamlike way, expanded to accommodate a kaleidoscope of images of the entire city and its surrounding green fields." Migration means learning not to take for granted what/who allows one to belong and practicing self-analysis through an "inward" vision. Furthermore, due to her "multidimensional vision," Feroza also immediately realizes that "there were many splendid cities beneath the same caressing sun that she wanted to look at, many new faces in the teeming world she wished to know and love as much as she loved her classmates and her family." Concurrently "in a tumult of nostalgia and fantastic anticipation" (47), the character easily imagines herself belonging in the future in multiple locations and within multiple communities even before she immigrates to the United States, revealing a flexibility that prepares her well for the challenges of becoming American.

In an interesting theoretical parallel to Sidhwa's fiction, when theorizing about border writing and performativity, D. Emily Hicks invokes "multidimensionality" in ways that may shed light on the effects of Sidhwa's fiction. Hicks posits that multidimensionality reflects "a democratic thought process; it avoids a single perspective, such as a middle-class Western cultural bias" (xxxi). While Feroza's multidimensional perspective is limited by her inexperience and by her upbringing in a community with its own types of chauvinism, *An American Brat* nonetheless stresses how an "accommodating mind" (242) allows her to transport herself between different types of situatedness. As a diasporan, she was always already part of several imagined communities prior to her immigration and assimilation experiences in the United States. As an immigrant, she has a further expanded self-perception.

Like the other female characters described in this chapter, there is no doubt that Feroza suffers due to exclusionary power practices, both because of her "dark femaleness" in the United States and because of Zoroastrian doctrine that uncompromisingly declares, "Once a Parsee-Zoroastrian marries a non-Zoroastrian, he or she is deemed to have renounced the faith and ceases to be a Parsee-Zoroastrian" (305). She rejects this orthodoxy by insisting that, "as for her religion, no one could take it away from her; she carried its fire in her heart" (317). Although the local Lahore fire temple may no longer welcome her, Feroza decides that she will visit Bombay if need be in order to strategically subvert this ethno-religious coercion to assimilate. It is through such tendencies for creative self-positioning that the protagonist accommodates herself to America and her diaspora, while inviting them to accommodate her as well.

The uncomfortable sense of being "foreign" which the fictional Feroza experienced as a Parsee teenager in Lahore and relived as a nonwhite immigrant college student in Idaho is therefore vital to her ability to recognize and resist injustice (both among Americans and Parsees) as an adult in the United States. With her firsthand experiences in South Asia and North America added to the collective history of the Parsee diaspora, Feroza learns to accommodate certain practices and ideologies prevalent in her new nation but refuses others that elicit feelings of *not* belonging for immigrants and other minorities.

Writing beyond the Ending

Read in conjunction with one another, these Americanization narratives about "dark femaleness" offer important insights about contemporary politics of belonging in the United States by depicting the ways in which newcomers to the nation may be able to choose among versions of

Americanization that they deem more empowering, inclusive, or socially just than others. Readers' responses to these stories, exemplified especially heatedly in literary debates about Bharati Mukherjee's writing, celebrate as well as question the feminist or antiracist politics of certain accommodations to nation. As noted in the introduction, this reinforces the reality that individual stories of Americanization will never speak to every American's experiences, nor will they predictably resist intolerance even if they challenge particular types of oppression. Instead, these literary texts demonstrate that each new immigrant contribution prevents the story of Americanization from reaching closure, a characteristic of all national narratives even if they often imagine an "ideal" or standard citizen.

In chapter 4, by closely reading independent cinematic stories about second-generation South Asians in America, I ask how film characters invent identities in ways that are related to but distinct from the literary narratives. Fluid interpretations of selfhood that are notable aspects of the texts examined in this chapter become even more conspicuous when they are part of the visual technology associated with popular culture. Actors reading scripted parts in South Asian independent films are also acting out gendered, ethnic, national, and diasporic affiliations. The ways in which these performances are informed by discourses of authenticity or cultural purity[49] are my central interests in my next chapter about ambivalence and belonging.

4 / "How to Be Indian": Independent Films about Second-Generation South Asian Americans

> *"She's been here so long it's almost like she was born in this country. And you know how these 'American' women are, always bossing you, always thinking about themselves. . . .*
> *It's no wonder we call them ABCDs."*
>
> CHITRA DIVAKARUNI, *ARRANGED MARRIAGE*

Chapter 1 of this book acts as a foundation for prominent discourses concerning assimilation and diasporization. Building on this foundation, in chapters 2 and 3, I differentiated particular sets of South Asian stories that highlight unique aspects of various politics of belonging. In this chapter, I shift the focus again and offer another vantage point for reconsidering narratives of national assimilation by looking at fictions which take place on the screen instead of on the page. This attention to a different medium is paired with explicit attention to second-generation stories in order to suggest some of the long-term implications of immigrant assimilation experiences, as the second-generation stories influence future generations in no less complicated or significant ways than those of the first generation. The contrasting types of narrative (i.e., ethnography, fiction, film), the distinct emphases in the stories, and the specific contextualization of diasporic histories in each chapter of this book reflect my purposeful assembling of heterogeneous accounts of the South Asian community as an antidote to implying that any one experience is the norm. Another result of combined attention to these stories is to collectively denaturalize and demythify the concept of Americanization and expose various political stakes that assimilation narratives represent. Having mapped some of the layered histories informing South Asian American stories in the previous discussions, I work in this chapter to augment these histories while also disrupting or troubling assumptions about belonging. In a book that undermines essentialist ideologies by focusing on "mixed" metaphors, hybridity, and multidimensionality, it is important to move toward a conclusion without asserting a rigid epistemology that only replaces, rather than meaningfully complicating, existing paradigms of belonging. Just as I began the book's chapters by tracing scholarly theories, I end them by sketching out my own theoretical framework for reading South Asian and other contemporary (trans) national narratives of belonging.

Four recent feature-length South Asian films which were independently produced—*Chutney Popcorn* (1999), *ABCD* (1999), *American Desi* (2000), and *American Chai* (2001)—are very useful to examine in relation to the other narrations of Americanization laid out in earlier chapters. These films about second-generation Indians[1] in the United States emphasize different tropes of belonging than those which were most prevalent in GuyaneseOpportunities, discussed in chapter 2, or in published literature, treated in chapter 3. Some of these thematic variations are attributable to the possibilities and limitations particular to film. At the same time, there are significant commonalities across these media in their representation of negotiations that individuals undertake in relation to the nation and to *other* imagined communities. Rey Chow has described film as "an opportunity to rethink other modes of discourse" (*Primitive Passions* 26), and in the present context, one can examine the significance of film performances as narratives of national and diasporic belonging. Even though the fictional film characters imagine identities beyond the national, a myth of the return to one's homeland is peripheral or even nonexistent, and this departure from traditional renderings of diaspora is my starting point for analyzing Americanization in these contributions to public culture.[2]

In this chapter, I describe films by and about South Asian Americans in which children of immigrants construct a sense of both "Indianness" and "Americanness" through imagining diaspora and engaging popular culture, as particularly befits film narratives. The film narratives highlight the dialectic of authenticity and "invention" rather than emphasizing the classic diasporic binary of homeland versus host country. Practices of performativity[3] which are inherent to cinema reward a methodology that makes visible the "regulatory grids of intelligibility" (Butler, *Gender Trouble* 166) according to which signifying practices make sense and have effect in the world, as compared to approaches which naturalize the workings of gender, race-ethnicity, or culture. Emphasizing tensions between expected and enacted scripts of belonging, major tropes discussed in this chapter include invented identities, code-switching, ethnic loyalty, and "drag" as a discourse of belonging.

Often with recourse to such strategies, by deploying recognizable narratives of authentic Indian identity or in failing to do so, the characters in all of the films call attention to the constructed nature of those scripts rather than convincing viewers of their veracity. Varying in tone from the sublimely ridiculous to the highly solemn, ethno-cultural performances in the films include voice-over monologues, staged music, celebrations such as Gujarati garba-raas, arts including photography, dressing "up," religious rituals, cultural programs, and marking gender. Speaking the lines that are scripted for them in different scenes, the actors are performing identities that are always invented, even in "real" life. These inventions have meaning insofar as they are interpreted by audiences as narratives of recognizable identities. In my discussion of these films, I remain committed to the analysis of how South Asians in America choose to narrate ethnicity, nation, and diaspora, rather than to studying the technologies of the medium. It should be noted that each filmmaker portrays Indian American identities somewhat differently through distinct choices concerning themes such as internalized racism, alternative sexualities, marriage and death, reproductive choices, and artistic expression. What they have in common is that all of the films portray Americanization by putting children of immigrants at the center of the narratives, exposing how these characters locate themselves in-between their parents' versions of "Indianness" and their own participation in multiple popular cultures. While depicting stories unique to the lives of Indian Americans, the films also revisit issues that can be found throughout Americanization fictions, including differences between generations of immigrants and their children, expectations of assimilation that heighten challenges to belonging, conflicts between community and individuality, and challenges to managing difference.

My strategy for "reading" these films is to weave together their themes to show how characters are creatively engaging in inventions and performances of Americanness through culture, gender, and sexuality. The chapter is therefore constructed similarly to my ethnographic readings in pairing aspects from the films together rather than separating out my analysis of each work from the others, as I do with the published novels in chapter 2. The connections between those preceding chapters and the present chapter are particularly significant in the context of cultural studies. For instance, Chow notes that institutional boundaries continue to separate film and ethnography in ways that should be resisted. She advocates that anthropology should "include within its definition of ethnographic practice the culture-collecting capacities, accomplishments of film," and film study should "consider the cross-cultural, anthropological, and ethnographic implications of filmmaking and film watching" (*Primitive Passions* 28). An ethnographic approach in relation to these particular films suits fictional worlds in which characters are in similar age groups, settings, and social situations and even plots are fairly closely aligned. Of course, analyzing films is a different task than unpacking interview transcripts or literary passages since one cannot easily share parts of the primary sources, as they are usually experienced, with the audience. With this in mind, I have elected to juxtapose particular scenes from the different films that are productively comparable because they similarly focus attention on certain processes of Americanization. Although the film protagonists are the children of immigrants rather than immigrants themselves, I nonetheless read these tropes as narratives of immigrant belonging and assimilation because the frameworks that engender such responses are through and through informed by communities migrating from one location to another.

In such portrayals, second-generation Indian Americans display behaviors reflecting how they make choices that affect their abilities to belong both in their ethno-cultural, diasporic communities and in the nation. Lisa Lowe defines immigrant acts as "practices constituted through dialectics of difference and disidentification," rather than constituted in sameness, and she posits that such acts end up calling critical attention to "horizontal relations between subjects across national boundaries" (267). Lest we too quickly celebrate this kind of border crossing and the power of the imagination in resisting either a nation- or diaspora-defined sense of selfhood, it is important to note that (trans)national relations do not prevent Asian Americans from pressing up against rather rigid expectations of ethnicity and culture, especially those based on "vertical determination by the state" and mainstream cultural forms (Lowe 267). Broadly speaking, in American public culture, deeply entrenched attitudes and institutionalized racial hierarchies project insurmountable differences rather than allowing for a completely free play of identities chosen by individuals or communities, certainly for racial minorities but in actuality for all Americans. But "dialectics of difference and disidentification" allow for some active choices within this national context.

I argue in this chapter that, in the case of films about second-generation South Asian Americanization, interactions between ethnic essentializing and immigrant "acting" bring into view yet another dialectic of ambivalence, that of authenticity and invention. These narratives concerning diasporization transcend the classic binary of deracinated immigrant assimilation versus paralyzing exilic nostalgia, as many theorists believe is true of contemporary transnationalisms more broadly. They also destabilize authenticity discourses, as do concepts theorized in the previous chapters (i.e., diaspora, mixing, and hybridity), by emphasizing changeability and heterogeneity rather than culturally static communities or identities. These films reveal that individuals will encounter multiple hails to cultural assimilation *at the same time* and experience anxieties concerning authenticity rather than sureness about belonging. Similarly, historian Eric Hobsbawm writes in his introduction to the influential collection of essays *The Invention of Tradition* that, even though expectations of certain types of patriotism might have been ill defined, "the *practices* symbolizing it were virtually compulsory. . . . The crucial element seems to have been the invention of emotionally and symbolically charged signs of club membership" (11). Although many (though not all) traditions might fit this description, Hobsbawm points out that cultures in moments of transition are especially informative about processes whereby investments are made in particular types of signs that prove belonging. Patterns of immigration that regularly effect dramatic change in the country make the concept of invention especially relevant in the United States. For instance, Lowe writes about Asian American "culture" that "the ways in which it is imagined, practiced and continued . . . is not something which already exists, transcending place, time, history and culture. Cultural identities come from somewhere, have histories. But, like everything which is historical, they undergo constant transformation" (64). This description of culture matches the ways that all of the narratives represented in this book are dynamic and changing ones that can nonetheless be carefully historicized in order to understand their broader implications.

And, as mentioned in relation to race and cultural hybridity in the previous chapter, Asian American studies, postcolonial theory, and feminisms of other types have developed their own paradigms concerning invented identities. Focusing on different topics, these share Lowe's commitment to insisting that identities are discursively constructed rather than coherent or fixed. In another representative moment, Stuart Hall advises from a cultural studies perspective,

> Perhaps instead of thinking of identity as an already accomplished fact, which . . . new cultural practices then represent, we should think, instead, of identity as a "production" which is never complete, always in process, and always constituted within, not outside,

> representation. This view problematizes the very authority and authenticity to which the term "cultural identity" lays claim. ("Cultural Identity and Diaspora" 234)

Hall here traces intertwined issues of performativity, authenticity, and authority which result in unpredictably inflected identities rather than indisputable facts; to focus on process and the context for identity texts is to question the power to name culture as an unchanging given. Related interventions are usually influenced by postmodernism, Derridean poststructuralist notions of *différance,* and/or Judith Butler's "troubling" of gender truths alluded to in the preceding chapter. In Butler's seminal study that deconstructs the "fact" of gender, *Gender Trouble,* she argued that gender as a narrative allows for its own deconstruction. When she concludes, "Gender can be neither true nor false, neither real nor apparent, neither original nor derived" (141), Butler rejects the notion that gender is innate or essential, which suggests possibilities for reading other axes of identity as active choices, as well.

Since the films discussed here also foreground invented identities, they destabilize "Americanness," which itself cannot be validated through recourse to genuineness, since there is no "original" standard to use as a comparison but rather shifting cultural investments. (Trans) national belonging in such a context requires constant repetition and often requires rehearsal, to use the language of performativity, which consequently means that the parts people play are noninevitable and may include tragedy, comedy, romance, or yet another genre. In a discussion about inventing Asian/American identities which emphasizes contradiction, unevenness, and ambivalence, Palumbo-Liu uses the phrase "staging realities" (43) as a way to mark how identity performances must negotiate contingencies of history and institutions. This formulation importantly points out that *no* expressions, representations, or what I am calling inventions of identity can escape the contexts in which they take place.

The film portrayals of Indian Americanness should thus be read as equally abiding and as ephemeral as any other performances, rather than as corroborations of static national homogeneity. Reinforcing this reading, while one of the films (*American Desi*) prominently displays American iconography (such as the national flag hanging in the protagonist's bedroom), none of them seriously engages with *that* story which has so often molded assimilation, the American Dream. This points to a paradox which is very suggestive about the continually "mixed" metaphors that inhere to Americanization, which I noted in chapter 2: for allegedly "successful" Americans, the American Dream is an *immigrant* investment which may be recalled by later generations without representing an appropriate script of Americanization for them. In the case of middle-class South Asian second generations whose struggles to belong are arguably defined less in material and institutional terms than for immigrant or other minority Americans, there may be an implicit sense that the American Dream has *already* been achieved and other types of assimilation concerns therefore seem more pressing.

Explicit attention to such complexities and contradictions in stories about second-generation Indians in the United States is not the norm in American popular culture. Instead, as Sunaina Maira sees it, "the image of India in the American public imagination, in the popular media and in literature, has often been tinged with exoticism and colored by the mysticism associated with Orientalized versions of Asia" (136). This type of exoticized image has interacted in sometimes unpredictable ways with how, over time, South Asian Americans of the post-1965 generation have often become associated with the model-minority myth, as a group representing high median family incomes and educational attainment. According to American television, most Indians are immigrant doctors. Or, in an alternative stereotype that has been common, South Asians are represented as certain types of caricatures, perhaps most famously as Apu Nahasapeemapetilon from *The Simpsons*, a convenience-store clerk with an unpronounceable last name, a thick accent, and ridiculously frugal ways—who nonetheless turns out to be highly educated. Contending that characters such as this have "standardized" Indian immigrants for television culture, Shilpa Davé explains that "the term 'brown voice' identifies a specific racializing of South Asians which simultaneously connotes foreignness and class and cultural privilege" ("Apu's Brown Voice" 314). Conjoining "color" and "voice," which are analogous (although not reducible) to race and narrative, Davé here documents how fortified stereotypes come to obscure complex diasporic ethno-cultural histories.

In American pop culture, Indian Americans continue to be under- or misrepresented, because only a narrow range of stories about them are broadly circulated and those tend not to be deeply examined. Davé concludes that there is a type of cultural shorthand for what South Asian immigrants represent in America: "to be heard and read as foreign but also to register a highly specialized educational, class, and historical status that is seldom associated with other Asian American immigrant groups" ("Apu's Brown Voice" 326). Along with playing Apu-like characters or assimilationist professionals, another major performance with which South Asians have become associated is as alienated, traditionalist, and anti-Western Others. South Asian actors take bit parts on television, as likely as not representing different racial-ethnic communities than their own, but one rarely sees productions devoted to their stories in the United States.[4] Even as an actor such as Kal Penn is recognizable as a former regular on the popular television series *House* and is a "crossover" hit—starring in independent South Asian American cinema, the stoner comedies featuring Harold and Kumar, guest appearances on episodes of major television series, and the mainstream blockbuster *Superman Returns*—stories focused on second-generation Indians in relation to their diasporic communities have been the least well known of his works. With the highly successful film adaptation of Jhumpa Lahiri's *Namesake* (2006), starring Penn, different types of stories about Indian Americans may have bigger audience draw in the future. Such a development will help to counteract the current proliferation of assumptions that identities can so seamlessly fit with either "Americanness" or "Indianness" that the other categorization is irreconcilable.

Troubling such assumptions, the four Indian American films discussed here follow traditions of Americanization stories, as well as touching on more universal life experiences, but even their titles mark ethno-cultural distinctiveness through diasporization and (trans)nationalism. Rajini Srikanth argues for analogous phenomena in literature as representing a sensibility for the "interconnected histories of nations" which "is present to some degree in almost all South Asian American writers—even those of the second generation, born and raised in the United States" (10). One film signals such a sensibility clearly, if primarily for South Asian Americans, with its use of the acronym ABCD, which signifies "American-Born Confused Desi" (in which "desi" represents a person from the "homeland"). *ABCD* is a film directed by Krutin Patel that contrasts various versions of national and cultural assimilation through its main characters. At the center of the film are two siblings, "the good son" Raj and "the wild child" Nina (DVD jacket), who are strikingly different but remain connected in their closeness to their widowed mother, Anju, played by Madhur Jaffrey of Indian cookbook fame. The winner of the Best Picture award at the Austin and Houston film festivals, the film takes the tag line, "It's about choices," highlighting the degree to which the characters must choose from among "confused" affiliations. The emphasis in the narrative is on romantic relationships both within and beyond one's ethno-cultural community, in addition to some rather moving scenes representing sibling affection and processes of grieving.

Released in the same year, the comedy *Chutney Popcorn* combines in its title two food references associated with India and America to represent the hybrid identities it narrates. Chutney, a sauce that combines sweet, savory, or spicy flavors, is a type of mixture which does not allow the resegregation of the original ingredients, potentially invoking melting-pot imagery—but with an ethno-cultural difference. Partly because the film's main character is so matter-of-fact about being a lesbian, this is the most overtly nonnormative of the four films. Directed by Nisha Ganatra, the film stars the director as Reena, opposite Jill Hennessey (who later became famous as the eponymous heroine of NBC's forensic drama *Crossing Jordan*) as Lisa. *Chutney Popcorn* has received numerous awards at international film festivals from audiences and for best feature, including in Berlin, Madrid, and Paris, as well as several festivals in California. According to the DVD jacket, "the cultural divide between Reena's Indian family and their lesbian lifestyle hits home" in a story about "the cultural struggles between immigrant parents and their Americanized children." It is billed as "a refreshing look at one contentious and loving family reinventing itself." Along with the romantic plot, another major storyline concerns Reena's heterosexual sister Sarita and her husband, Mitch, and the couple's attempts to conceive a child. Connecting all of these characters is the family matriarch, Meenu, who is once again represented by Madhur Jaffrey.

The third film, the aforementioned *American Desi*, has a title that transforms the homeland from India to America but nonetheless maintains the diasporic link through the Indian word *desi*. Directed by Piyush Dinker Pandya, this is probably the best known of the films among Indian communities in the United States and had extended local cinema runs in the New York metropolitan area. Packaged as a "cross-cultural comedy" that "mixes the elements of an American romantic comedy with the unique flavor of the Indian experience," the film is the only one of the four to neatly resolve the narrative conflicts represented by the tag line, "Can our guy become a true 'desi' and get the girl?" It thus holds few surprises for audiences used to happy endings in both Hollywood and Bollywood, such that the college boy (Kris) gets his girl (Nina), defeats the bad guys, and learns to "balance" his identities with the help of his "zany" Indian roommates (DVD jacket). The film's yoking together of a fairy tale about love overcoming all with Americanization tropes are suggestively juxtaposed against scenes paying homage to Bollywood styles.

American Chai is a slightly more recent film which, like *Chutney Popcorn,* hybridizes language in its title by associating a drink from India with the modifier "American." "American Chai" is also the name of the protagonist's band, which represents a new fusion sound,[5] appropriate in a film subtitled "A Non-Traditional Blend." Written and directed by Anurag Mehta, the dramatic comedy won the Audience Award at the Slamdance and Gen Art film festivals, and it had a fairly long run at Towne 3, a classic small theater in San Jose, California. Also like *Chutney Popcorn,* which highlights Reena's henna drawings and photography, the film uses the trope of performances (in this case, music) to narrate cultural conflicts as experienced by the college-age Sureel. It is described on the DVD jacket as a love story which is "funny, feel-good, coming-of-age" and focused on "rock and roll dreams." Audiences can expect a film that "celebrates the virtues of the American melting pot with truth, respect and lots of humor." Sheetal Sheth, the actress who starred as Nina in *ABCD,* reappears in this film in a very different part that suggests much less cultural alienation or "confusion." One of Nina's love interests in *ABCD* is played by Aasif Mandvi, who has a role in *American Chai,* as well. Ajay Naidu, who appeared in *Chutney Popcorn,* is again somewhat disreputable in this film, but in an arguably more sympathetic part. The variability in the types of performances by these actors in the same few films only heightens an awareness of the many different roles South Asian Americans *can* play.

In addition to the appearance of certain actors in more than one role and the films' commonly hybrid titles, the films share other notable characteristics, some of which are discussed in the remainder of this chapter and others which would benefit from future analyses. One theme in these films that is not elaborated in this discussion is the imagined roles of mothers, given that two of the narratives develop around absent fathers. In addition, the repeated significance of romance, especially as related to marriage possibilities, would be well worth spelling out, as an aspect of coming-of-age experiences as well as for implications concerning social institutions. Sandhya Shukla describes "race as a site of desire" (241) and, in *Sexual Naturalization: Asian Americans and Miscegenation,* Susan Koshy historicizes certain types of racial mixing in the United States, which are types of readings that might be illuminating in this context. Another notable element of the movies that would be rewarding to examine more closely is how other racial performances interact with inventions of Indianness, particularly "blackness," which is so crucially informative about the construction of American identities in general. Although technical details, such as camera work or lighting effects, do not stand out for me in any of the films, interpretations about the use of music and other technologies in these cultural products might also prove informative.

How to Be: Neither Hollywood nor Bollywood[6]

The current analysis focuses on the ways in which the four films collectively show that "how to be Indian" and how to be in diaspora are determined *in America* as the major characters engage with dominant national narratives through both conformity and resistance. This recalls the varying inventions of "Indian" identity that were common to the Guyanese American stories of chapter 2. These various processes must be interpreted as different sets of identities than those concurrently emerging from the subcontinent, which means recognizing permutations of Indianness without authorizing some more than others. Shukla, for instance, opts to associate "India" as a concept not with "a precise location of homeland, nor a singular motivating impulse, but instead with a heterogeneous imaginary that draws energy from historical formations of colonialism and postcolonialism, discourses of diversity, and exercises of bureaucratic power" (3). I am much more persuaded by such readings of Indian identities than ones that insist on a universal type.

In order to understand the kinds of imagined belonging which different South Asian Americans may choose or have chosen for them, it is important to interrogate the assimilationist "authenticity" ideologies which prop up an impossibility such as "100 percent" American or Indian. It is useful to recall Benedict Anderson's *Imagined Communities* here, because of the ways in which he shifts attention *away from* tendencies to measure whether or not certain identities seem legitimate. He clarifies that "communities are to be distinguished, not by their falsity/genuineness, but by the style in which they are imagined" (6). It is indeed in "the style" of their imagining that the films discussed in this chapter proffer different versions of assimilation and diasporization which link second-generation South Asian Americans—through family and immigrant communities—to the Indian subcontinent even as they are also indelibly "Americanized." In a discussion of black music, Paul Gilroy concludes that we can see creative activities of this sort as analogies "for comprehending the lines of affiliation and association which take the idea of the diaspora beyond its symbolic status as the fragmentary opposite of some imputed racial essence" (95).

My use of the phrase "how to be Indian" in the title of this chapter therefore highlights how performativity not only is an obvious element of any cinema and a prominent theme in South Asian American narratives but also has important ontological implications—since the passive "to be" contrasts with the active strategizing suggested by the provisionality of "how to be." As Chow puts it, the import of ethnic practices "lies not in their authenticity but in the mode of their signification" (*Primitive Passions* 144), as confirmed by the need to decide "*how* to be Indian." The allusion in the chapter title is from a scene in *Chutney Popcorn,* in which Sarita complains to her Anglo-American husband, "I don't need [my sister] Reena showing me how to be a woman and you showing me how to be Indian." The line comes at a poignant moment, when Sarita is discovering that her assumptions about family, agency, and femininity are all in jeopardy. Her plaintive and resentful outburst thus usefully invokes some of the major ideas in this chapter. To allude to the "how" of being a woman and being Indian recalls, à la Simone de Beauvoir's famous declaration, that one is not born either of these things but instead is made and becomes them according to a variable combination of social expectations and self-determination.

The other three films also reflect how certain (trans)national identities seem to beg for legitimizing, and this is reinforced by the films themselves being cultural products that are arguably without official derivation. None of them was a major release, although each has done well within particular milieus, for example as part of Asian American or international film festivals. They have also been screened at local community theaters, such as those that are now devoted to Indian-theme films in central New Jersey.[7] Yet none of the films has truly "made it big" in either Hollywood or Bollywood, for some reasons which Jigna Desai discusses in *Beyond Bollywood,*[8] even though either cinema arguably has ready-made audiences for the stories being told. Briefly put, it seems that the films have not been considered contributions to Bollywood (i.e., the Indian film industry dominated by Bombay which produces the most films of any cinema in the world),[9] because they do not meet certain generic conventions that include length, musical and dance numbers, and a tendency to melodrama. Furthermore, their locations of production/distribution and a focus on stories within America differentiate them from the bulk of Bollywood cinema. (The last may gradually be changing, since some recent Bollywood films depict diasporic experiences beyond the subcontinent, as documented by Rajinder Kumar Dudrah.) The films are currently also not of mainstream Hollywood ilk because they were made independently of a major studio, usually represent a director's first project out of film school, and involve varying levels of professional acting.

This lack of fit is relevant because film studies have historically taken "national cinema" as the frame for understanding creative production. However, globalization has arguably eradicated borders such that discrete nationally defined cinematic audiences no longer exist.[10] Certainly, films from Bollywood cross borders daily, with an estimated "enraptured global audience of over a billion people" (Chute 36), while American films threaten to outdo indigenous productions throughout the world, from the United Kingdom to many postcolonial countries and beyond. Not having benefited from major studio interest, and even if DVD releases lead to greater dissemination today than would have been possible even a decade ago, South Asian American independent films such as those discussed here have not had mass distribution. Hamid Naficy characterizes such cultural products as a type of "accented cinema"; he contends that films such as these should be considered "at once an allegory of both exile and cinema" (46) because they are outside of the normal distribution and production infrastructures of cinema and are simultaneously about individuals who are cultural Others. This results in films that are in many ways tangential to mainstream industries and that may suffer from not being part of a distinct national cinema or even contemporary globalized film machinery. As Desai points out in "Bombay Boys and Girls," such films are "independent" in paradoxical ways, not usually able to depend on major support but nonetheless needing some access to "pre-established networks of exchange" in order to reach any audiences (52).

Similarly to the lived experiences of Asian Americans and other marginalized communities, these films can be considered to be a part of and "yet apart"[11] from the national imaginary. Even though Bollywood is gaining significantly more attention in the American mainstream these days, as Dudrah argues, movies about the children of Indian immigrants which are being independently produced, directed, and released in America are usually familiar only to limited audiences in either region. This is true despite evidence of consistent interpenetration of American and Indian cinema from years of "borrowed" plots and translated choreography (more often from the former to the latter), as well as from blockbuster films such as *Moulin Rouge* inspiring comparisons to Indian cinema. When Ashutosh Gowariker's 2001 film *Lagaan* was nominated for an Oscar for Best Foreign Language Film, Bollywood came "West" for some audiences (for more on this, see Dudrah 15–35). Jenny Sharpe writes, more generally, that "Bollywood has more recently begun to infiltrate a Euro-American consciousness through what can be identified as a new transnational cultural literacy" ("Gender, Nation, and Globalization" 59). Still, what is the fate of films inspired by both Hollywood and Bollywood that are neither representative of nor represented by them?

Since the films are *neither* Bollywood nor Hollywood, they call direct attention to interstitiality. In an interview with Koshy ("Turning Color"), Gurinder Chadha gestured to the political and artistic implications of this when describing her own situation as a British Asian filmmaker.[12] With the major international distribution of her two films *Bend It Like Beckham* (2002) and *Bride and Prejudice* (2004) since the time of that interview, Chadha can be considered an international success. However, she says that she previously felt, "I represent a problem for the industry; people didn't know what to do with *Bhaji* [*on the Beach*]," her film from 1993 (Koshy, "Turning Color" 158). After setting one of her films in America in the late 1990s and finding that audiences responded with discomfort, Chadha concluded,

> I think when most people in America consider a film with people of different races in it, they expect the drama to come out of friction between black and whites. Most films that are coming out of L.A. (mainstream Hollywood films) are drawn with those kinds of divisions around race. Either that or they are totally about Asians. (160–61)

In the circumstances Chadha describes, readings of popular culture rest on industry assumptions that there is *only* one audience (black, white, or Other) who might be interested in a film. She says, "While I'm trying to blur those boundaries, I find the market thrives on them" (161). Unpacking such contradictory impulses, literary scholar Amit Rai analyzes the historical and institutional role of Asian diasporic films and writes, "Asian American films can usefully be situated as a non-dominant cinema" (14). By labeling such cinema as "non-dominant," Rai suggests that their position is a minority one in the same manner that the characters in the films are minoritized. This implies that, despite (or because of) these films' lack of major distribution, the thematic and material representations of blurred borders in them are very telling, however widespread or localized their audiences are.

That the films I discuss do not properly belong to either Hollywood or Bollywood—and are about ABCD characters who do not belong to *either* America or India, but rather to both—foregrounds some specific implications of diasporization. The films can usefully be described, in the manner that Naficy explains "accented" cinema, as being located in cultural spaces that are overlapping yet unique, "because they are created astride and in the interstices of social formations and cinematic practices. Consequently, they are both simultaneously local and global, and they resonate against the prevailing cinematic production practices, at the same time that they benefit from them" (4). Such a methodology of situating films as being "both/and" (instead of "neither/nor") acknowledges influences from multiple sources rather than opting for one or another;[13] it also suggests that there are productive as well as limiting aspects to the cultural or ethno-cultural "confusion" of immigrant positionalities and cinemas. As Shukla advises in her discussion of two earlier films about the Indian diaspora, Chadha's *Bhaji on the Beach* and Mira Nair's *Mississippi Masala,* "generation also is central to how we might think of the production of a kind of cinematic Indianness in diaspora" (236).

Naficy's and Shukla's analyses are well paired because they speak to a transnational context for "accented" cinemas that represent interstitiality, as well as the need to historicize the particular accent that is produced. When we do this, we can read Indian identities after immigration as being invented through consensus but also in "a field of conflict," rather than through the evocation of an "idealized community" (Shukla 239). Identifying "accented" performances of belonging and recognizing "fields of conflict" is a very different proposition than deeming certain Indians more representative than others. Since the power to define an ethno-cultural community can be limited to a few individuals (e.g., elders, often male), second-generation South Asian Americans may be left facing few options for "invention." In the national context, analogous politics of authenticity, which are elaborated shortly, have had dramatic historical implications as means to consolidating power through law and "sciences" of race or gender, for example, in many nation-states. The films expose similar processes at work in contemporary Americanization experiences.

The scholars who have paid the most focused academic attention to South Asian films in global contexts are Desai, Dudrah, and Gayatri Gopinath. In the intersection of their readings of Bollywood, diasporic, and other cinema created by and/or narrating stories about South Asians, these critics have carved out an intellectual space in which to examine the narrative effects of new technologies and new mechanisms of globalization. Their discussions act as a backdrop for my own original analyses of South Asian American films, an analysis which emphasizes tropes of assimilation and belonging.

Ambivalent Assimilation and "American-Born Confused Desis"

There is one dominant image common to these films that most directly symbolizes intersections of nationality, diasporization, and invention. That is the icon of the "American-Born Confused Desi" mentioned earlier. The acronym, familiar to most South Asian Americans, refers to those who are from the *desh,* or homeland, originally meaning India but now applied to different groups associated with the subcontinent. The joke is that second-generation Indians in America are all "ABCDs" (some enterprising wits have even extended it out to the letter Z) and the label works to reinforce the binary of diasporic homeland versus an American present. Mixing languages in the label negatively labels "mixed-up" Indians. Maira was one of the first to gloss this "pejorative label" in an academic study and to describe how it signals that traditional identifications are supposedly "waning in the second generation, reproducing the trope of the second generation as culturally confused" (132). The ABCD allegedly cannot identify to which culture he or she belongs or owes loyalty. As Maira clarifies the acronym, it is clear that several sets of binaries come into play: "The underlying idea is that two cultural poles are available to the second generation, 'Indian' and 'Western,' and that the former is clearly tied to a superior, truer ethnic identity" (132). When labeled as ABCDs, second-generation Indians in the United States may find that other members of their diasporic community do not read them as belonging according to certain definitions of "cultural" identity, at the very same time that they are deemed neither "real" nor certainly "typical" Americans according to historical apparatuses for managing race.[14]

By foregrounding ABCD quandaries, the four coming-of-age films (which represent bildung, or "formation," just like the literary narratives discussed in chapter 3) thus portray ethno-cultural performances that either facilitate or impede a sense of assimilating to and/or belonging within changing (trans)national contexts. In each film, the central character is portrayed in significant moments when he or she fails to be culturally appropriate, is unable or refuses to authenticate Indian ethnicity, or does not meet the expectations associated with particular American situations. The major narrative conflicts are thus between different affiliations, while the films' resolutions model how individuals might negotiate the challenges of accommodating various identities. Each filmmaker imagines something unique in the way ethno-cultural identity and gender are invented (with, unfortunately, very little attention to the racial economics that were so central in Guyanese American stories), but all maintain a central focus on understanding the mutual influences of "American" and "desi" for supposed "American-Born Confused Desis."

Key scenes in the film narratives represent second-generation Indian Americans confronting expectations of authenticity or accusations of inauthenticity, frequently from their families or ethnic communities. In the discussion referenced earlier, Gilroy notes that the "politics of racial authenticity" often emerge as "highly charged and bitterly contested" engagements within communities (96). These engagements result in readings of ethno-cultural identities that are conflicting and ambivalent, implying that belonging is negotiable if one conforms to certain expectations while sometimes simultaneously assuming unaltering cultural "essences" or ethnic instincts. In an example of the latter assumption, Reena in *Chutney Popcorn* is encouraged to dance at her sister Sarita's wedding reception because, after all, she has "Punjabi blood." However, Reena's look of surprise and confusion informs the film's audiences that blood does not always "tell." At the same time, according to an alternate, coexisting script, characters may be expected to simply don ethnicity as if deciding what to wear. In an experience similar to Reena's in which a character is considered ethnically "confused," in *ABCD,* when Nina attends a friend's wedding, one of the other guests wonders, "What is she *wearing?* Didn't she know it was an Indian wedding?" And the bride, an Indian American woman who is planning on relocating to India after her "traditional" Indian wedding held in the United States, dismissively responds, "Typical ABCD." Also pointing to the cultural work accomplished by such naming, in *American Desi,* Nina melodramatically rebuffs Kris's romantic overture, informing him that her interest in him is altruistic rather than sexual. After slapping him, she impatiently advises him, "I figured it would be nice for you to learn something about your own culture," but he expresses disdain for "Indianness" and dismisses a country in which he claims modern amenities are a "myth" and outdated traditions such as arranged marriages still prevail. She begins to retort, but he interrupts her and angrily demands, "What are you going to call me, Nina—an ABCD?" because he anticipates the power that she can assume by labeling him as the "confused" one.

Closely reading the film narratives exposes many such conflicts concerning cultural knowledge, authenticity, and accommodation of affiliative expectations. In *Chutney Popcorn,* for instance, although it is Sarita who expresses overt anxiety about "how to be Indian," the film narrative consistently represents both sisters as needing to learn about their culture, to the extent of being schooled by Sarita's husband, Mitch, who is not "even Indian." As a funny case in point, when a family friend urges Reena to dance, Reena embarrasses her mother in front of the other guests by naively responding, "Are we Punjabi?" to which her mother Meenu replies, "You know absolutely nothing!" before stalking off. In *American Chai,* Sureel's early voice-over lays out the issues even more pointedly; he confesses to the audience, "See, I was born in America, which makes me American. My parents were born in India, which makes me Indian American. They raised me in this country with the values and beliefs they established in their time, in their world, which makes me crazy." While the contrast between "born" and "makes" points to dilemmas of differentiating innate and constructed subjectivities, Indianness is tied to "values and beliefs," which are never really specified (but are, the movies show us, clearly familiar inventions) but which the second generation is often expected to know, anyway. The themes of confusion ("which makes me crazy"), alienation, and ignorance are repeated in each film around the figure of the ABCD, whose relationship to ethnic or cultural communities is potentially always in question.

Anxieties of Authenticity[15]

The prevalence of the ABCD trope in these films confirms what I argued in chapter 1, that varied narratives of Americanization have similarities, but they develop through very specific engagements with the community histories in question. Characters in the films are portrayed inventing identities but also being constrained by certain idealized images, such as truly "Indian," "American," "woman," or "straight." The protagonists repeatedly fail to meet others' expectations or have to impossibly "stretch" to fit a certain image, in a way that mirrors the protagonists in the published fictions discussed in chapter 3 about "dark femaleness." It becomes quite clear in the films as well as in the novels that logics of authenticity require negotiation *between* and *among* members of certain identity communities in ways that can be quite conflictual. Davé, when reading second-generation South Asian participation in American beauty pageants as a politics of belonging, describes "idealized performances" which "privilege a specific type of cultural performance," underlining how important it can seem for immigrants that their children "act" in recognizable ways. In such a "site of contention" ("Community Beauty" 337–38), possibilities for ethno-cultural performances raise a number of major questions, including, Who is "real" or "genuine"? What is the "original" type against which others are measured? How does one prove one's provenance? The opposite of the authentic must also be considered, since being deemed inauthentic comes to represent something invalid, falsity, a lack of authority, or a copy rather than an (often-mythical) original.

This list of consequences for "inauthenticity" reveals that the political terrain for deciding who "truly" experiences, understands, or can describe cultural phenomena continues to be complicated and contested. Sociologist Sharmila Rudrappa traces a genealogy of "authenticity" and considers different ways that American immigrants have historically imagined its expectations; she believes that what is at stake includes

> something that has fidelity to actuality, compatible with a certain source or origin, in accordance with tradition, or something that exists in sincerity without feigning or hypocrisy. It endows an object or practice with acceptability because the object conforms to standards of fact and reality and is not contradicted by evidence. It is trustworthy, credible, and convincing. . . . It is real, genuine, original. (133)

As this description shows, "authenticity" brings with it a lot of cultural baggage: it raises concerns about loyalty, "reality," and the preservation of traditions, which is a repeated theme in South Asian stories of diasporization. This description also suggests that lack of conformity to an expected practice may mark a moral or ethical failure, since it can be read as *not* sincere or trustworthy, thus presumably prone to lies and falsehoods. Perhaps the most telling aspect of Rudrappa's definition is her conclusion that something deemed authentic cannot be questioned; as she writes, the "thirst for authenticity remains unquenched because it tantalizes Indian Americans with promises of access to full citizenship and personhood" and allows them to "author themselves into being" (139). As a seeming antidote to anxieties that immigrant communities encounter due to displacement and cultural marginalization, authenticity can thus seem to represent a great many possibilities even while being based on rigid dichotomies.

Strategies emphasizing invention or performativity stand in stark contrast to anxieties of authenticity and help to reveal what Lowe calls "politicized cultural work" (9) within varying frames of reference. As mentioned in chapter 3, it has been suggested that an emphasis on hybridity and change can lead to an affirmation of the agency of subjects as they negotiate different aspects of social identity without being bound by one, unchanging script. In this vein, Homi Bhabha described in such pieces as "Of Mimicry and Men" how the performativity demanded by colonial encounters—in which "the fetishized colonial culture is potentially and strategically an insurgent counter-appeal" (*Locations of Culture* 91)—was precisely the ground on which the differentiation between colonizer and colonized might be destabilized. Adding an important caveat to this important insight about power's vulnerability, although some readers of Judith Butler's writing overlook it, she insists that "*gender* is not a noun, but neither is it a set of free-floating attributes, for we have seen that the substantive effect of gender is performatively produced and compelled by the regulatory practices of gender coherence" (*Gender Trouble* 24). It is never inevitable that embracing the discursive nature of identity will be empowering; playing different roles also opens one up to risk and may undermine politics of identity that are often necessary elements in activism. There are very real dangers that, for marginalized groups, either relying on or rejecting authenticity outright can serve to legitimate hegemonic authority. Might not any immigrant, for example, ultimately fail on all fronts, neither fully American by virtue of race and ancestry nor fully "ethnic" by virtue of living in America?

Since postmodern deconstructions of master narratives dismiss notions of the authentic Self as aspects of Enlightenment solipsism, this might convince some people that all claims to authenticity are not only suspect but also unnecessary. However, since agency is never limitless, it is important to accept challenges to authenticity and authority provisionally and, in the interests of social justice, to remember that denying selfhood to historically disprivileged populations within dominant nationalisms is perhaps merely to compound inequalities. Despite theoretical claims about the death of the Subject, concerns about authenticity in the context of rights and representation reflect on complicated issues that must be addressed not only for minority groups but more generally, as well. This is because important concerns raised in relation to authenticity include the challenges of contradictory allegiances or loyalties; the complexities surrounding unequal power relations between different constituencies; the reliability of an individual's cultural knowledge, especially if there is either too little or too much (negatively or reductively) popularly associated with his or her community; and the dangers of consuming or co-opting "exotic" Otherness.

Based on the various types of anxieties associated with authenticity, evaluating its role in relation to knowledge production continues to create tensions among academics and activists, notably within postcolonial and ethnic studies. These tensions arise as responses to many different types of cultural processes, including investments in purity (as historically represented by policies such as antimiscegenation laws in many modern nation-states), movements for social equality through identity politics (represented in many civil rights projects), and conferrals of authority (which can mean cultural as well as material capital). Gayatri Spivak's famous question "Can the subaltern speak?" may never be satisfactorily answered since our very epistemologies are founded on authorizing certain representations of identity that are always already mediated by institutions of power. Spivak herself, as a famous academic personality, seems to mark the near impossibility of hearing the voices of the nonelite. When one participates in highly theorized, intellectually demanding discussions that attempt to represent the subaltern—in the English language, in the American academy—it is perhaps inevitable to be accused of merely projecting our voices instead of hearing those of Others.

Thus, as well as marking a "generational debate" (Katrak, "Changing Traditions" 76), authenticity wars reflect serious (often highly contradictory) ideologies related to distributions of power across nation-states, regions, and the globe. Questions of loyalty in the wake of modernity are often understood to represent conflicts between emergent national allegiances and "traditional" familial, tribal, ethnic, or religious obligations. Regarding contemporary xenophobic nationalisms, Ratna Kapur (the director of the Centre for Feminist Legal Research in New Delhi) reminded an audience at the Presidential Forum of the 2005 MLA convention, "Today, assimilation involves strict compliance with the new legal criteria for citizenship and nationality proliferating in Europe and elsewhere—a walking, talking, 'almost white but not quite' standard. Fealty is a critical feature of these new standards, where even one visit to the motherland can render you an imposter" (24). When citizenship is seen as a reward for certain kinds of "fealty," meaning sworn obligation to a state, then immigrants must be able to prove their national authenticity by somehow meeting an unattainable standard for belonging. As long as some national subjects are defined as "almost white but not quite," there is a supposed lack of fit whereby every choice, activity, behavior, or movement has the potential to disprove legitimacy.

Clearly, authenticity, like Americanization, is imagined within dynamic fields of meaning reflecting how contemporary transnational subjects may be required to negotiate contradictory politics of belonging. Peter van der Veer therefore claims that the "question of authenticity and continuity can be interpreted, to an important extent, as a question of discursive and performative power" ("Introduction" 11). The key things to notice about this reading of authenticity are the ways in which continuity or tradition are interpreted not as set but instead as willfully created in language and action and having implications for the exercise of authority or influence. One of the most important questions to ask about authenticity claims or demands is whose will-to-power frames the fields of meaning. Even while there are constant theoretical as well as practical challenges to "the cult" of authenticity and similar fictions constructed in discourse, there are political and social consequences associated with being *in*authentic. These can range from actual deportation and excommunication to more symbolic types of exclusion or invisibility. Searching for proof of authenticity may well be a fruitless task that hampers our recognition of the decided heterogeneity of all individuals and groups. Yet it is hard to deny that implicit expectations of authenticity consistently come into play in the interactions between diverse communities within the United States and other multicultural/multiracial nations.

Even as the consequences are not as materially consequential, in the films, issues of authenticity are fittingly represented in various contradictory and ambivalent ways. For example, second-generation characters rehearse the relationships between national and ethno-cultural identities rather than assuming them, taking the ABCD's cultural "confusion" as the momentum for self-identification. In contrast, the first generation is often deeply invested in maintaining immigrant traditions (such as arranged marriages and certain religious practices) as a way of rejecting (Anglo-American) normative national culture and securing cultural authenticity for the second generation. Associated activities signify a sense of cultural distinctiveness, even superiority, at home, as contrasted with ethnic minoritization outside the family or community space. For the second generation, this tendency in parents can contrast sharply with their own ethno-cultural inventions if they wish to "be just like all the other kids," as Sureel confesses at one point in *American Chai,* rather than mark themselves as culturally or racially different.

Although anxieties of authenticity are not only relevant for immigrants negotiating assimilation processes or communities in diaspora, conditions of Otherness seem to render the process more conspicuous and urgent, as was obviously the case for the protagonist in *Manhattan Music,* for whom "nothing felt right" (9). In the field of film, postcolonial scholar Patrick Williams suggests that cinema may be especially revealing of such issues since it can be viewed as *the* "Western-produced genre, born at the high point of rapid European colonial expansion, massively dependent on (Western) technology and capital investment, bringing with it an even worse ideological package than the novel" (455). This history raises questions about "colonized" populations and their abilities to make use of such ideologically laden technologies without becoming complicit in traditional hierarchies of power. Discourses of authenticity are pervasive in public culture, even if they often go unremarked, but they are also differently deployed in various contexts, so that the important issue Williams raises may be of little relevance for second-generation Indian Americans, who may consider themselves no less "Western" than other Americans. This change is reminiscent of the ways in which debates about using the English language in former colonies no longer seem to arouse quite as much heat as in famous exchanges between Chinua Achebe and Ngugi wa Thiong'o.[16] It seems that "chutnification" of English by "natives" such as Salman Rushdie provides enough evidence to convince many people that this is now a nonissue.

As revealed in concerns about who use utilizes what technologies or languages, "authenticity" problematically presupposes oppositional identities and discrete "ownership" of cultural practices or objects. Through the type of cultural studies methodology common to all the chapters of this book, I read anxieties of authenticity as mechanisms via which individuals or communities assert affiliations that can be recognized within specific contexts. Anthropologist John L. Jackson Jr. affirms this when, with painstaking care, he traces ideologies of authenticity and reads them as "attempts to predetermine social possibility" for racial minorities in the United States (13). It seems to me that, in the Foucauldian sense of identifying the limit through its transgression, those expressions of ethnicity that are taken for granted as authentic are not as revealing as those that are scrutinized because they fail to meet some implied ideal. Thus, it is under those conditions when there seem to be questions about authenticity, rather than an implicit assumption of it, that the consequences are most obvious. And in situations of cultural displacement or marginalization, authenticity gestures to a perceived lack or absence which immigrants and their children may hope to recuperate in order to identify an appropriate narrative of belonging.

Therefore, discourses of authenticity—at the nexus of our notions of affiliation, community, and legitimacy—are often the testing ground for cultural fidelity disguised as a desire for "genuineness." There are incentives for individuals to monitor and discipline not only their own narratives of cultural affiliation but also those of others in their communities. In this sense, authenticity discourses suggest "how loyalties are nurtured and attenuated," as well as "the very structure of allegiance," in Leslie Bow's words (15). Bow is interested in "the charge of cultural betrayal as it seems to regulate group belonging," which she believes "does not simply contest the authenticity of one's identity or commitment whether in regard to alliances characterized by biological inevitability or those politically chosen, but instead becomes a potent *rhetorical* figuration deployed to signal how affiliations are formed and then consolidated" (8, 11). Her study emphasizes the extent to which authenticity is "figured," or discursively imagined, as cultural loyalty and thus becomes a critical measure of belonging. One can leverage claims of authenticity to justify participation within an identity community or, alternately, make a charge of betrayal in order to limit who belongs. As Bow concludes, "the question of identity is also invariably one of loyalty" (177). This statement helps to clarify some of the ways in which assimilation to the nation—often identified as "loyalty" and patriotism—is also a reading of one's identity. Furthermore, according to many people, for identities to be legible, they supposedly cannot be constituted from discrete (seemingly contradictory) sources.

This makes it obvious that *expectations* of authenticity—rather than empirical evidence of it—overdetermine understandings of identity, especially for minority groups within a nation. In critiquing "authenticity," it is certainly possible to expose expectations of prescripted ethnic (and other) identities as unsatisfactory strategies for understanding and managing difference, but it is rather impossible to do away with authenticity entirely.

Filming Femininity and Masculinity Desi Style

Various scenes in the four films confirm that anxieties of authenticity are relevant for all members of shared identity groups, for men as well as for women. There are some notable cinematic moments concerning women's ethno-cultural performances that I discuss later, but male characters are also conscripted according to narrow readings of Indianness and Americanness. Such representations provide a valuable counterpoint to the female narratives of assimilation considered in the previous chapter. For example, both Sureel in *American Chai* and one of Kris's roommates in *American Desi* struggle with expectations from their fathers about appropriate future careers and life partners for Indian "boys," exposing the infantilizing and "feminizing" that can take place when men do not conform to ethno-cultural scripts. For example, Kris's roommate Jagjit predicts that his father "would take out his *talwar* and cut off [Jagjit's] balls" if he discovers that Jagjit is majoring in art rather than engineering, which is a suitable career according to his family. The repetition in *American Desi* of images such as having one's "balls in a sling" are crude but effective representations of the men's fears of emasculation if they disappoint parental demands for "authentic" behavior.

In a rather more nuanced gender narrative, in *ABCD,* if Nina is the "wild child," this is especially striking *in contrast to* her brother Raj as the "good son." Raj's story seems less dramatic than Nina's partly because his character is portrayed as the more stable, protective older sibling in contrast to her abrasive assertiveness and self-centeredness. However, his story—like all others—is not that simple. After their mother's death, Raj breaks off his engagement to Tejal, a "traditional" Indian woman, quits his job, and decides to travel indefinitely. He had earlier explained to a co-worker, "[My fiancée] expects a lot out of me. Like my mom, she puts a lot of value in my success in business." He quickly qualifies that neither of them judges him, but he has already exposed his tendency to fulfill his mother's and future wife's expectations of him as an Indian son and future husband who will act in predictable ways, both responsibly and dependably.

The trigger for Raj's transformation seems to be his recognition that playing the "proper" roles, as he has been assuming them, may well have cost him a promotion for which he has been hoping. When the promotion is instead offered to his friend and co-worker Brian, Raj questions his boss about it; Raj is informed that he is a better accountant than Brian, but not as outgoing or social—"it's a personality thing." Interpreting this as potential racism but being assured by Brian that that could only be the case "if [he] were black, maybe," Raj finally seems to confront the implications of his own assumptions about race and gender. That he breaks with all of the institutions which provide familiar context represents a radical decision to reassess and seemingly start from scratch in inventing himself, as Jasmine does at the end of the Mukherjee's story of an immigrant "maximalist," discussed in chapter 3. As was true in that narrative, it is unfortunate that, in *ABCD,* what seems to be a liberating act of deconstructing expectations of "authenticity" potentially comes at others' expense. One of the ways in which this becomes clearest in the film narrative is through the consequences faced by Raj's fiancée. Since one of Raj's heroic new decisions is to break up with Tejal, the film suggests that she will pay a serious price for his self-discovery: she fears that her chances of a "good marriage" are ruined because she accepted a long engagement (meaning she is now "older") and allowed Raj to seduce her under the assumption that they would marry.

Even as there are clear implications for desi male identity, this is nonetheless one of many narrative instances depicting how anxieties of authenticity and purity are especially heightened for women. Recalling John Berger's famous analysis that, in Western art traditions, men do the gazing while women are gazed *at,* one can imagine how this tendency is further emphasized in film performances, especially in depictions of female bodies. In films that are centrally about characters' confrontations with accommodating American and Indian expectations of authenticity, the identities and bodies presented are both literally and figuratively bearers of culture. Traditionally in Bollywood films, meanwhile, female chastity has been of such central significance that one major trope into the late twentieth century was the suggested, but not pictured, on-screen kiss, so that sexuality in conjunction with female leads was never more than discreetly hinted at, unless sexual dishonor was recontained through an "honorable" death, often figured as suicide. In the past decade, outrage inspired by the increasing suggestiveness of clothing and salacious representations of female sexuality in Indian movies merely highlights how significantly the national "body" continues to be a contested site in relation to specifically *gendered* bodies, as discussed in chapter 3.

In *American Desi,* it is one of Kris's roommates, Selim, who develops a sympathetic understanding of the expectations of authenticity which, broadly speaking, inform middle-class Indian female identities in the United States. At the beginning of the film, Selim frequently and loudly announces his conviction that Indian women are "ruined" and "corrupted" by America because they do not know how to cook Indian food, prefer *goras* (white men), and are man-hating feminists in any case. Upon surprising a fellow student, Farah, at the mosque, Selim realizes that he has misjudged her based on knee-jerk assumptions when he assumed she was one of "these ABCDs." Luckily, Selim is persuaded by Farah's religious "piousness" that his stereotype is inaccurate. Just like Kris, Selim is redeemed in the film narrative once he recognizes that Farah can be both American and Muslim, that in fact there may be more complicated demands for authenticity placed on Indian American women than he has previously acknowledged. This recognition is dramatized when he must veil himself in a burqa to trick her parents into believing that he is her roommate; her fears for the consequences should they catch him in her room in the all-girls dorm are convincing based on the rules of her family script, as was also evidenced in the example of Tejal in *ABCD.* Selim benefits from experiencing for himself what it means to perform this type of gendered identity; he humbly apologizes to Farah: "This is going to sound crazy, but the other night was the first time I thought about what it must be like for you as an Indian woman."

In *American Desi,* Selim comes to recognize that his own deployment of Muslim American male identity has been problematic, but gender inconsistencies in relation to anxieties of authenticity are less neatly reconciled in *ABCD.* A telling scene from the latter movie portrays some rather intractable attitudes toward perceived inauthenticity in Indian women in America. At one point in the film narrative, Nina tries to disentangle herself from Ashok, a recent immigrant, after a passionate few weeks together, because he seems too serious and perhaps "too" Indian. When Ashok asserts that he is in love with her and resists her rejection, their interaction contrasts his patience and earnestness with her ambivalent, capricious, and even dictatorial behavior toward him. When reluctantly agreeing to meet him and discuss their romantic troubles, for example, she insists on setting arbitrary rules, such as eating at a fast-food place which is far from friendly to vegetarians such as Ashok; when he confusedly asks why, she flippantly replies, "I don't know. Call it a craving," seeming to continue a pattern of leveraging potentially sexualized power to offset perceived social disadvantage or discomfort. A man in a newsstand kiosk observes their interaction and turns out to be a recent Indian immigrant, evidenced by his sense of newness, his accented English, and his tendency to use an Indian language with customers who look like desis. When attempting to establish a cultural connection with Nina and confronting her immature and patronizing response, he calls her a "bitch." He later warns Ashok to be cautious of her, because "she has been in this country too long": "Believe me. She's a whore. They get that way here." In this scene, the newsstand voyeur evokes an unfortunately familiar conflation; if Shukla points out that it is problematic when "sexuality becomes a sign of 'Westernness'" (242), it is as often the case in South Asian narratives that putative Westernness (here, more specifically Americanness) becomes a signifier of sexuality in a highly negative manner. Bow argues that similar conflations in other contexts "clearly serve to regulate female sexuality" and "police and uphold the identifications necessary for affiliation and connection" (8). Thus, the Indian newsstand character in *ABCD* attempts to reassert himself in the face of Nina's dismissal by characterizing her Americanization as a deviation from the pure or chaste womanliness presumed to exist in Indian women who stay in the homeland. Like any essentialist gender or racial stereotype, this is an inadequate generalization about diasporic Indian women, but the alleged immorality of Americanness nevertheless becomes the scapegoat for "unwomanly"—thus inauthentic—cultural qualities.

Scripts of sexual(ized) normativity operate in all cultural landscapes and they interact with national narratives in dynamic ways, since, for example, Americanization has a *history* of being associated with sexual and racial impurity. The Hollywood movie machinery, in spite of its contemporary prominence, used to suffer in the eyes of the Old World because of the perception that there was no coherent national identity in the United States that might produce "high" culture. On this subject, Ian Jarvie summarizes certain strains of European intellectualism for which "the invasive and disruptive threat of movies from a nation that did not have a single culture . . . was a danger: American movies depict[ed] a society that was emphatically egalitarian in outlook, even if not in outcomes, democratic to a populist T, and manifestly multicultural" (85). Jarvie concludes that this was one of the reasons that the word "mongrel" so often came to be associated with the New World, in a way that destabilized "purificatory nationalisms and tends therefore to undermine them" (85). In the films currently under discussion, we might say that characters, especially men, who worry about the purity of Americanized women are echoing the threat of "mongrelization" that has haunted America since its inception. And this in turn parallels the fear of hybrid reproduction that pervaded colonial encounters, as documented by postcolonialist Robert J. C. Young in his important book *Colonial Desire*. Although people in many different geopolitical spaces cling to the idea of unalloyed national loyalty and ethnic consistency, Young and others reveal that no group has ever likely been as "pure" as its members might prefer.

Due to the ambivalence Nina experiences regarding her diasporic, national, and ethno-cultural affiliations in *ABCD*, the character's performances of gender are in fact often paradoxical and invite multiple interpretations. The narrative recalls Butler's observation that gender "ought not be construed as a stable identity or locus of agency from which various acts follow" (*Gender Trouble* 140), and the fictional Nina admits that there is no coherent narrative to explain her actions. In certain scenes, Nina is sexually aggressive or profane in seemingly willful efforts to deconstruct stereotypical images of Indian femininity. At the start of the film, for instance, she forcibly ejects a non-Indian lover from her apartment after he jokes, "I thought you Indian women are supposed to give your man whatever he wants." Nina's actions might reflect historical and activist realities in which women from the South Asian diaspora "forcefully intervene in masculine productions of Indianness" (Shukla 246). However, Nina somewhat unexpectedly reconciles with her former fiancé Sam, whose Anglo-American mother earlier fell into "a depressed funk" upon learning of their engagement because Nina did not conform to her expectations for a daughter-in-law.

Further, Nina's decision to marry Sam despite this reaction and her insistence on wearing a white dress in an "American" ceremony in a church ("where everybody is happy," she remarks) makes such a reading unconvincing. In choosing America (Sam) over India (Ashok), Nina could arguably be rejecting "the patriarchal heavy-handedness of Asian" identities (Bow 164). Perhaps love and national affiliations can be read separately? Even more likely, based on the chronically angry way in which Nina is portrayed in the film, some part of choosing Sam seems to be a desire to live the American Dream by marrying the all-American suitor. Nina's choices certainly implicate complicated politics of sexual capital, a term which Koshy uses as a shorthand for "the aggregate of attributes that index desirability within the field of romantic or marital relationships in a given culture and thereby influence the life-chances and opportunities of an individual," especially in the context of Asian American women and white men (*Sexual Naturalization* 136). The somewhat unpredictable ways in which *ABCD* portrays the character of Nina certainly work to frustrate expectations of authenticity that surround her, although it is not quite clear what the tone at the end of the film is meant to be. There is future promise in reconciliation between the siblings, but so many other things remain unclear, which arguably reinforces the themes of "confusion" and ambivalence represented by the film's title.

Inauthentic . . . or in "Drag"?

With the example of *ABCD* in mind, it becomes possible to reclaim the term "ABCD" by noting that identity inventions can be usefully linked to practices such as code-switching or drag—which are subversive because they not only acknowledge but actually *presuppose* a lack of strict conformity or genuineness and thus undermine discourses of authenticity. Although the scene of Selim's cross-dressing in *American Desi* is detached from queer politics (and is furthermore bracketed by drunken high jinks), it shows that film engaging in related politics of ethno-cultural invention. Even more significantly, there is a thoughtful scene in *Chutney Popcorn* that made me recognize the appropriateness of using the trope of "drag"—violating gender norms, "cross" dressing, queerness[17]—as an illuminating analogy for understanding authenticity and invention in this collection of films. This is certainly not meant to duck the historical specificity of what writer Jeffrey Hilbert reads as "the politics of drag" but, instead, to borrow a metaphor for certain kinds of cultural performativity that insistently strain against normativity and rigid standards by which we measure different ideals of gender, race, class, beauty, and so on. It furthermore seems excusable to the degree that some of the same urgencies of achieving civil rights inform both LGBTQ and ethnic-minority communities. The positions of disempowerment are not identical, but they are at times structurally similar in that they both involve institutional biases and exclusion. Anthropologist Rosalind Morris discusses why, as metaphors of drag have become so central to theories of performativity, it is necessary to ask which performances are about what; for instance, she suggests that performances of gender/sexuality are "racialized" just as race performances are "genderized" (585). So when film characters simultaneously perform gender, sexuality, and ethnicity, it becomes even easier to notice how different ethno-cultural scripts influence and inflect one another.

To invoke "drag" in the context of ABCD films is to suggest that episodes of what Desai calls "postcolonial diasporic mimicry" (*Beyond Bollywood* 107) or parody, camp,[18] and identity play are potentially active ways of responding to impossible demands for authenticity. Similarly, Gayatri Gopinath argues that "a consideration of queerness" in the context of public cultures challenges nationalisms, even of the diasporic variety, because "queerness is to heterosexuality as the diaspora is to the nation" (11). What Gopinath implies is that to disrupt the master narratives of nation associated with purity, authenticity, and heterosexual "productivity" (both procreational and economic, I would add) means posing a critique of them and also "exploding binary oppositions between nation and diaspora, heterosexuality and homosexuality, original and copy" (11). Thus, in the space-time between acting and acting *again*, there is the chance that nonnormative performances will take center stage and create more permanent disruptions to the familiar scripts.

For instance, following Sureel's typically comedic announcement in *American Chai* that being Indian American makes him "crazy," there is a scene of a family meal during which an obvious contrast is set up between ethno-cultural spaces and that of Sureel's undergraduate college, which stands in for mainstream America in the film. Sureel's father casually mentions the possibility of an arranged marriage for his horrified son, his mother feeds him "healthy" Indian food laden with ghee, and the family communicates in both English and Gujarati. Transitioning from these depictions of "Indianness," Sureel flashes back to a conversation with childhood friends, who were both white Americans, as a means of explaining the "identity crisis" that he claims resulted from being part of the only Indian family in town. Informed by one playmate that he must choose between being either Christian or Jewish, ("I'm Jewish. It's better," she declares) and faced with the other's equal confusion at his darkness ("Are you a Negro?") and his claim to being Indian ("What tribe are you from?"), he concludes, "By the age of ten, I had become the world's first Indian Jewish Native American Negro." When Sureel humorously narrates his friends' inability to properly define or label him, the film suggests that embracing the actual messiness of identity through parody is a useful strategy for responding when anxieties of authenticity come into play.

In response to such convoluted sociopolitical negotiations, characters in the films paradoxically claim authenticity by *performing* ethno-cultural identities, as usefully represented by such phenomena as code switching.[19] Code-switching occurs in the scene mentioned earlier from *American Chai*, when the father transitions from speaking to his sons in English to Gujarati without missing a beat. More generally, code-switching can refer to instances or extended periods in which individuals may consciously or unconsciously signify *differently* based on specific contexts and consequences. Naficy alludes to such practices in terms of polyphony, heteroglossia, and multilinguality in ethnic-minority and diasporic films that "destabilize the omniscient narrator and narrative system of the mainstream cinema" (25). As with performances of identity more broadly, then, code-switching calls attention to the "impurity" of cultural positionalities, since individuals speak multiple languages, enact ethnicity variously, and shift modalities of representation. Denying that this suggests a free field of cultural performativity, Maira cautions about remix youth culture that "the performance of a visibly hybrid ethnicity occurs in specific contexts and is not always optional; it belongs to a range of performances of cultural scripts in everyday life" (45). This caveat reminds us that within uniquely bounded cultural spaces, which codes make sense or can effectively be interpreted certainly inform the possibilities for individual actors or communities.

Whatever choices individuals make when faced with the possibility of moving into and out of ethnically or culturally symbolic spaces, the need to make such a decision is common to the film protagonists and reveals the ongoing process of deciding which "voice" (more properly, voices) one wishes to claim. Code-switching potentially allows individuals to tell stories in a different way, changing their import or effect and sometimes decentering normative understandings of insiders/outsiders. The term "switching" describes speech acts as well as various other instantiations of ethno-cultural identity. It includes contexts in which multiple languages are in play, which is pertinent to many minority communities in the United States and others throughout the world, as well as possibilities for moving into and out of certain roles by virtue of dress, accent, idiom, and the like. So, for example, when determining the import of switching between languages (in these films, English and Indian ones) without subtitles, a viewer recognizes that one important effect is to imagine speaking to at least two audiences simultaneously. And audiences who understood both languages are privileged over all others with respect to the films' accessibility. The practice thus also implies mastery over two or more cultural registers.[20] In the films' direct engagement with such doubling—inevitably "inauthentic"—they narrate what it means to successfully switch between cultures, to fail in proficiency, or even to reject opportunities to code-switch. When asking "which languages 'speak'" certain cultural productions, different contexts "provide different and differently available symbolic systems of race, ethnicity, and nationhood," as Shukla writes (244).

It is within such varying contexts that Indian American identity is performed *again* but with a difference in each of the films. For instance, the overarching conflict of authenticity in *American Desi* involves the main character's renunciation of his putative "Indianness" in favor of performing a thoroughly "American" part. He insists that people call him Kris rather than his given name, Krishna, because the latter emphasizes his ethno-cultural and religious difference. At the beginning of the film, Kris is associated with multiple things conspicuously symbolizing his Americanness, including an image of the U.S. flag in his room, his New

York baseball jersey, and "Young Americans" playing as he leaves home for college shouting, "Freedom!" It is instantly apparent to viewers that the dominant theme in the movie is Kris's disdain for all things Indian, which he overcomes through his inadvertent attraction to an Indian American woman and through the earnest-but-bumbling assistance of his trio of Indian American roommates. Nina and the roommates teach Kris that his anti-Indian sentiments are in fact self-hatred; by the end of the film, it is his willingness to participate in the others' code-switching (thus, to be a "true" desi) that allows him to win the girl while defeating the villain. Helpfully, one of the characters compares the finale to a happily-ever-after Bollywood narrative, affirming the viewer's interpretation that Kris has been symbolically assimilated to and redeemed within his diasporic community. He achieves this feat by combining his role as a "typical" American college student with a newly gained cultural competence in Bollywood and other Indian activities, which Jigna Desai considers a type of cultural "reconciliation" mediated by pleasures and desires figured in Bollywood imagery (118). What is revealed in Kris's interactions with other desis in the film is that communities maintain significant enough investments in certain kinds of ethno-cultural expression that they "help" each other rehearse how to behave. Since code-switching and other types of performance dominate the film narratives, however, we can infer that anxieties of authenticity may not always be as neatly resolved as in *American Desi*, and this is especially true regarding gender or sex norms, as described earlier.

Indeed, it may more often be the case that anxieties—and, more generally, inventions—of identity are constantly replayed and rehearsed without reaching neat closure, as is nicely illuminated by a scene from *Chutney Popcorn* in which the main character acknowledges that she *is* "confused" and, in fact, *in*authentic. This scene can usefully be unpacked with reference to Naficy's recognition that "mimicry, passing, posing, camp, drag, sly civility, doubling, and masquerade depend on the existence of an original something that is turned into something else, a copy of the original. Put another way, they depend on repeating an original as the same with a difference—a difference that often implies criticism" (270). In a moment that speaks directly to such processes, Reena, after frustrating her mother at her sister's wedding reception, is asked if she has gotten any good photos; she shrugs uncomfortably and tells her girlfriend, Lisa, "I can't. . . . It's like, I feel like I'm in drag, you know." It is as if her sense of not fitting in also disrupts her ability to record the scene in front of her meaningfully. In response, Lisa laughs and says, "Actually, you look like you are in drag." Reena smiles in response, seemingly relieved, and says, "Thanks," with her ability to document the party on film restored. The implication of this scene is that Lisa helps Reena remember the artifice of identities, rather than encouraging her to try to assimilate to the assumptions that proliferate throughout the movie. This epiphany is pointedly emphasized when, concurrent with this conversation, a non-Indian guest at the reception demands that one of the other guests must have a "real," "Indian" name other than Monica, followed by a woman (likely the latter's mother) yelling, "Moneekaa," with a conspicuously Indian inflection, in the girls' direction.

Of the four films, *Chutney Popcorn* is the most self-conscious in showcasing performances of palimpsestic identities. By playfully deconstructing most of the identity categories that confront them, characters in the films self-consciously invent identities in ways that have serious implications. The narrative does not relate Reena's realizations about inauthenticity only to ethno-cultural identification but repeats the theme in various scenes depicting her with a circle of non-Indian friends. These women self-identify as lesbians and engage in a running commentary about who is or is not "a dyke," playing with the rules of categorization and humorously identifying the contingencies associated with all identity labels. For example, one of their friends chastises them when they seem surprised about a character's sexual identity by retorting, "Bi-phobia is *so* 1995." Like ethno-cultural belonging in the film, lesbian identifications seem to include many possibilities; furthermore, cross-cutting these positionalities are various aspects of human experience that are irreducible to them. Treating questions of reproductive choices, family and genealogy, and personal agency in intertwined ways that are tragic as well as comedic, the film represents identities that are dynamic rather than being simplified narratives affirming authenticity. The ethnic, gender, and sexuality performances in the film collectively work to destabilize normative notions of Indianness, Americanness, femaleness, and heterosexuality. This is a similar process to those which Gopinath identifies as "impossible desires" in South Asian public cultures; she concludes her study on that subject by discussing how "queer diasporic cultural forms suggest alternative forms of collectivity and communal belonging that redefine home outside of a logic of blood, purity, authenticity, and patrilineal descent" (187).

Interestingly, by the end of *Chutney Popcorn*, the narrative implies that *everyone* in the film is influenced by analogous alternative forms, and thus actually "in drag," encouraging us in the audience to see ourselves this way, as well. When Butler concluded that, "*In imitating gender, drag implicitly reveals the imitative structure of gender itself—as well as its contingency*" (*Gender Trouble* 137), she suggested a useful way to read gender and sexuality in this film. Exposing "imitative structures," the film closes with Reena's mother, Meenu, at least tacitly accepting her daughter's sexuality by positioning Reena's girlfriend, Lisa, "like the husband" during a Hindu religious ceremony. Meenu at the same time places Reena's sister Sarita "like the brother" who will protect Reena. As Meenu proceeds with a ceremony to bless her forthcoming grandchild, whom Reena will bear after artificial insemination of Mitch's sperm, she reveals to both daughters and their partners that she herself is imitating something rather than acting on certain knowledge. Meenu makes several vague gestures and grimaces as she asks at one point, "But what to do?" because she does not know how the ceremony goes despite her claim to have done this "twice before." Anupama Arora reads this scene as paralleling multiple moments in which the film "queers" expected diasporic rituals: she argues, "Like Sarita's inability to bear a child and Reena's surrogate motherhood, Meenu is, however, unable to simply 'reproduce' Indian rituals, in the process highlighting tradition itself as denaturalized" (39). This convincing reading suggests that tradition itself is no less invented than the identities of second-generation characters.

Announcing to viewers that such "denaturalizing" does not have to be an unrelentingly grim experience, Meenu becomes reconciled to her daughter's "inauthentic" identity in a lovely, hilarious scene in which Reena reminds her mother that any person in the family could have been gay because "you never know." Startled, Meenu responds, "—you talking about my mother? She would never wear those shoes," as she points at Reena's feet. In this moment, *Chutney Popcorn* affirms what Kulvinder Arora claims about other South Asian diasporic films in terms of "alternative narratives of belonging": a same-sex story is about "more than sexual preference. It is a desire to affiliate strongly with other women based on both commonalities and differences" (244). Reading queerness in South Asian cultural products, Kulvinder Arora reinforces scholarly conclusions reached by Anupama Arora, Desai, Dudrah, and Gopinath, which posit that nonconformity to one type of conventional script (such as heteronormativity) implicitly has the ability to destabilize other binaristic epistemologies. Kulvinder Arora thus reads independent South Asian diasporic films as "counter-narratives to assimilationist narratives" (222). Emphasizing the queer counternarrative in the scene just described, Meenu stares at the Statue of Liberty and gaily announces to

Reena that "even she is wearing a sari," suggesting that one of the most enduring symbols of Americanization is actually in ethnic drag. In an analysis of German theater, Katrin Sieg points out that, "as a simulacrum of 'race,' [drag] challenges the perceptions and privileges of those who would mistake appearances for essence" (3). Despite her very different focus, Sieg, like me, historicizes assimilation discourses in a specific national space (see 233–53) and traces "the intricate ways in which race, nation, and sexuality are predicated on each other in ethnic drag" (23). Sieg's suggestions about drag, as the appropriation and critique of systems in which there are unequal powers to narrate, are useful to consider in light of ABCD film performances of invented identities.

Concluding Scenes

Reading "drag" across distinct geopolitical contingences makes it especially obvious that the four film narratives presented here, which conspicuously presence diasporic belonging, are insistently *American* films depicting private, middle-class identity negotiations. These latter tendencies are also generally true of the fictions of chapter 3, but not of the GuyaneseOpportunities Americanization program, with its pseudo-official status and targeted demographic. Juxtaposing the three sets of narratives is therefore important in understanding the broader implications, as noted throughout this book. Specifically, all four films discussed in this chapter represent immigration and assimilation in a relatively narrow range of sites; except for *American Chai,* they are set primarily in East Coast suburbs such as those inhabited by professional Indian communities starting in the 1980s and 1990s. The films also collectively narrate processes of Americanization in terms that are largely familial or romantic such that conflicts are usually worked out one-on-one. The films do not generally concentrate on the ways in which assimilation is an official, public, national issue. Instead, identity negotiations and performances are undertaken in localized settings, most notably in the private sphere of families, sometimes broadened to ethnic communities, college settings, and social organizations constructed around "culture." Furthermore, the films conform to a pattern that Shukla describes, in which class status is "a relatively uncharted territory in diasporic representation. . . . Well-credentialed and wealthy Indians who embody the 'American dream' hold a large purchase on the popular imagination" and may themselves effectively deny the diversity (whether economic, social, and cultural) of Indians in America (241). Indeed, except for a few brief asides and minor characters, none of the films complicates the class privilege that the protagonists generally enjoy.

Although each complicates notions of "how to be Indian," these films are therefore not explicitly oppositional in political[21] or plot terms, which one might also conclude about the published fictions or ethnographic interviews described in the other chapters of this book. With regard to form, the films cannot be considered experimental; for instance, each is firmly within a realist mode of representation and emphasizes verisimilitude in constructing a mostly linear narrative. With their inclinations toward comedy, the film narratives (except possibly for *ABCD*) primarily entertain their audiences. This is not necessarily a black mark against them. Although this study imagines the potential for narratives to destabilize certain normative assumptions, it does not suggest that all engagements with assimilation or other often-teleological discourses are resistant in nature. Naficy connects the expectation of resistance in such cultural products to anxieties of authenticity, when he writes that "defensiveness and the desire for counterhegemonic representations" often create "communal pressure" for films to be "fully" representative of a diasporic community (65). Indeed, for viewers, like myself, who may initially hope for narratives which radically transcend limiting discourses of authenticity, it is necessary to recognize how each film performs certain deconstructions of Indianness without expecting that any of them is able somehow to escape entirely the contingencies of its own imagined film world or the global capitalist market in which films circulate today. Reading the meaning behind the inventions of ethno-cultural identities by artists, actors, and authors allows us instead to acknowledge anxieties of authenticity and other narrative implications that are themselves revealing about contemporary ethno-cultural experiences.

Therefore, these films are best regarded as examples of ambivalent Americanization, since they portray normative assimilation while simultaneously troubling expectations of authentic ethnic, national, or diasporic selves, revealing complicated processes of accommodation rather than simplified narratives of in- or exclusion. Even the arguably least complicated of these film narratives, *American Desi,* calls attention to inventions of identity that undermine static representations of immigrants. In the character of one of Kris's roommate, *American Desi* suggests potentially radical deconstructions of the racial status quo in the United States. Kal Penn plays Ajay, an admittedly over-the-top and caricaturish Indian "homie," who instructs Kris, "I'm just trying to keep it real. Blacks and Indians got a hell of a lot more in common than you think. We share a common ancestry.... You know India used to be part of Africa.... We were one land, one people.... I'm just rediscovering my original roots." One of the many prods in the film for Kris to abandon his project of internalized racism, this scene (like others in the film) is potentially touching and politically thought-provoking, but played in a rather juvenile manner.

In a related manner, each of the four films narrates assimilation to national, ethno-cultural, and generic expectations but also undermines them, sometimes dramatically but often playfully. For example, *American Chai* concludes with several types of narrative uncertainty, with Sureel heading to London hoping to find love and musical success but assured of neither. Following his leave-taking from his parents, who have assimilated themselves to what they perceive as unconventional choices, Sureel fantasizes about a romantic reconciliation, the second time in this film that Bollywood cinema is invoked. The scene shows Sureel and Maya running toward one another across an open field, yelling each other's names, and then meeting for a deflected kiss when she demurely turns away. But in this reprisal of Bollywood convention, the two actors openly kiss each other, subverting the expected development of the scene, rewriting a familiar script for those viewers familiar with Indian cinema. In a similar move of undercutting expected "authentic" representations, in *ABCD,* Nina stands on the steps of a church wearing a white wedding dress and ties a *rakhi* on her brother's wrist. This symbol represents a Hindu tradition honoring the bonds between brothers and sisters; even though their mother's death means there is no longer parental pressure or reminder, Nina commemorates the holiday as a way of reconnecting with her brother through this ethno-religious gesture. Even as she seems to have assimilated, choosing to perform a modern "American" wedding as compared to the childhood friend whose "traditional" Indian ceremony she had earlier attended, this scene marks even Nina as incompletely Americanized.

Thus, in these films about children of South Asian immigrants, although characters may in some ways *appear* to be assimilated, invented identities including "Indianness" dramatically shape the narratives. This is true even though "the nation-state of Indian is absent" (Shukla 244). The films, especially *ABCD* and *Chutney Popcorn,* do not always provide satisfying closure and do not fit any one canonical film story. Yet in their material existences tangential to the world's major cinemas, the films remind us of the presence—in the cultural margins and borderlands—of communities such as Indian immigrants and their descendants.

Ironically, being neither Hollywood nor Bollywood may be an empowering position, encouraging filmmakers to elude some of the weighty baggage of a colonizing influence that could too forcefully influence the stories told in their films. Because of the films' very interstitial nature, perhaps they (like the characters they portray) retain more obvious incentives for resisting the hegemonies of either America or India. Therefore, it seems to me that our work as viewers of these films, as well as audiences for other related cultural productions, is to make productive meaning from the interstitial positioning that they portray.

Critically examining American films about South Asians ideally furthers projects for understanding how immigrant communities can belong both here (in the United States) and elsewhere (as part of an imagined diaspora). As Naficy notes, "immigrants everywhere have been key players in the development of the literature and cinema of their adopted countries," and American cinema was from the start "immigrant, transnational, and American all at the same time. . . . From cinema's inception, émigré and ethnic filmmakers attempted to make films for their own specific audiences, with little sustained success or with mixed results" (7). The limited distribution of these films speaks to the underexposure of diverse immigrant experiences in American cinema, but the sustained effort to tell these stories—as noncanonical and thus hard to categorize as they are—also speaks to the grand traditions that continue to shape American and desi stories into the twenty-first century. Even though (or precisely because?) South Asian American films do not fit within a major national cinema, they help define the boundaries of what Michael Rogin calls "American self-making" (1057) by reflecting the unique experiences of one immigrant group among many others.

Neither Hollywood nor Bollywood, but borrowing from and contributing to both cinematic traditions, these are stories of diasporic and ethno-cultural identity construction in a medium that shares some characteristics with literary production but also allows for different emphases. As a "popular" culture form, movies may be arguably more accessible than the written word. Yet these are films with fairly circumscribed audiences, as with South Asian Americanization stories more broadly. And even though films are made by groups of people and cannot be considered any one author's vision, the resulting composite product can nonetheless be "read" for its narrative implications. Furthermore, whereas one is bound by chronology and continuity when attending a theatrical release, film viewing on a videotape or DVD can be more individualized, allowing the audience to customize the experience, just like reading a book. In this sense, films about ABCDs are certainly important contributions to collections of stories about diasporic South Asians.

When viewing these films with combined attention to imagined diaspora, assimilation processes, ethnic inventions, and discourses of authenticity, it is hard to deny that Americanization is but one among many processes by which individuals and communities narrate experiences of belonging under conditions of (trans)nationalism today. The films reveal that being an American *always* means participating in performances of identities.

Conclusion: Ambivalent Americanization and South Asian Narratives of Belonging in Diaspora

As suggested by the analyses in this book, when investigating assimilation stories and related narratives of belonging in the United States, one finds that multiple other discourses are inevitably implicated. Authenticity expectations are relevant for national belonging as well as for other systems of self-naming, including religion, diaspora, region, and so on. Each narrative of Americanization and belonging discussed in the preceding chapters illuminates the others as provisional and consistently multivalent, portraying multiple inventions of Americanness. Despite this, (trans)national communities come to invest so much in certain self-narrations that contradictions and ambivalences may go unaddressed. In contrast, by shifting our attention away from categorical imperatives to how national and other stories are always and already intertextual, since they are influenced by narratives from the past and inform future versions, it is possible to seek out the layered meanings of narratives of belonging rather than flattening out dynamic and fluid processes.

Accordingly, in this study, by looking at three distinct groups—post-1965 immigrants relocating from the South Asian subcontinent, Indo-Caribbeaners enacting secondary migrations, and second-generation ethnic Indians—within the larger demographic of South Asians in America, I have sketched out a set of narratives that, in juxtaposition, emphasize differences as well as calling attention to similarities. While describing the unique historical, political, and social conjunctures crucial to each by studying them in separate chapters, I have pointed out how varied narratives of affiliation also mirror each other in certain moments and specific ways. There are common resonances in these stories, particularly concerning such things as the active efforts required to "become" (or be recognized as) American, tensions as well as mutual support offered by other members of one's chosen communities, and a lingering sense that the "becoming" is never a completed process but rather a vital redefining in constant flux.

"Belonging" is the central trope that I have closely read in these stories in relation to prominent dialogues in several disciplines. To belong is to be a member of a group, to be suitable or fit to be part of something, usually described as a feeling or experience. The actuality of belonging (or not belonging) is a universal experience for every individual subject confronted with the world outside of one's own consciousness, beyond one's own body. In this study, I have looked at belonging in terms of cultural investments accruing to interpretations of race-ethnicity, gender, class, immigration, assimilation, nation, diaspora, hybridity, and authenticity. Across these differently salient processes, the shared experience of negotiating belonging which occurs in the lives of all people within (and even marginal to) societies is one that can help us recognize a common humanity; however, "belonging" is as often a source of conflict, anxiety, fear, and anger, surrounding questions about who really belongs versus who, by nature of not belonging, is a potential threat or a rival. The complicated and intertwined processes informing belonging thus lead to what I have called the ambivalences of assimilation. These have been the figures through which I have exposed engagements with belonging, a desire which continues to be one of the most significant but arguably least actively articulated aspects of global contemporaneity.

Nor is "belonging" merely to do with individual feelings and sensibilities; as my discussion develops in the chapters of this study, I make the point more and more emphatically that belonging is also about cultural histories, political capital, intellectual priorities, and even actual materiality, including economics. Belonging is the interface for groups to self-consciously name themselves or be named, as well as to organically come into being as time and geography shift the realities according to which people live. As such, belonging points to central aspects of being human, and studying it clears a space for fuller questioning of and decision-making about how such naming functions. If naming people, as well as things and ideas, shapes reality, then it is critical that we ask pointed questions about its working, including, What names do people use to describe themselves and others? *Who* usually does the naming? Which names have political and historical weight as compared to those that—even if considered appropriate within a group—may not fit hegemonic narratives, as happened with the Guyanese communities represented in chapter 2? What are possible responses when a particular name or narrative becomes an obstacle, as was the case with the "dark femaleness" which I discussed in chapter 3? In chapter 4, I trouble the very act of naming itself, by pointing out that expectations of an authentic fit (i.e., seamless belonging) are always bound to meet with disappointment because identity categories are themselves unstable constructs which work only as shorthand in specific moments and sites. As with the elusive particle, tracking in time *and* space is impossible when individuals and communities continue to migrate across the globe as well as symbolically.

That story—it is one we all know in America. By the early twenty-first century, you do not even have to be in the United States to crave the American Dream, although it was uniquely shaped in this nation through repeated stories of a fuller, happier, and "richer" life. The paradox is that this vision excludes the majority of people in the nation, but the myth of the American Dream has sustaining power which empirical evidence cannot seem to belie. If ever America were freer and more capable of fulfilling dreams than anywhere else, it is only because of how many and how much immigrants have believed the mythology. If pushed, most Americans would likely agree that we do not have the classless society of which some pilgrims dreamed, but it *is* better than anywhere else, right? How collectively, not just individually, we should characterize "better" is perhaps the least well specified aspect of American national dreaming, which reinforces centuries of history in which Americanization never came to be definitively named.

What my study demonstrates is the ways in which different versions or sets of stories suggest what America and the American Dream *may* be, just as British author Joseph Conrad's narrator Marlow in *Heart of Darkness* envisions an episode's meaning best being revealed through indirect lighting, "as a glow brings out a haze" (4). To make sense of the possibilities, I attend to what is at stake in related narratives, what role the dream plays in connecting diverse immigrants, through the imagination, into a potential "nation" of self-chosen types. Contextualized within a broader history of Americanization, the South Asian stories represented in this book collectively work to help define what seemed indefinable to my class on the American Dream, as described in chapter 1. In chapter 2, I questioned how this dream (more properly, dreams) shaped the quotidian experiences of an immigrant group in its efforts to integrate into a small U.S. city. In chapter 3, I examined related metaphors of belonging within the frame of coming-of-age narratives, tracing how individual identities are profoundly linked to shared stories about nation and diaspora. In chapter 4, by examining symbols and scripts from popular culture, I consolidated the findings from the previous discussions in order to expose how stories are as much constructed performances as they are "real," meaning that there is room for dynamic expressions of agency as well as sometimes rigid expectations affecting how and why people belong.

In light of my extended analysis of such phenomena in relation to the experiences of certain diasporic immigrants, this is the most vital insight: as long as the modern nation-state persists, instead of achieving a "successful" or "completed" sense of belonging, not just immigrants but *every* American (arguably every person) is constantly negotiating assimilation to the changing narratives of his or her (trans)national communities. "Americanization" is a customized version of a broader set of processes representing how people negotiate hails to become part of a larger collective, whether defined by nation, race, diaspora, or something else. What this represents is not an actual achievable goal, contrary to what Americanization programs of the past and ongoing uncritical acceptance of the American Dream imply. Instead, we must *always* be ambivalent toward Americanization, as with all demands for national or other types of assimilation, because they are best viewed as mechanisms obscuring particular investments rather than stories showing us how to live "happily ever after" (Sexton 57).

Accordingly, "ambivalence" is a response which I have privileged throughout this book, pointing out that it is a powerful tool for the types of deconstructive thinking that are absolutely necessary for projects of social justice, which begin with our ability to imagine the world differently than before. If (neo)colonial and other chauvinistic discourses and policies from the past continue to overdetermine power relations in the present, then we must be able to develop intellectual and other strategies for undoing their seemingly "disinterested" logic. Ambivalence means paying attention to "mixing" rather than fruitlessly searching for an authentic original (e.g., American, Indian, or anything else) that has never existed. Paying attention to layers of narrativity, history, meaning, and affiliation instead of focusing on oppositional binaries means complicating familiar stories like the American Dream. The anxiety and fear that such complexity might invoke should not prevent a recognition of the concomitant increase in possibilities—what the dream seems to have always meant, across many differences of interpretation. The American Dream, Americanization, and other stories of national assimilation are all narratives constructed through heteroglossia, with many diverse voices contributing to their development. When these voices speak with different, transnational "accents," it behooves one to listen closely in order to recognize how even those stories that seem unassimilably Other play a part in shaping the possibilities, thus realities, of a shared planet. For Americans, on whose stories this book concentrates, doing so means appreciating belonging to the "fullest," as James T. Adams idealistically imagined the American Dream. As mentioned earlier, reading ambivalence in the American Dream is therefore a methodology for making it *more* rather than less relevant to Americans as a whole.

Another important element of this book is the repeated act of "reclaiming" words and images—for example, "ambivalence," "confused," "Americanization," "the American Dream"—that have come to be viewed suspiciously because of the cultural and political weight which they represent. This is not merely a theoretical trick; instead, it represents an active strategy for denaturalizing the language used to describe belonging so that Americans can analyze the cultural and material investments that inform various narratives. Rather than expecting immigrants or any citizens to meet impossible expectations of authenticity in order to gain rights, resources, or respect, Americans should instead bravely confront national ambivalences and those ethno-cultural histories that have imbued them with power.

As these more general implications reveal, the particularity of South Asian narratives represents another opportunity for Americans in general to examine their most revered or contested idea(l)s of national belonging by testing the limits of citizenship, posing transnationalism alongside nationalism, and decentering (formerly) familiar stories to include the previously marginal. The resulting insights are valuable not only for the immigrant group in question but also for all those seeking a more realistic, fuller, and richer understanding of "We the People."

Notes

Introduction

1. Benedict Anderson uses the phrase "imagined community" to interrogate nationalism as a cultural artifact, but his paradigm of imagined communities analogously applies to diasporas because of the "profound emotional legitimacy" commanded by particular versions of "communion" which are not necessarily bounded by time or place (4, 6). The analogy is limited, since diasporas are products of different historical effects and are furthermore not "sovereign" and "limited" (6), as per Anderson's influential definition of the nation.

2. Some scholars include other nations such as Afghanistan within this categorization, but that is not a universal trend. The history of the subcontinent (both in ancient and modern times, under the Mughal Empire, the British Raj, and after independence) reveals religious and ethnic communities migrating across areas that are now territorially marked as sovereign. They created complex webs of interconnections that can sometimes be hard to separate, even as national identities often emphasized differences throughout the twentieth century and created divergent modern realities. The dispersal of South Asians around the world amplifies such affects on a global scale. Since Indians form the largest group of South Asians both numerically and with regard to political clout in the United States, "South Asian" is often conflated with "Indian," which Anita Mannur calls a "logic of Indocentrism" (8). This is not unlike the historical association of "Asian American" with "Chinese American" in the academy and popular discourse. Although it is regrettable to repeat this trend, the bulk of published materials concern Indians in America, especially in terms of literary works. In focusing on assimilation, I have also had a topical reason for narrowing my choices but remain alert to the semantic limitations when naming the communities I discuss. See chapter 1 for a further discussion of the term "South Asian."

3. Although there have been South Asians in the Americas since the eighteenth century, they have only been notably visible with what is usually considered the second major wave of immigration, after 1965. For analyses of earlier

Indian immigrant groups, see Mazumdar; Koshy, "Category Crisis"; Shankar and Balgopal.

4. See Rajini Srikanth's introduction to *The World Next Door* (1–2) on the problematic history of equating "America" with the United States. As aware as I am of this limitation, I maintain this usage here to reflect the common parlance in the narratives I examine, without intending to replicate a linguistic erasure of the rest of the Americas.

5. "Race" and "ethnicity" are obviously loaded terms that are, unfortunately, used very inconsistently even by scholars. Common definitions of "race" assume shared biological ancestry, while "ethnicity" may more often suggest cultural characteristics of particular groups. In this study, I use "ethnicity" to represent the processes by which different communities are identified, which usually includes some combination of geographical origin, ancestry, and culture. I tend to employ "race" when I am pointing to hierarchies of oppression and institutional structures. Given the uneven use of these terms in different discourses and by different individuals, I count on context to make the broader significance clear. Certain discussions have particularly influenced my usage, including Werner Sollors's distinction concerning the terminology of "race" versus "ethnicity" (*Beyond Ethnicity* 21–24, 36–39) and Aisha Khan's analysis of Indo-Caribbean communities. Khan usefully describes a strategy of using categories without relying on them: she writes that one can treat "race" and "religion" "as descriptive according to local criteria generated within certain kinds of power relations, rather than as prescriptive, predicting a priori what those relations ought to be" (5). See also Khan's overview of how racial discourses developed in Europe in the sixteenth century (32–33).

6. "Class" is used in the current study to designate the combined positionality by which individuals or groups are associated with capital of both the material and cultural sorts. Several authors theorize at greater length about "class" in relation to South Asian communities, including Koshy, "Category Crisis"; Maira; B. Mani; and Rajan and Sharma, chap. 1.

7. Following Arjun Appadurai and Carol Breckenridge, public culture can be understood as "a *zone* of cultural debate" which "has much to do with the tensions and contradictions between national sites and transnational cultural processes" (5). This zone encompasses "discursive formations" ranging from "the explicitly theoretical and literary, to the visual, the spectacular, and the experiential" (3). Also see Jigna Desai, *Beyond Bollywood*; Gopinath; and Werbner, *Imagined Diasporas.*

8. For some of the most influential analyses of diaspora, see Cohen; Radhakrishnan; and the essays collected in Braziel and Mannur. On the relationship between "nation" and "diaspora," see Lowe's first chapter. For historical overviews of the concept of diaspora, see Desai's first chapter in *Beyond Bollywood*; Hu-Dehart; Ong, intro.; and Werbner, *Imagined Diasporas.* Inderpal Grewal lays out some of the tensions that have historically been theorized and realized between nationalisms—which are based on bordered communities—and diasporas, which describe global, seemingly unbordered rubrics, especially in the chapter "Becoming American: The Novel and the Diaspora" (*Transnational America*). On the topic of differentiating immigrant and diasporic identities in relation to power politics, also see Clifford 307–10; he warns that "theories and discourses that diasporize or internationalize 'minorities' can deflect attention from long-standing, structured inequalities of class and race" in countries such as

the United States (313). On the South Asian diaspora in particular, see Samir Dayal's "Min(d)ing the Gap" (in which he discusses how choosing to emphasize diaspora is often a strategy for ignoring racism or other institutional problems, thereby affirming national hegemony, the bourgeoisie, and the status quo) and Vijay Mishra, who theorizes the "new" Indian diaspora.

9. Generally speaking, I use the word "identity" to describe cultural groups with which individuals and communities are associated. Rather than rehash many excellent discussions on the meanings of "identity" which have influenced this book, I direct the reader to Anderson, "Nationalism, Identity, and the World-in-Motion"; Gilroy; Gupta and Ferguson; H. Moore; Rajan and Sharma, "Theorizing Recognition"; and Werbner (while Werbner addresses the topic in most of her writing, her discussion of "arguments of identity" is particularly revealing, in *Imagined Diasporas*).

10. See Amardeep Singh's deconstruction of the 2010 census categories, for his blog on the Sepia Mutiny website.

11. A phrase which I invoke several times in this study, *In the American Grain* is, of course, the title of William Carlos Williams's 1925 book of essays. In that work, Williams critiqued expatriate modernists, including T. S. Eliot, Ezra Pound, and H.D. Along with Marianne Moore, he insisted on "Americanness" as an important element of his modernist writing. I use the phrase to recall the tensions in (trans)nationalism that were implicit in Williams's expression while also deconstructing it by suggesting that globalism *is* in the American grain.

12. See Clifford Geertz's classic piece "Thick Description" for a discussion of how ethnography "benefits from collecting possible meanings for concepts and locating webs of significance to reflect the complexity of cultures" (28). Applying such a strategy to South Asian studies, Arjun Appadurai sketches a notion of "thickness with a difference" (55).

13. Hitchcock offers an illuminating argument against "fetishizing of agency in an institutional framework" such that we assume textuality and other influences are equivalent (see especially 61–62). The concept of agency has been both crucial and contentious in feminist and antiracist discourses, but it may well have been overemphasized. I use the term in the present study in the very narrow sense of individuals acting in self-defined interests.

14. For important statements in the development of cultural studies, see Jameson; and Johnson.

15. See Judith Butler's "Merely Cultural" on this subject, specifically regarding the relationship between culture, queerness, and political economies. Meanwhile, E. San Juan Jr. offers a sustained critique of the directions in which cultural studies have moved and the challenge of connecting textual analysis with "real-world" change, in his chapter "Questioning Contemporary Cultural Studies."

16. Geertz, "Deep Play" 448, 452.

17. Ifekwunigwe 198.

18. For some particularly suggestive definitions of "culture," see Bauman, "Culture and Management" and *Liquid Modernity*; Gilroy, intro.; Hall, "Living with Difference"; Johnson; Lowe; and Spivak, "The New Subaltern." Also, Aihwa Ong's conclusion summarizes her treatment of culture "as a contingent scheme of meanings tied to power dynamics" (243).

19. For critiques of globalization, see Appadurai, chap. 2; and Tomlinson.

20. These include Lowe's notion of "Asian American cultural politics," Gayatri Gopinath's analysis of "South Asian public cultures" through "an alternative set of reading practices" (20–21), and Susan Koshy's call for a "transnational literacy" that heeds "the new and shifting relationships between ethnic, area, postcolonial, or globalization studies" ("The Postmodern Subaltern" 111).

21. A "palimpsest" refers to layered writing in which previous layers are never fully covered over. In addition to the frequent use of this imagery by influential writers such as H.D., Meena Alexander (one of the authors discussed in chapter 3) talks about "a palimpsest of self" in an interview with Zainab Ali and Dharini Rasiah (71), and sociologist Pnina Werbner alludes to the usefulness of the metaphor for "multiplex" identity struggles (*Imagined Diasporas* 75).

22. Jean Yu-wen Shen Wu and Ming Song reprint "Success Story of One Minority Group in U.S.," a 1966 article from *U.S. News and World Report* which they claim pinpoints "when the currently widespread concept of Asian Americans as the model minority was conceived." In the language of the article, "At a time when it is being proposed that hundreds of billions be spent to uplift Negroes and other minorities, the nation's 300,000 Chinese-Americans are getting ahead on their own, with no help from anyone else." As Wu and Song summarize, "many historians and social scientists agree that the message in the piece—namely, that the Asian American case demonstrates that a racial minority can 'make it' in America with hard work and sacrifice—was designed to scold other disenfranchised racial minorities, especially vocal African Americans," by implying that "if they fail, the fault lies in their lack of initiative and not in the deep structural inequalities based on race" (158).

23. A term coined by Israel Zangwill, in his 1909 play with that title, that has become synonymous with American assimilation.

24. Margaret Gibson makes a similar gesture with the title of her study, *Accommodation without Assimilation.*

25. In *Allegories of Empire,* Jenny Sharpe draws a similar conclusion about colonial racism, which she reads as "a defensive strategy that emerged in response to attacks on the moral and ethical grounds of colonialism" (6).

26. There are clearly overlapping areas of interest in studies of cosmopolitanism and diaspora, but I avoid discourses of cosmopolitanism in this study because of a series of debates which are usefully summarized by Rajan and Sharma's introduction to *New Cosmpolitanisms,* Cheah's and Robbins's introductions to *Cosmopolitics,* and Hitchcock. In these discussions, the scholars reclaim "cosmopolitanism" or offer a neologism to escape problematic implications, but I prefer "diasporization" as a central concept because, notwithstanding differences of opinion about its import, "diaspora" nonetheless suggests to me a wider field of possibilities that do not need quite as much qualification. Most recently, John C. Hawley glosses some of what seems to be at stake in competing theories of cosmopolitanism.

27. Ghosh, "The Diaspora in Indian Culture" (78).

28. Appadurai.

29. Bhabha, *The Location of Culture.*

30. For a particularly good example of this "turn," see Huang.

31. "Ambivalent" is also a common way of characterizing South Asian public cultures. See, for example, Desai, who writes that "South Asian/American cosmopolitanism is deeply rooted in ambivalence" ("Bollywood Abroad" 133), and Bakirathi Mani,

who claims that "the location of 'South Asia' is marked by ambivalence, nostalgia, and desire" (720). In an overview of Bapsi Sidhwa's writing, Robert L. Ross also stresses that ambivalence is integral to her novel of Americanization ("The Search for Community in Bapsi Sidhwa's Novels"). Additionally, Jaspal Kaur Singh writes that "for identity to be empowering, the postcolonial notion of ambivalence must be used" (58), specifically tying ambivalence to political agency.

32. Ghosh posits that heteroglossia is particularly relevant to the case of Indian diasporization ("The Diaspora in Indian Culture" 75).

33. See, for example, Harry F. Wolcott's discussion of ethnographic research that utilizes key informants and brief case descriptions for the purposes of interpreting culture (102).

1 / Reading Assimilation and the American Dream as Transnational Narratives

1. For an informative discussion of how the meanings of the play have often been simplified over the intervening years, see Sollors, *Beyond Ethnicity* 97. Leviatin and Lallas also make this point. Nonetheless, for many Americans, the concept of the "melting pot" stands for a highly problematic attitude of color-blindness toward historical differences among groups, a use that is not directly related to the play that made the concept famous.

2. This dialectic has become a central focus in transnational studies; see, for instance, Braziel and Mannur, intro.; Gupta and Ferguson; jain, "Theorizing South Asian America"; Lionnet and Shih; Lowe, chap. 1; Tomlinson; and Werbner, "The Materiality of Diaspora."

3. Shilpa Davé in "The Doors to Home and History," analyzes this concept in relation to South Asian American literature.

4. In this context, Anannya Bhattacharjee traces some of the problematic ways in which certain groups of immigrants construct the American nation, due to habits of ex-nomination, or the "the bourgeoisie's power to remain ideologically un-named" through processes such as essentialism and nationalism (234). For middle-class South Asian immigrants, Indians in particular, Bhattacharjee feels that they seek "economic advancement through the model of the envied West and cultural preservation of the Indian essence. In the emerging binary India signifies nation, culture, tradition, God; and the United States signifies material prosperity, participation in legislative politics, economic advancement, and industrial and technological advancement. In this, immigrant Indian constructions of national identity are revealed to be predictably similar to dominant nationalist thought in India" (236), and in America as well, I would add.

5. For more on the significance of political naming, see Radhakrishnan's response to envisioning the future of Asian American studies. He argues, "There is no representation without 'naming' (Asian-America as a name creates a certain interrelationship among the parts that constitute it), and 'naming' as a process is symptomatic of a tension between epistemology and politics. If radical epistemology insists on a deconstructive and open-ended process, politics advocates strategic closure." In other words, being hard to name can create challenges to belonging but offers a potential resistance to "prescriptive singularity" (251–52). See my conclusion for some further thoughts on this subject.

6. Urvashi Butalia's *The Other Side of Silence* does the important work of bringing

gender to the analysis of what Sangeeta Ray calls "the apocalyptic event for the subcontinent" (*En-Gendering India* 126). Butalia writes that approximately twelve million people moved between the newly created India and Pakistan and that probably one million were killed, and about seventy-five thousand women "are thought to have been abducted and raped by men of religions different from their own" (3). In *Cracking India,* Bapsi Sidhwa describes some of the efforts to "recover" such women, whose eventual circumstances are still an ongoing concern on the subcontinent.

7. In important comparative approaches, Gilroy considers Jewish and pan-Africanist politics, and Stéphane Dufoix discusses Jewish and black/African diasporas in his first chapter.

8. Spivak makes a severe criticism of the ways in which positioning women in discourses of transnationalism may actually serve to further obscure subalterns and affirm "the financialization of the globe" at the cost of "social distribution in developing nations" and the success of "civil social structures" ("Diasporas Old and New" 248–49). Her comments remind us of the continued "historical silencing of the subaltern" (263). My analyses of metaphors of transnationalism as narratives of nation, though I do not suggest that they offer a solution to this dilemma, instead pose questions about diasporas differently, hopefully with productive (if highly circumscribed) ends.

9. See, for instance, Braziel and Mannur.

10. This difference is the premise for Fareed Zakaria's short piece "To Become an American," in *Newsweek*; he notes how the German government in the early twenty-first century encouraged foreign workers to visit the country without holding out any hope for them to be integrated into the society, a model that he claims did not help its recruitment efforts.

11. Patricia P. Chu provides the following précis for Americanization in her discussion of Chinese American literature: "the immigrant passes from an old world defined as a dystopia of exhausted possibilities and tragic narrative outcomes to the utopian new world, where opportunity and happy endings beckon" (146–47).

12. Kazal, citing Milton Gordon, contrasts "Anglo-conformity" with "the melting pot" and "cultural pluralism" as major ideologies of assimilation (442).

13. Sociologist Denis-Constant Martin describes how relationships between individuals and nations lead to particular possibilities for "choices" of identity, made in relation to power and organized around whichever affiliation an individual selects as most relevant.

14. John Higham influentially defined nativism as "intense opposition to an internal minority on the grounds of its foreign (i.e. 'un-American') connections" (4).

15. Priscilla Wald describes such "official stories" as narratives that constitute America "because of the authority they command, articulated, as they are, in relation to the rights and privileges of individuals. They determine the status of an individual in the community. Neither unvarying nor monolithic, they change in response to competing narratives of the nation that must be engaged, absorbed, and retold: the fashioning and endless refashioning of 'a people'" (2).

16. Ronald Takaki and Gary Gerstle are among scholars who help to demolish the stereotype that European immigrants arrived in America in order to relocate, as compared to Asian immigrants, who are often assumed to be sojourners intending short stays.

17. For example, see Dublin.

18. See Brownstein.

19. Butler, "Merely Cultural."

20. See Mannur.

21. On this topic, in "The Local and the Global: Globalization and Ethnicity," Stuart Hall notes, "The erosion of the nation-state, national economies, and national-cultural identities is a very complex and dangerous moment. Entities of power are dangerous when they are ascending and when they are declining. . . . So when I refer to the decline or erosion of the nation-state, I do not mean that the nation-state is bowing off the stage of history" (177). Similarly, Sangeeta Ray cautions that we heed "the continuing presence of the nation in discourses that seek to supersede and subvert its constrictive confines such as internationalism, transnationalism, global capitalism, academic multiculturalism, and even corporate-style multiculturalism" (*En-Gendering India* 2).

22. See Mae M. Ngai's important historicizing of immigration in an understudied period, from 1924 to 1965; her epilogue also provides an overview of the past decade of immigration in the United States.

23. See *In Other Worlds: Essays in Cultural Politics,* 197–221.

24. See Koshy, "Category Crisis"; Mazumdar.

25. For more on this topic, see Jacobson; and Roediger.

26. See Katrak, "South Asian American Literature"; Niranjana; Puri; Rustomji-Kerns; Shankar and Srikanth.

27. See Leonard, *Making Ethnic Choices*; Shankar and Balgopal.

28. Ngai situates this important immigration act in relation to other major historical shifts, especially in chap. 7.

29. For more detail about post-1965 immigration, see, for instance, Grewal's chapter "Becoming American: The Novel and the Diaspora" (*Transnational America* 35–79) or Maira's introduction to *Desis in the House.*

30. For different interpretations of this history, see Koshy, "Category Crisis"; and Mazumdar.

31. See Desai, *Beyond Bollywood,* chap. 3; Koshy, "Category Crisis" (especially 285); Ngai 5–7; and Srikanth on "the idea of America" (33–37).

32. See Demetrios J. Lallas for a corrective to tendencies to attribute the phrase to Adams, when it was actually first used by Walter Lippman in a 1914 critique of laissez-faire capitalism.

33. The degree of privilege associated with voluntarily migration into the American middle class should not be taken for granted. It must be acknowledged that the process of immigration for South Asians with professional skills valued in both India and the United States is very different from other patterns in which immigrants are forced into certain low-paying sectors of the workforce that often compound other types of oppression that they experience through migration. For more on this topic, see Glenn.

34. For an interpretation of opportunistic minoritization, see Samir Dayal's discussion of how South Asians may "perceive or imagine advantages to accrue from a calculated self-positioning as diasporic" because "immigrant" can also signify "minority" and thus racial inferiority ("Min(d)ing the Gap" 236). Also see Monisha Das Gupta's explanation that South Asian immigrants "transferred skills learned in independent India to their new environment, a transnational process used in this case to promote

a sense of belonging to the United States. Even though they faced discrimination in the United States, this did not shake their faith in abstract liberal citizenship. In India, they were its primary beneficiaries.... [They] struck the accommodating medium between the reinfusion of U.S. society with culturally different immigrant workers and their (tentative) absorption in the national body through their participation in conventional politics" (53–54).

35. South Asians who migrated to the United States after the 1980s often did not share these conditions, and analyses of their stories are important contributions to the scholarship that is emerging. For example, "the arrival of the later group of South Asian immigrants has been governed by a very different set of immigration laws and citizenship criteria. The immigrants who arrived after the mid-1980s are more likely to have lower levels of education and show greater concentration in blue-collar jobs" (Purkayastha xii). On this subject, also see Rangaswamy. For examples of brief pieces that reflect working-class South Asian experiences, see the anthology *Contours of the Heart,* edited by Maira and Srikanth.

36. Grewal argues that the American dream explicitly and problematically links national belonging to consumer culture, which is dispersed beyond U.S. borders through globalization (*Transnational America*, 206).

37. The term "desi" (which I discuss in chapter 4) alludes to the Hindi word for "homeland," *desh.* It is a prevalent signifier for South Asians, especially Indians. See Prashad's article "Desh: The Contradictions of 'Homeland.'"

2 / They Came on Buses

1. I have struggled to determine the best terminology to use for the subjects of this chapter, given that my argument is that no existing nomenclature is quite the right fit. Following the way in which they generally spoke about themselves, I tend to refer to the community as "Guyanese." The initiatives that I discuss also termed the population they targeted "the Guyanese," but implicitly they meant only Indo-Guyanese, which is why I use that construction in the section on racial economics. However, a few of my interviewees strongly objected to the term "Indo-Guyanese" based on the multiculturalism implicit in Guyana's designation as the land of six peoples. This tendency was confirmed during my visit to Guyana, where racial differences were certainly very prominent, but people did not generally describe each other to me as "Indo" or "Afro."

2. For studies of Hmong assimilation, see Chan; Faderman and Xiong; and Koltyk. On Hmong cosmopolitics, see Schein.

3. Gopinath also writes about "impossibility" or "the unthinkability of a queer female subject position within various mappings of nation and diaspora" (15).

4. Haunting contemporary anthropologies are the histories of ethnographic work undertaken in colonizing interests, against which I offer my own readings. As an example of the former, Rey Chow calls it the "most basic anthropological scenario.... The Western anthropologist must insert himself and his social practices (such as "scientific" observation and recording) into these 'primitive' contexts. In spite of the grandiose salvational motives of his profession, the very presence of the Western anthropologist means, effectively, that these 'other' cultures are changed and displaced forever from their 'origins'" (*Primitive Passions* 176–77). See also Mankekar, chap. 1.

5. Except for the case of Schenectady's mayor (who met with me in his capacity as

a public official) and others who publicly identified themselves, I have avoided using names in order to maintain the confidentiality of those with whom I spoke. Over the course of three years, I interviewed numerous people in Schenectady, meeting with individuals for at least half an hour and, at times, for over two hours. These were people of Guyanese descent, long-term non-Guyanese Schenectady residents who interacted with Guyanese immigrants, and people who were directly involved with GuyaneseOpportunities initiatives. I do not provide demographic information here because my goal is not statistical analysis; instead, I highlight repeated themes from these interviews, particularly common stories about the assimilation processes affecting Guyanese immigrants in Schenectady. In those cases in which an interviewee expressed an attitude that was unique but seemed noteworthy, I have pointed that out in my analysis.

6. Although I do not think there was one official title used in all cases, the name of the website is useful in referring to a series of efforts that were both systematic and ad hoc in cultivating the growing Indo-Guyanese community in Schenectady. Warren Woodberry, a journalist for the *Daily News*, described it as a "Dream City" project, but the use of this term has not been widespread.

7. As described in literature provided in Schenectady to visiting Guyanese immigrants, the SEDC "is the clearinghouse for economic development projects within the county. [SEDC] is a private, non-profit corporation cooperatively supported by local government and the business community. SEDC's mission is to promote and develop a strong, viable economy in Schenectady County."

8. These included local newspapers, news programs, and online forums. The online sites which had the most discussion about GuyaneseOpportunities were the port80cafe message board, the Schenectady, New York Public Forums, and the *Times Union* (Albany, NY) online communities.

9. My students agreed to comply, as I did, with regulations for human subject research, in consultation with the Union College Human Subjects Research Review Committee, which approved expedited review.

10. During Stratton's campaign to become Schenectady's mayor, he asserted that he would not "target any particular nationality or race" (Goodwin, "Guyanese Wonder: Where Are the Candidates?"). Leading up to his resumption of Jurczynski's "push," Stratton announced, "Without question, the influx of Guyanese and others relocating to Schenectady from the western Caribbean is making a positive impact on our society, as these new families invest in the community, reclaim homes, and work to improve the quality of our neighborhoods" ("Diversity Touted"). This statement was made upon the appointment of Kamla Sahabir, a Guyanese American woman, to the City Planning Commission.

11. For one example, the collection *The New Second Generation* (1996), edited by Alejandro Portes, represents some of the most prominent contemporary researchers of immigrant assimilation in America, including Patricia Fernández-Kelly, Richard Schauffler, Rubén Rumbaut, Mary Waters, and Min Zhou. Other notable contributions to ethnography studies have been made by anthropologist George Marcus; sociologists Nancy Foner, Herbert Gans, and Eva Morawksa; and political scientist Aristide Zolberg.

12. For instance, professor of education and anthropology Margaret Gibson (cited in chapter 1) analyzes Sikh high school students and assimilation in the late 1990s.

More recent work in sociology includes two other studies also cited earlier, namely, Rudrappa's on Chicago immigrants and ethnic institutions and Purkayastha's on second-generation Americans from across South Asia. In more specialized analyses, Sunaina Maira describes Indian "youth culture" in club scenes in New York City, and Sheba Mariam George documents South Indian female nurses who preceded their families in immigrating. Journalist S. Mitra Kalita interviewed working-class Gujarati families in central New Jersey, and historian Madulika S. Khandelwal (like Rangaswamy, who was also mentioned in the introduction) studies immigrant communities in more metropolitan areas. In a comparative project, meanwhile, anthropologist Sandhya Shukla has investigated Indian diasporic communities in England and America.

13. See Clifford, "Mixed Feelings"; Huang; Lowe; Niranjana; and Ong.

14. See Chow, *Primitive Passions,* for a discussion of what she calls "a new ethnography" in which the ethnographer—in this case, Zhang Yimou—is a part of the culture he is analyzing, which does not result in a representation of the "real" China any more than Orientalist representations did. Instead, she reads his films as self-reflections with their own idealizations and ideological implications (see especially 143–45).

15. I regret not being able to say more about gender in these stories, because I agree with Spivak that "it is around the issues of democratization and gender-and-development that the question of subaltern consciousness most urgently arises" ("The New Subaltern" 332). Furthermore, Gerstle's point is well taken that there are still "relatively few studies of gender and American identity" that focus on assimilation (547). GuyaneseOpportunities worked to recruit families and homebuyers such that gender assumptions were certainly made in terms of "traditional family values." For an analysis that explicitly analyzes gender in relation to Guyanese communities, see Peake and Trotz. For an analysis of South Asians that usefully seeks out exceptions to American immigrant history in which "it is unusual for women to be the first immigrants and primary breadwinners for the family," see George (2).

16. Many contemporary discussions of American politics and identity certainly combine economic and race-based analysis, although I do not believe the term "racial economics" has been consistently applied to these analyses. I develop my original use of this concept throughout the chapter.

17. I have listed the three affiliative categories in alphabetical order, to avoid choosing one as the primary label.

18. I. M. Cumpston provides information from similar reports in an article from the mid-twentieth century.

19. See Robert A. Carlson on the altruistic nature of some Americanization programs in the late 1800s (442–44), as well as the backlash toward Progressivist projects in the 1920s that led to immigration restrictions. See also Rudrappa for an overview of "theories on assimilation" (165–69).

20. Among others, Speek lists the following ways of defining nationality: similarity of ideals, beliefs, and customs; common cause; consciousness of kind related to a definite home country; a group of people carrying on a collective life by mental interaction; "organic community and continuity of interests"; values developed through experience; an agreed-upon means for gratifying "certain fundamental wishes"; habits in common (246–48).

21. See Kalita 43–46.

22. The following situations in other small cities offer comparisons and contrasts to the initiatives in Schenectady, with respect to their decisions regarding contemporary immigrants and assimilation processes. The atmosphere became racially quite tense in Lewiston, Maine, when the mayor wrote an open letter requesting that Somali immigrants halt their migration to the city ("Two Cities, Two Immigrant Landings" in the *New York Times*). Similarly, Michael Powell and Michelle Garcia reported in the *Washington Post* about Hazleton, Pennsylvania, when the mayor and others wanted to be the "toughest place on illegal immigrants in America," through harsh (potentially illegal) ordinances that other municipalities in the country considered adopting. In upstate New York, the Arthur Levitt Public Affairs Center at Hamilton College sponsored several reports and projects concerning immigrant integration issues. Focusing on Bosnian refugees, the "Levitt Reports" available on the center's website include analyses of cross-cultural transitions and financial implications.

23. See Speek 239; and Carlson 444.

24. Jurczynski recounted his visit in the editorial "Trip to Guyana Brought Home the Connection to Schenectady," in Schenectady's *Sunday Gazette*, in which he triumphantly noted that in Guyana "only New York is a better-known American city than Schenectady." Also see Goodwin, "Immigrant Appeal Intrigues Mayor."

25. These words are most often associated with civil rights leader Dorothy Height, who maintained that black Americans are not "problem people" but rather people with problems, like all others (218). Also see Cornel West's discussion of this race "problem" in the introduction to *Race Matters*.

26. For a powerful critique of the politics of color blindness, see Patricia J. Williams.

27. This is made clear in Ramasami's undergraduate thesis in political science at Union College titled "The Multi-Dimensional Racial Tension in Kenya" (1999).

28. For background on the use of lies and pretense to "recruit" Indian laborers to Guyana, see Carter and Torabully 20–26.

29. I allude here to Sollors's well-known model of consent and descent, which differentiates between "achieved" and "ascribed" identity (*Beyond Ethnicity* 37).

30. For making these differences clear by describing the conclusions she reached through original research in Kenya, I am grateful to Hemwatie Ramasami, who accompanied me on the research trip to Guyana in 2004.

31. Former president of Guyana Cheddi Jagan, in his important book on the history of Guyana, *The West on Trial*, is highly critical of America and the effect that U.S. Cold War policies had on the newly independent Guyanese nation. This sentiment was inconsistently represented by Guyanese Americans with whom I spoke, who were nonetheless often very proud that Guyana's first president had been of Indian descent. See also Suzanne Wasserman's 2003 film *Thunder in Guyana*, in which she describes how Janet Jagan, a Jewish American woman, assumed Guyana's presidency after her husband's death. Wasserman notices how certain types of anticommunist pressure from America undermined efforts at improving conditions in Guyana.

32. For one explanation, see Joseph Berger, about the degree to which other Indian communities do not always consider Guyanese to be "real" Indians.

33. See Mike Goodwin's reporting for Albany's *Times Union*, especially "Tax Hikes, Political Scandal, Snow Batter Mayor."

3 / "Stretched over Dark Femaleness"

1. The three authors represent choices I made in a field limited by what is published and widely available in the United States. The rubric I used was to include South Asian writers with established literary careers whose novels that were within the novelistic tradition in English focused on one character's responses to Americanization processes. Other prominent South Asian writers who have written fiction set in the United States are Anita Desai, Chitra Divakaruni, Jhumpa Lahiri, and Salman Rushdie.

2. A notable exception is Carmen Faymonville's article about *Jasmine* and *An American Brat.*

3. See Jussawalla on what she identifies as the tradition of the postcolonial bildungsroman: the character "has made his journey from the initial culture contact, the absorption into the colonizers' frame of mind, a move towards hybridity and a final coming to a recognition of himself belonging to the culture that he started from" ("Kim, Huck, and Naipaul" 37).

4. See, for example, Feng.

5. In an informative and rather unusual examination, in "Who Wants Pale, Thin, Pink Flesh?" Ruth Maxey discusses both Alexander's and Mukherjee's writing in terms of their "Othering of *white* bodies" (530, emphasis added).

6. On interracial relationships, see Chu; Koshy, *Sexual Naturalization.*

7. This passage about racialized gender identity points to a pronounced difference in the way stories have been associated with South Asian women or men. Whether this is primarily a reflection of editorial choices for publication or which stories different writers choose is outside the purview of the current discussion; for a brief discussion on the "literary marketplace" in relation to South Asian Americans, see Katrak, "South Asian American Literature" 195–96. In any case, novels by South Asian Americans fit a highly gendered pattern of female authors portraying immigrant experiences in the United States and male authors usually focusing on the subcontinent, on which Ross comments ("'Haunting Presence' and 'Broken Identities'" 97). This trend may change as the publication of South Asian stories diversifies and second-generation South Asians more frequently publish their narratives.

8. William Safran has influentially described the Jewish diaspora as the "ideal type" (84). In *Diaspora and Multiculturalism,* Monika Fludernik elaborates on this theme in *Manhattan Music.* Also, on the broader topic of Jewish diasporization, see Kurien; and Palumbo-Liu (344–45). The relationship of Jewish American assimilation to other minority integration in the country is important, in relation to both classic models of dispersal and the relationships between race, ethnicity, religion, and culture.

9. This monstrousness is reminiscent of the tropes Sandra Gilbert and Susan Gubar trace in *The Madwoman in the Attic: The Woman Writer and the Nineteenth-Century Literary Imagination,* in which they made the now-classic argument that, because women writers have historically been the Other to the normative male writer, they were positioned as "infected" or "dis-eased" monsters.

10. Lallas critiques Adams's rendition of the American Dream for being "racially insensitive" (6) and "compromised by racist overtones" (13).

11. In this chapter, I discuss race-ethnicity as combined identities because institutional hierarchies, ancestry, and culture are all reflected in South Asian "dark femaleness" as a contrast to "whiteness."

12. Exclusion of course operates on other axes, including sexual identity, religion, and ability. These topics are not as prominent in the texts discussed in this chapter, however.

13. See Crenshaw.

14. For a reading of Mukherjee's maximalism as an interventionist political stance, see Grice.

15. See Cheah 292–303.

16. For more elaborated discussions on how scientific and other languages are reflected in discourses of cultural hybridity, see Fludernik, *Hybridity and Postcolonialism*; and Friedman.

17. See Nelson Vieira's "Hybridity vs. Pluralism" for a discussion of the relationship between these two concepts, specifically in the context of Brazil.

18. For more on debates surrounding hybridity theory, see Katharyne Mitchell, who writes that the concept of hybridity "relies on an abstraction from the material social relationships and practices" produced in real spaces (91).

19. See Stoneham.

20. Draupadi traditionally represents the power of good to overcome evil as a mythic wife who resisted temptations, such as lust and impulses to anger, despite her many tribulations. As she is portrayed in the epic *Mahabharata,* she was the daughter of King Drupad of Panchala who became the wife of the Pandavas, five brothers who "won" her in battle and promised their mother, Kunti, that they would share the spoils before they knew it was a woman. Considered to be not quite human, Draupadi kept these brothers united to fight against evil. In future adventures, she maintained her own resistance to immorality despite being wagered and lost in a game of dice and exiled. An uncommon wife, Draupadi therefore conforms to certain conventional notions of "woman" while also being an empowering model for the character in *Manhattan Music.* Lavina D. Shankar provides an extended reading on how Alexander playfully reinvents the Draupadi myth ("Postcolonial Disaporics 'Writing in Search of a Homeland'").

21. Citizenship is of course one of the main ways to officially belong to a country, a privilege which is granted to Sandhya because of the greater emphasis in post-1965 U.S. immigration policies on family (re)unification programs, as compared to other countries. At the same time, *Manhattan Music* does not focus on obstacles to official citizenship, since Sandhya's immigration bypasses the many barriers faced by others seeking inclusion in the United States, for example, South Asians of the working or lower classes, unwanted refugees from certain parts of the world, Mexicans from across the border, and many other groups. Sandhya's middle-class status in particular affords her more options for becoming American than are available to many other immigrants.

22. Diwali, or "divali," as it is alternatively spelled, commemorates the return of Rama after a fourteen-year exile, in the Hindu epic *Ramayana,* signifying the reestablishment of good in the myth.

23. This is one example of textual evidence that leads me to disagree with Jaspal Singh's readings of *Manhattan Music.* Singh claims that "Draupati [*sic*], the hybridized and diasporic subject, permitted everything, must bring Sandhya, the oppressed Indian women, into her sexuality and identity as defined by her Westernized intellectual self" (183). Singh's overall project involves locating "postcolonial female narrative

voices within . . . conflicted spaces . . . to critique them through the political and cultural conditions that produced them in the first place" (2), and she usefully theorizes the difficulty of representing resistance to gender normativity when one's terms are already fully shaped by (modernist) norms. However, her reading of *Manhattan Music* is not persuasive, given the emphatic way that Sandhya, by the conclusion of the novel, announces her need to find her own narrative rather than simply to be guided by Draupadi's.

24. On many of the topics discussed in this section, there are related analyses in *Bharati Mukherjee: Critical Perspectives,* edited by Emmanuel Nelson, to which I would draw the reader's attention: for instance, see Brenda Bose on the American dream and reincarnation; Pushpa Parekh on names; and Debjani Banerjee on reinvention.

25. Mukherjee's editorials from the late 1980s and '90s—for example, "Immigrant Writing: Give Us Your Maximalists!" in the *New York Times* and "American Dreamer" in *Mother Jones*—have contributed to a strong association of the author with redefinitions of America and minorities within it.

26. While Mukherjee describes *Wife* as a novel that was as much shaped by her feelings of alienation in Canada as by her subsequent sense of belonging in the United States, I discuss it here as a novel about America rather than about Canada since it invokes specifically American geographies and icons. For more information on Mukherjee's perception of the novel, see Andrea Dlaska (45).

27. For exceptions, see Susan Koshy's chapter "Sex Acts as Assimilation Acts" in *Sexual Naturalization*; Katrak, "South Asian American Literature"; and Shankar, "The Limits of (South Asian) Names and Labels."

28. See Schultheis.

29. As many critics have noted, Mukherjee's passionate defenses of America and the opportunities it affords immigrants sometimes appear apolitical and dehistoricized when she does not acknowledge her own elite class background or South Asian patterns of integration as privileged compared to other minorities in the United States. For example, can American Indians or African Americans claim an American "intensity of spirit" despite historical oppression, or is this only the case for newer immigrant groups?

30. Singh includes Meena Alexander in this critique, pointing to Alexander's position in the Western academy as evidence of the author's reinforcement of (neo)colonial power and questioning Alexander's claim to marginalization. This reading is not as convincing as some of Singh's other interpretations, since she describes how "the immigrant's resistance to and compliance with the hegemonic discourses change with the context of oppression" (62). Pointing to what she finds missing in Mukherjee's writing in this quotation, Singh does not seem to apply the same logic to Alexander's fictions or actual subjectivities, which she nonetheless seems to agree are oppressed never in a simple way but in complicated structures engendering different types of agency and resistance.

31. "Re-reading beyond Third World Difference."

32. See Rajan; Dlaska.

33. Woolf writes against the consignment of women within houses and family, with expectations of Victorian respectability that meant they were to suppress their artistic, intellectual, and sexual feelings. Woolf says that women were confronted with a phantom angel—the internalization of these expectations—who encouraged them to be pure and womanly at the expense of asserting agency.

34. Sita is one of the most frequently evoked Indian symbols for womanhood. See Kulvinder Arora on this topic and other mythologies of female sexuality. Padma Rangaswamy writes that an "image of womanhood that has a profound effect on the Indian psyche is that of Sita, the heroine of India's most beloved epic, the *Ramayana*. Sita's chastity, obedience, and unflinching loyalty to her husband represent the ideal path for an Indian wife. This ideology survives even among modern, upper-class Indian women who defer to their husbands in an almost instinctive way" (145). Rangaswamy offers the important caveat that there are also many mythic Indian images of female dynamism and power, arguing that Indian women are not merely submissive and tractable. Also arguing this point, many feminists in India challenge the pervasiveness of Sita worship.

35. Lavina D. Shankar disagrees with this reading when she argues that the narrative voice is "supercilious" and paints Dimple as "a stereotypically dumb wife" ("Postcolonial Disaporics" 296–97). This is too brief a gloss on *Wife*, in an article focusing on Alexander's writing, to be entirely persuasive.

36. Feminisms in the past thirty-five years (at least) in the United States have developed by constant reassessment of the similarities and differences between groups of women, including a critique of white and middle-class biases in earlier theorizing. While assuming a "universal" female experience is one potential difficulty in talking about women around the world and diverse women in the United States, another is to see the West as more free from patriarchy than supposedly more traditional Eastern cultures, whose women need "rescuing" by Western feminism.

37. I appreciate Chu's reading of "the novel's failures as a 'realist' or 'domestic' novel" (97). She concludes that this failure exposes the limits of the traditional bildungsroman genre for Asian American subjectivity. Others have argued, by contrast, that multiethnic bildungsromane in the late twentieth century often actively subvert the conventions of realism in narrating minority subjectivity. See, for example, Karafilis.

38. See Ray's critique of Mukherjee's depiction of interethnic violence and demonization of the Sikhs, who agitated for a separate nation of their own after Partition. The critic sees this as a partisan representation of communal violence in India ("The Nation in Performance" 228).

39. *Sati* is the practice of Hindu widows immolating themselves on their husband's funeral pyre. Jasmine says about her decision to come to the United States, "This was the place I had chosen to die, on the first day if possible. I would land, find Tampah, walking there if necessary, find the college grounds and check it against the brochure photo. . . . I had dreamed of arranging [Prakash's] suit and twigs. The vision of serenely lying on a bed of fire among the palm trees in my white sari had motivated all the weeks of sleepless, half-starved passage" (107). Although *sati* is an important trope in the novel since Jasmine eventually decides to live rather than to sacrifice herself, it is nonetheless not particularly well developed in the narrative. For a famous comment on *sati*, see Gayatri Chakravorty Spivak's analysis in "Can the Subaltern Speak?" in which she problematizes understandings of *sati* from the perspective of Indians, the Raj, and globally. Also, Wickramagamage notes ideologies that maintain the tradition discursively, if not in actual practice, in her discussion of *Jasmine* (184–87).

40. While Braendlin's argument is highly relevant to *Jasmine*, it is important to note that "social determinism" for black or Chicana characters such as she discusses does not take the same form as for many South Asian protagonists. There are different

narratives of America available to women of different groups, based on their particular histories in the United States as well as their race, class, and sexuality, which must be noticed even as similarities in minority positions are also analyzed.

41. See Faymonville for an examination of how "frontier" imagery is represented in *Jasmine* and also in *An American Brat.*

42. Many critics object to the way such an allusion in the novel echoes Mukherjee's famous claim that her "Indianness is now a metaphor, a particular way of partially comprehending the world" (*Darkness* xv). For example, Ranee Kaur Banerjee writes, "Inconsistencies, the blatant disregard for facts, the callous remaking of histories, these are qualities and characteristics not only of Mukherjee's characters but of the author herself in her occasional disregard for accurate detail in her rendering of a fictional world" (199–200). Unlike many other scholars, Banerjee recuperates this tendency in the fiction by concluding, "Facts don't matter. . . . Realities and identities are artifacts to be made and unmade, over and over again. What is all-important is the essential transfigurative yet tenacious nature of the migrant and the fascinating, compelling stories (s)he has to tell" (200).

43. The alternative spelling, "Parsi," may be gaining currency, but here I have chosen to use "Parsee," which is Bapsi Sidhwa's usual spelling. For readings of the Parsee and Pakistani diaspora, see Rajan and Sharma's *New Cosmopolitanisms,* especially Karen Leonard's chapter on South Asian religions (103–4).

44. The dates of the Parsee expulsion from ancient Iran vary from source to source. Whereas Sidhwa writes in *An American Brat* that it was "fourteen hundred years ago" when the Parsees "fled to India as religious refugees after the Arab invasion of Persia" (68–69), others such as Luhrmann date their dispersal to as late as the tenth century AD (78).

45. See, for example, Luhrmann; and Kulke. Also, William Safran summarizes, "The diaspora of the Parsis is in several respects comparable to that of the Jews: its members have been held together by a common religion, and they have engaged in commerce and the free professions, have been pioneers in industrial innovation, and have performed various useful services to the ruling class. Like the Jews, the Parsis have been loyal to the government. But unlike the Jews, they are not widely dispersed. . . . Moreover, they have no myth of return to their original homeland, Iran, whence they emigrated in the eighth century. The weakness of the Parsis' 'homeland' consciousness can be attributed in part to the caste system of India and the relatively tolerant attitudes of Hinduism, both of which made for a greater acceptance of social and ethnocultural segmentation and made Parsis feel less 'exceptional'" (89).

46. Luhrmann describes this as "the most famous story of Parsi history" (78). It is widely circulated and can be found in most criticism about Sidhwa, with the details of the story changing very little between accounts.

47. It should be noted, however, that ethnocentricity is not foreign to the Parsees, whose most orthodox members vehemently oppose exogamy and advocate the excommunication of Parsee women who marry "nons." There has been a great deal written on endogamy as one of the causes of the potential extinction of the Parsees; for example, it is a prevalent concern in the articles in *The Novels of Bapsi Sidhwa,* edited by R. K. Dhawan and Novy Kapadia, since intermarriage is considered one of the primary themes in Sidhwa's writing. Also, among many references to Parsee restrictions on intermarriage throughout *The Parsis: Madyan to Sanjan,* edited by Kapadia and

A. G. Khan, see Kapadia's "A Suitable Parsi Boy" (115–26). For a discussion of Parsee attitudes toward marriage in general, see Luhrmann 168–70.

48. Chandra Mohanty convincingly deconstructs stereotypical imagery of "the Third World woman" in her seminal and frequently reprinted piece "Under Western Eyes."

49. Although it cannot be pursued in the present study, the theme of "cultural purity" might also be usefully addressed in relation to the novels. For example, in relation to Sidhwa's work, Jill Didur points out that the "obsessive concern with contamination and degeneration of the community's bloodline stemmed from the precarious position of authority that Parsis occupied in the colonial order of things" (75).

4 / "How to Be Indian"

1. These films share a narrative focus with the ethnographic stories and novels of my earlier chapters, leading me to use the term "South Asia" when talking about the broader communities in question. In my earlier chapters, I have made attempts to clarify what culture, race, or ethnicity represent in those particular discussions. Unlike my previous texts, in these films, the main characters are identified as Indian and do not generally seem to represent other parts of the subcontinent, which is why I use "Indian" in relation to the film narratives. Since the films do not conspicuously work to separate the cultural from the ethnic or the diasporic, I use the term "ethnocultural," although the conflation of the terms has implications that I problematize in other places. In this case, as best I can, I provide cues for the varied definitions of "Indianness," as culture and as ethnicity, which are alluded to in the films. In a related discussion, Khyati Y. Joshi sketches some of the complexities of authenticity in relation to what she calls "ethnoreligious" identity (52–53).

2. While Christiane Schlote's point is well taken that second-generation South Asians do not stand in the same relation to (trans)nationalism as the immigrant generation does, I depart from her when I argue that a transformed analysis of diasporization is still a useful model for reading their stories.

3. For overviews of the concept of performativity and its ambivalent politics in different disciplines, see Morris; and Scheie.

4. For more detailed information, consult the list compiled by the South Asian Journalists Association (SAJA).

5. For a critique of "fusion" talk, see Katrak, "Changing Traditions."

6. For historicizing discussions on Bollywood, see Desai, *Beyond Bollywood*; Dudrah 34–36.

7. See Naficy's section "Accented Mode of Production" (43–46) for a discussion of such niche screenings.

8. In her chapter titled "Between Hollywood and Bollywood" (emphasizing a betweenness I would argue is not really there), Desai briefly cites each of the films on which I focus.

9. *Film Comment* devoted a special issue to "Bollywood 101" in summer 2002, in which the guest editor David Chute provides some useful information about the role of Bollywood in international cinema and introduces a number of articles on specific topics.

10. See Hjort and MacKenzie's *Cinema and Nation* for many useful discussions about the value and limitations of linking film to national identity and belonging.

11. See Shankar and Srikanth.

12. See Yasmin Hussain's chapter about how Chadha's films represent "desification" of British cinema (71–90).

13. Mani makes a similar argument about Miss India USA winners, whom she argues will "always straddle two spatially and temporally disjunctive narratives of citizenship and national subjectivity" (737).

14. For a brief overview of the ideologies that positioned Indians in America as related to other Asian groups, see Palumbo-Liu, who notes that South Asian American and Pacific Rim diasporas may be mutually informative, although he defers the discussion (39–40, 392).

15. Although it is impossible in literary stud ies to forget Howard Bloom's *Anxiety of Influence* concerning the overweening pressure represented by literary "forefathers" or the analogous "anxiety of authorship" experienced by women writers, as described by Gilbert and Gubar, I do not directly reference either of those paradigms in this chapter. My discussion is more relevant to Priscilla Wald's notion of the "anxiety of identity," as discussed in the introduction.

16. See Loomba for an informative analysis of this exchange.

17. On combining Asian American and queer studies, see Bascara (119). Lest this discourse be considered a "Western" one which is a sign of Americanization, Ruth Vanita in the introduction to her edited volume critiques how "lesbian and gay studies in the Euro-American academy by and large take the view that same-sex desire has historically been unrepresented in South Asian languages, and that its representation appears only in the work of recent Indian writers in English, many of them diasporic" and "a particular feminist view of Indian 'tradition,' especially religious tradition, as repressive of desire, pleasure, and freedom" (2). As a corrective, the essays in her collection work at "tracing and interpreting a range of discourses on same-sex love, often within religious traditions, through South Asian history": "We found many texts that represent same-sex relations" and "that constitute a continuity of discourse, by speaking to one another across time within particular linguistic and literary-critical traditions" (2).

18. For an analysis of "camp" and "kitsch" in Bollywood, in terms of queerness and cultural politics, see Dudrah 118–20.

19. For analyses of code-switching in terms of sociology, see Maira; in terms of anthropology, see Kirin Narayan.

20. Maira's portraits emphasize compartmentalized identities, which are also elements of the films I discuss, but the film narratives conclude with attempts to combine rather than separate identities. In doing so, they provide some interesting contrasts between self-narrations and film portrayals of South Asian Americans. Coming-of-age stories as a genre may invite such resolutions between individual and community, as the bildungsroman has historically been understood to end.

21. For a suggestive comparison, see how Hussain describes the political "assertiveness" of second and later generations of British South Asians (25–28).

Works Cited

ABCD. Dir. Krutin Patel. Laxmi Pictures, 1999.

Abel, Elizabeth, Marianne Hirsch, and Elizabeth Langland, eds. *The Voyage In: Fictions of Female Development.* Hanover, NH: University Press of New England, 1983.

Adams, James Truslow. *The Epic of America.* Boston: Little, Brown, 1937.

Afzal-Khan, Fawzia. "Women in History." *International Literature in English: Essays on the Major Writers.* New York: Garland, 1991. 271–81.

Alba, Richard D. and Victor Nee. *Remaking the American Mainstream: Assimilation and Contemporary Immigration.* Cambridge, MA: Harvard University Press, 2003.

Alexander, Meena. *Fault Lines: A Memoir.* New York: Feminist Press at the City University of New York, 1993.

———. *Manhattan Music.* San Francisco: Mercury House, 1997.

———. *The Shock of Arrival: Reflections on Postcolonial Experience.* Boston: South End, 1996.

Ali, Zainab, and Dharini Rasiah. *Words Matter: Conversations with Asian American Writers.* Ed. King-kok Cheung. Honolulu: University of Hawaii Press, 2000. 69–91.

Allen, Diane S. "Reading the Body Politic in Bapsi Sidhwa's Novels: *The Crow-Eaters, Ice-Candy Man* and *An American Brat.*" *South Asian Review* 18.15 (1994): 69–80.

American Chai. Dir. Anurag Mehta. Dream Merchant Pictures, 2001.

American Desi. Dir. Piyush Dinker Pandya. American Desi Productions, 2000.

Anderson, Benedict. *Imagined Communities: Reflections on the Origin and Spread of Nationalism.* Rev. ed. London: Verso, 1991.

———. "Nationalism, Identity, and the World-in-Motion: On the Logics of Seriality." Cheah and Robbins 117–33.

Aneja, Anu. "*Jasmine,* the Sweet Scent of Exile." *Pacific Coast Philology* 28.1 (1993): 72–80.

Anzaldúa, Gloria. *Borderlands/La Frontera.* San Francisco: Aunt Lute, 1987.

Appadurai, Arjun. *Modernity at Large: Cultural Dimensions of Globalization.* Minneapolis: University of Minnesota Press, 1996.

Appadurai, Arjun, and Carol Breckenridge. "Public Modernity in India." *Consuming Modernity: Public Culture in a South Asian World.* Ed. Carol Breckenridge. Minneapolis: University of Minnesota Press, 1995. 1–19.

Appiah, Kwame Anthony. "Cosmopolitan Patriots." Cheah and Robbins 91–111.

Arora, Anupama. "Rituals of Queer Diaspora in Nisha Ganatra's *Chutney Popcorn.*" *South Asian Popular Culture* 5.1 (2007): 31–43.

Arora, Kulvinder. "The Mythology of Female Sexuality: Alternative Narratives of Belonging." *Women* 17.2 (2006): 220–50.

Arthur Levitt Public Affairs Center, Hamilton College. "Levitt Reports." The Trustees of Hamilton College, 2006.

Ashcroft, Bill. *Post-colonial Transformation.* New York: Routledge, 2001.

Bahri, Deepika, and Mary Vasudeva, eds. *Between the Lines: South Asians and Postcoloniality.* Philadelphia: Temple University Press, 1996.

———. Introduction. Bahri and Vasudeva 1–32.

Bakhtin, M. M. *The Dialogic Imagination.* Ed. Michael Holquist. Trans. Caryl Emerson and Michael Holquist. Austin: University of Texas Press, 1981.

Bales, Kent. "Walt Whitman's Daughter; or, Postcolonial Self-Transformation in the Fiction of Bharati Mukherjee." *Daughters of Restlessness: Women's Literature at the End of the Millennium.* Ed. Sabine Coelsch-Foisner, Hanna Wallinger, and Gerhild Reisner. Heidelberg: Universitätsverlag C. Winter, 1998. 187–201.

Bammer, Angelika. Introduction. *Displacements: Cultural Identities in Question.* Ed. Bammer. Bloomington: Indiana University Press, 1994.

Banerjee, Ranee Kaur. "'Singing in the Seams': Bharati Mukherjee's Immigrants." *No Small World: Visions and Revisions of World Literature.* Ed. Michael Thomas Carroll. Urbana, IL: National Council of Teachers of English, 1996. 189–201.

Bascara, Victor. "'Within Each Crack/A Story': The Political Economy of Queering Filipino American Pasts." Davé et al. 117–36.

Bauman, Zygmunt. "Culture and Management." *Parallax* 10.2 (2004): 63–72.

———. *Liquid Modernity.* Malden, MA: Blackwell, 2000.

Beauvoir, Simone de. *The Second Sex.* New York: Knopf, 1989.

Benjamin, Joel, Lakshmi Kallicharan, Ian McDonald, and Lloyd Searwar. "In the Eyes of Others: Introduction." Benjamin et al. 11–16.

———, eds. *They Came in Ships: An Anthology of Indo-Guyanese Prose and Poetry.* Leeds, UK: Peepal Tree, 1998.

Berger, Joseph. "Indian, Twice Removed: Guyanese Immigrants Cautious about Being Labeled." *New York Times* 17 December 2004.

Bhabha, Homi. *The Location of Culture*. London: Routledge, 1994.

———. *Nation and Narration*. London: Routledge, 1990.

Bhattacharjee, Anannya. "The Habit of Ex-nomination: Nation, Woman, and the Indian Immigrant Bourgeoisie." Gupta 229–52.

Bloom, Harold. *The Anxiety of Influence: A Theory of Poetry*. New York: Oxford University Press, 1997.

Bow, Leslie. *Betrayal and Other Acts of Subversion: Feminism, Sexual Politics, Asian American Women's Literature*. Princeton, NJ: Princeton University Press, 2001.

Braendlin, Bonnie Hoover. "*Bildung* in Ethnic Women Writers." *Denver Quarterly* 17 (1983): 75–87.

Brah, Avtar. *Cartographies of Diaspora: Contesting Identities*. London: Routledge, 1996.

Braziel, Jana Evans, and Anita Mannur. "Nation, Migration, Globalization: Points of Contention in Diaspora Studies." Braziel and Mannur 1–22.

———, eds. *Theorizing Diaspora*. Malden, MA: Blackwell, 2003.

Brennan, Timothy. *At Home in the World: Cosmopolitanism Now*. Cambridge, MA: Harvard University Press, 1997.

Brownstein, Ronald. "Is the American Dream a Myth?" Review of *Creating an Opportunity Society*, by Ron Haskins and Isabel Sawhill. *National Journal* 17 October 2009.

Bulosan, Carlos. *America Is in the Heart: A Personal History*. New York: Harcourt, Brace, 1943.

Butalia, Urvashi. *The Other Side of Silence: Voices from the Partition of India*. Durham, NC: Duke University Press, 2000.

Butler, Judith. *Gender Trouble: Feminism and the Subversion of Identity*. New York: Routledge, 1999.

———. "Merely Cultural." *Social Text* 52–53 (1997): 265–77.

Carlson, Robert A. "Americanization as an Early Twentieth Century Adult Education Movement." *History of Education Quarterly* 10.4 (1970): 440–64.

Carter, Marina, and Khal Torabully. *Coolitude: An Anthology of the Indian Labour Diaspora*. London: Anthem, 2002.

Carved in Silence. Dir. Felicia Lowe. Felicia Lowe Productions, 1988.

Chan, Sucheng. *Hmong Means Free: Life in Laos and America*. Philadelphia: Temple University Press, 1994.

Chaturvedi, Vinayak, ed. *Mapping Subaltern Studies and the Postcolonial*. London: Verso, 2000.

Cheah, Pheng. "Given Culture: Rethinking Cosmopolitical Freedom in Transnationalism." Cheah and Robbins 290–328.

———. "Introduction Part II: The Cosmopolitical Today." Cheah and Robbins 20–44.

Cheah, Pheng, and Bruce Robbins, eds. *Cosmopolitics: Thinking and Feeling beyond the Nation.* Minneapolis: University of Minnesota Press, 1998.

Cheung, King-Kok, ed. *An Interethnic Companion to Asian American Literature.* New York: Cambridge University Press, 1997.

Chopin, Kate. *The Awakening: An Authoritative Text, Biographical and Historical Contexts, Criticism.* 2nd ed. New York: Norton, 1994.

Chow, Rey. *Primitive Passions: Visuality, Sexuality, Ethnography, and Contemporary Chinese Cinema.* New York: Columbia University Press, 1995.

———. *Writing Diaspora: Tactics of Intervention in Contemporary Cultural Studies.* Bloomington: Indiana University Press, 1993.

Chu, Patricia P. *Assimilating Asians: Gendered Strategies of Authorship in Asian America.* Durham, NC: Duke University Press, 2000.

Chuh, Kandice. *Imagine Otherwise: On Asian Americanist Critique.* Durham, NC: Duke University Press, 2003.

Chute, David. "The Road to Bollywood." *Film Comment* 38.3 (2002): 36.

Chutney Popcorn. Dir. Nisha Ganatra. First Look International, 1999.

Clifford, James. "Diasporas." *Cultural Anthropology* 9.3 (1994): 302–38.

———. "Mixed Feelings." Cheah and Robbins 362–71.

Clifford, James, and George E. Marcus, eds. *Writing Culture: The Poetics and Politics of Ethnography,* Berkeley: University of California Press, 1986.

Cohen, Robin. *Global Diasporas: An Introduction.* Seattle: University of Washington Press, 1997.

Comins, D. W. D. *Notes on Immigration from India to British Guiana, Jamaica, St. Lucia, Trinidad, and on Return Passages.* Georgetown, Guyana: National Archives of Guyana, 1893.

Conrad, Joseph. *Heart of Darkness.* Madison, WI: Cricket House Books, 2010.

"Consider This." Editorial. *Post-Standard* (Syracuse, NY) 2 August 2002: A12.

Continuous Journey. Dir. Ali Kazimi. Peripheral Visions, 2004.

Crenshaw, Kimberlé Williams. "Mapping the Margins: Intersectionality, Identity Politics, and Violence against Women of Color." *Critical Race Theory: The Key Writings That Informed the Movement.* Ed. Kimberlé Crenshaw, Neil Gotanda, Gary Peller, and Kendall Thomas. New York: New Press, 1995. 357–83.

Cullen, Jim. *The American Dream: A Short History of an Idea That Shaped a Nation.* New York: Oxford University Press, 2003.

Cumpston, I. M. "A Survey of Indian Immigration to British Tropical Colonies to 1910." *Population Studies* 10.2 (1956): 158–65.

Daly, Vere T. *A Short History of the Guyanese People.* Oxford, UK: Macmillan, 1975.

Das Gupta, Monisha. *Unruly Immigrants: Rights, Activism, and Transnational South Asian Politics in the United States.* Durham, NC: Duke University Press, 2006.

Das Dasgupta, Shamita, and Sayantani DasGupta. "Women in Exile: Gender

Relations in the Asian Indian Community in the U.S." Maira and Srikanth 381–400.

Davé, Shilpa. "Apu's Brown Voice: Cultural Inflection and South Asian Accents." Davé et al. 313–36.

———. "'Community Beauty': Transnational Performances and Cultural Citizenship in 'Miss India Georgia.'" *Lit: Literature Interpretation Theory* 12.3 (2001): 335–58.

———. "The Doors to Home and History: Post-colonial Identities in Meena Alexander and Bharati Mukherjee." *Amerasia Journal* 19.3 (1993): 103–14.

Davé, Shilpa, LeiLani Nishime, and Tasha G. Oren, eds. *East Main Street: Asian American Popular Culture.* New York: NYU Press, 2005.

Dayal, Samir. "Creating, Preserving, Destroying: Violence in Bharati Mukherjee's *Jasmine.*" Nelson, *Bharati Mukherjee.* 65–88.

———. "Min(d)ing the Gap: South Asian Americans and Diaspora." Shankar and Srikanth 235–65.

Dearborn, Mary. *Pocahontas's Daughters: Gender and Ethnicity in American Culture.* New York: Oxford University Press, 1986.

Deleuze, Gilles, and Félix Guattari. *A Thousand Plateaus: Capitalism and Schizophrenia.* Minneapolis: University of Minnesota Press, 1987.

Derrida, Jacques. *Of Grammatology.* Trans. Gayatri Chakravorty Spivak. Baltimore: Johns Hopkins University Press, 1976.

Desai, Jigna. *Beyond Bollywood: The Cultural Politics of South Asian Diasporic Film.* New York: Routledge, 2004.

———. "Bollywood Abroad: South Asian Diasporic Cosmopolitanism and Indian Cinema." Rajan and Sharma 115–37.

———. "Bombay Boys and Girls: The Gender and Sexual Politics of Transnationality in the New Indian Cinema in English." *South Asian Popular Culture* 1.1 (2003): 45–61.

Dewey, John. *The Middle Works, 1899–1924.* Ed. Jo A. Boydston. Carbondale: Southern Illinois University Press, 1980.

Dhawan, R. K., and Novy Kapadia, eds. *The Novels of Bapsi Sidhwa.* New Delhi: Prestige, 1996.

Diaspora: A Journal of Transnational Studies. Home page. http://www.utpjournals.com/diaspora/diaspora.html. 8 August 2008.

Didur, Jill. *Unsettling Partition: Literature, Gender, Memory.* Toronto: University of Toronto Press, 2006.

Divakaruni, Chitra B. *Arranged Marriage: Stories.* New York: Anchor Books, 1995.

"Diversity Touted with a New Appointment to Schenectady Post." *Business Review* (Albany, NY) 6 September 2005.

Dlaska, Andrea. *Ways of Belonging: The Making of New Americans in the Fiction of Bharati Mukherjee.* Vienna: Braumüller, 1999.

Dorr, Wendy. "Middlemen." *This American Life.* NPR broadcast, 15 October

2002.Drake, Jennifer. “Looting American Culture: Bharati Mukherjee’s Immigrant Narratives.” *Contemporary Literature* 40.1 (1999): 60–84.

Dublin, Thomas. *Immigrant Voices: New Lives in America, 1773–1986.* Urbana: University of Illinois Press, 1993.

Dudrah, Rajinder Kumar. *Bollywood: Sociology Goes to the Movies.* New Delhi: Sage, 2006.

Dufoix, Stéphane. *Diasporas.* Trans. William Rodarmor. Berkeley: University of California Press, 2008.

Dugger, Celia W. “U.S. Plan to Lure Nurses May Hurt Poor Nations.” *New York Times* 24 May 2006.

DuPlessis, Rachel Blau. *Writing beyond the Ending: Narrative Strategies of Twentieth-Century Women Writers.* Bloomington: Indiana University Press, 1985.

Edwards, Brent Hayes. *The Practice of Diaspora: Literature, Translation, and the Rise of Black Internationalism.* Cambridge, MA: Harvard University Press, 2003.

———. “The Uses of *Diaspora.*” *Social Text* 19.1 (2001): 45.

Edwards, Eric J. “City Discriminating by Importing Guyanese.” *Times Union* (Albany, NY) 13 April 2003: B4.

Egerer, Claudia. *Fictions of (In)Betweenness.* Gothenburg, Sweden: Acta Universitatis Gothoburgensis, 1997.

Ellison, Ralph. *Invisible Man.* New York: Random House, 1952.

Eriksen, Thomas. *Ethnicity and Nationalism: Anthropological Perspectives.* London: Pluto, 1993.

Faderman, Lillian, and Ghia Xiong. *I Begin My Life All Over: The Hmong and the American Immigrant Experience.* Boston: Beacon, 1998.

Faymonville, Carmen. “South Asian American Women Writers’ Cultural Dialogue with the Mythical West.” *Asian American Literature in the International Context: Readings on Fiction, Poetry, and Performance.* Ed. Rocío G. Davis and Sämi Ludwig. Hamburg: Lit, 2002. 247–61.

Feng, Pin-chia. *The Female Bildungsroman by Toni Morrison and Maxine Hong Kingston: A Postmodern Reading.* New York: Peter Lang, 1998.

Fludernik, Monika. *Diaspora and Multiculturalism: Common Traditions and New Developments.* New York: Rodopi, 2003.

———.“The Diasporic Imaginary: Postcolonial Reconfigurations in the Context of Multiculturalism.” Fludernik, *Diaspora and Multiculturalism* xi–xxxviii.

———, ed. *Hybridity and Postcolonialism: Twentieth-Century Indian Literature.* Tübingen, Germany: Stauffenburg-Verl., 1998.

Fraser, Cary. *Ambivalent Anti-colonialism: The United States and the Genesis of West Indian Independence, 1940–1964.* Westport, CT: Greenwood, 1994.

Friedman, Susan Stanford. *Mappings: Feminism and the Cultural Geographies of Encounter.* Princeton, NJ: Princeton University Press, 1998.

Frye, Joanne S. *Living Stories, Telling Lives: Women and the Novel in Contemporary Experience.* Ann Arbor: University of Michigan Press, 1986.

Geertz, Clifford. "Deep Play: Notes on the Balinese Cockfight." Geertz, *Interpretation* 412–54.

———. *The Interpretation of Cultures*. New York: Basic Books, 1973.

———. "Thick Description: Toward an Interpretative Theory of Culture." Geertz, *Interpretation* 3–32.

George, Sheba Mariam. *When the Women Come First: Gender and Class in Transnational Migration*. Berkeley: University of California Press, 2005.

Gerstle, Gary. "Liberty, Coercion, and the Making of Americans." *Journal of American History* 84.2 (1997): 524–58.

Ghosh, Amitav. "The Diaspora in Indian Culture." *Public Culture* 2.1 (1989): 73–78.

———. *In an Antique Land*. New York: Vintage Books, 1994.

———. *The Shadow Lines*. New York: Viking, 1989.

Gibson, Margaret A. *Accommodation without Assimilation: Sikh Immigrants in an American High School*. Ithaca, NY: Cornell University Press, 1998.

Gilbert, Sandra M., and Susan Gubar. *The Madwoman in the Attic: The Woman Writer and the Nineteenth-Century Literary Imagination*. New Haven, CT: Yale University Press, 1979.

Gilroy, Paul. *The Black Atlantic: Modernity and Double Consciousness*. Cambridge, MA: Harvard University Press, 1993.

Glenn, Evelyn Nakano. "From Servitude to Service Work: Historical Continuities in the Racial Division of Paid Reproductive Labor." *Signs* 18.1 (Autumn 1992): 1–43.

Glissant, Édouard. *Poetics of Relation*. Trans. Betsy Wing. Ann Arbor: University of Michigan Press, 1997.

Göbel, Walter. "Bharati Mukherjee: Expatriation, Americanality, and Literary Form." *Fusions of Culture*. Ed. Peter O. Stummer. Amsterdam: Rodopi, 1996. 111–18.

Goodwin, Mike. "Guyanese Wonder: Where Are the Candidates?" *Times Union* (Albany, NY) 23 October 2003: B1.

———. "Immigrant Appeal Intrigues Mayor." *Times Union* (Albany, NY) 20 January 2003: B1.

———. "Tax Hikes, Police Scandal, Snow Batter Mayor." *Times Union* (Albany, NY) 12 January 2003: D1.

Gopinath, Gayatri. *Impossible Desires: Queer Diasporas and South Asian Public Cultures*. Durham, NC: Duke University Press, 2005.

Govinden, Devarakshanam. "The Indentured Experience: Indian Women in Colonial Natal." Hawley 55–76.

Graham, Otis L., Jr., and Elizabeth Koed. "Americanizing the Immigrant, Past and Future: History and Implications of a Social Movement." *Public Historian* 15.4 (1993): 24–49.

Grewal, Inderpal. "Reading and Writing the South Asian Diaspora: Feminism and Nationalism in North America." *Our Feet Walk the Sky: Women of the*

South Asian Diaspora. Ed. Women of South Asian Descent Collective. San Francisco: Aunt Lute, 1993. 226–36.

———. *Transnational America: Feminisms, Diasporas, Neoliberalisms*. Durham, NC: Duke University Press, 2005.

Grice, Helena. "'Who Speaks for Us?': Bharati Mukherjee's Fiction and the Politics of Immigration." *Comparative American Studies: An International Journal* 1.1 (2003): 81–96.

Gupta, Akhil, and James Ferguson. *Culture, Power, Place: Explorations in Critical Anthropology*. Durham, NC: Duke University Press, 1997.

Gupta, Sangeeta R., ed. *Emerging Voices: South Asian American Women Redefine Self, Family, and Community*. New Delhi: Sage, 1999.

Hai, Ambreen. "Border Work, Border Trouble: Postcolonial Feminism and the Ayah in Bapsi Sidhwa's *Cracking India*." *Modern Fiction Studies* 46.2 (2000): 379–426.

Hall, Stuart. "Cultural Identity and Diaspora." Braziel and Mannur 233–46.

———. "Living with Difference: Extracts from a Conversation between Stuart Hall and Bill Schwarz." *Soundings*. February 2007.

———. "The Local and the Global: Globalization and Ethnicity." McClintock et al. 173–87.

Halter, Marilyn. *Shopping for Identity: The Marketing of Ethnicity*. New York: Schocken Books, 2000.

Haney-López, Ian F. *White by Law: The Legal Construction of Race*. Revised and updated ed. New York: NYU Press, 2006.

Havely, Cicely. "Patterns of Migration in the Works of Bapsi Sidhwa." Dhawan and Kapadia 61–70.

Hawley, John C., ed. *India in Africa, Africa in India: Indian Ocean Cosmpolitanisms*. Bloomington: Indiana University Press, 2008.

Height, Dorothy. *Open Wide the Freedom Gates: A Memoir*. Cambridge, MA: Perseus Books, 2003.

Herman, David, Manfred Jahn, and Marie-Laure Ryan, eds. *The Routledge Encyclopedia of Narrative Theory*. London: Routledge, 2005.

Hicks, D. Emily. *Border Writing: The Multidimensional Text*. Minneapolis: University of Minnesota Press, 1991.

Higham, John. *Strangers in the Land: Patterns of American Nativism, 1860–1925*. 1955. New Brunswick, NJ: Rutgers University Press, 1992.

Hilbert, Jeffrey. "The Politics of Drag." *Out in Culture: Gay, Lesbian, and Queer Essays on Popular Culture*. Ed. Corey K. Creekmur and Alexander Doty. Durham, NC: Duke University Press, 1995.

Hill, Howard C. "The Americanization Movement." *American Journal of Sociology* 24.6 (1919): 609–42.

Hitchcock, Peter. *Imaginary States: Studies in Cultural Transnationalism*. Urbana: University of Illinois Press, 2003.

Hjort, Mette, and Scott MacKenzie, eds. *Cinema and Nation*. London: Routledge, 2000.

Hobsbawm, Eric. "Introduction: Inventing Traditions." Hobsbawm and Ranger 1–14.
Hobsbawm, Eric, and Terence Ranger, eds. *The Invention of Tradition*. Cambridge: Cambridge University Press, 1983.
Hollinger, David A. *Postethnic America: Beyond Multiculturalism*. New York: Basic Books, 1995.
Holte, James Craig. "The Representative Voice: Autobiography and the Ethnic Experience." *MELUS* 9.2 (1982): 25–46.
Hsiao, Ruth Yu. "A World Apart: A Reading of South Asian American Literature." Shankar and Srikanth 217–34.
Huang, Yunte. *Transpacific Displacement: Ethnography, Translation, and Intertextual Travel in Twentieth-Century American Literature*. Berkeley: University of California Press, 2002.
Hu-Dehart, Evelyn. "Afterword: Brief Meditation on Diaspora Studies." *Modern Drama* 48.2 (2005): 428–39.
Hussain, Yasmin. *Writing Diaspora: South Asian Women, Culture, and Ethnicity*. Burlington, VT: Ashgate, 2005.
Hwang, David Henry. *M. Butterfly*. New York: Plume, 1989.
Ifekwunigwe, Jayne. "Returning(s): Relocating the Critical Feminist Auto-ethnographer." Braziel and Mannur 184–206.
Jackson, John L., Jr. *Real Black: Adventures in Racial Sincerity*. Chicago: University of Chicago Press, 2005.
Jacobson, Matthew Frye. *Whiteness of a Different Color: European Immigrants and the Alchemy of Race*. Cambridge, MA: Harvard University Press, 1998.
Jagan, Cheddi. *The West on Trial: My Fight for Guyana's Freedom*. Antigua: Hansib Caribbean, 1997.
Jaidka, Manju. "Hyphenated Perspectives on the Cracking of India: Bapsi Sidhwa's *Ice-Candy-Man*." *South Asian Review* 25.2 (2004): 43–50.
jain, anupama. "Re-reading beyond Third World Difference: The Case of Bharati Mukherjee's *Jasmine*." *Weber Studies* 15.1 (1998): 117–26.
———. "Theorizing South Asian America: The Praxis of Locating Communities Locally and Globally." *South Asian Review* 24.1 (2003): 220–36.
Jameson, Fredric. "On 'Cultural Studies.'" *Social Text* 34 (1993): 17–52.
Jarvie, Ian. "National Cinema: A Theoretical Assessment." Hjort and MacKenzie 75–87.
Johnson, Richard. "What Is Cultural Studies Anyway?" *Social Text* 16 (1986): 38–80.
Joshi, Khyati Y. *New Roots in America's Sacred Ground: Religion, Race, and Ethnicity in Indian America*. New Brunswick, NJ: Rutgers University Press, 2006.
Jurczynski, Albert J. Personal interview. 24 October 2002.
———. Personal interview. 9 July 2003.
———. "Trip to Guyana Brought Home the Connection to Schenectady." Editorial. *Sunday Gazette* (Schenectady, NY) 20 April 2003: C6.

Jussawalla, Feroza. "'Hybridity,' Our Ancestral Heritage: Minority 'Indian' Writers Speak of Their Diversity." Fludernik 199–218.

———. "Kim, Huck and Naipaul: Using the Postcolonial Bildungsroman to (Re) Define Postcoloniality." *Links and Letters* 4 (1997): 25–38.

———. "Navjote Ceremonies: The Location of Bapsi Sidhwa's Culture." Dhawan and Kapadia 80–87.

Kain, Geoffrey. "Rupture as Continuity: Migrant Identity and 'Unsettled' Perspective in Bapsi Sidhwa's *An American Brat.*" *Asian American Literature in the International Context: Readings on Fiction, Poetry, and Performance.* Ed. Rocío G. Davis and Sämi Ludwig. Hamburg: Lit, 2002. 237–46.

Kale, Madhavi. "Projecting Identities: Empire and Indentured Labor Migration from India to Trinidad and British Guiana, 1836–1885." Van der Veer 73–92.

Kalita, S. Mitra. *Suburban Sahibs: Three Immigrant Families and Their Passage from India to America.* New Brunswick, NJ: Rutgers University Press, 2003.

Kapadia, Novy. "Expatriate Experience and Theme of Marriage in *An American Brat.*" Dhawan and Kapadia 187–99.

———. "The Parsi Paradox in *The Crow Eaters.*" Dhawan and Kapadia 125–35.

———. "A Suitable Parsi Boy." Kapadia and Khan 115–26.

Kapadia, Novy, and A. G. Khan, eds. *The Parsis: Madyan to Sanjan (An Appraisal of Ethnic Anxieties Reflected in Literature).* New Delhi: Creative Books, 1997.

Kapur, Ratna. "Dark Times for Liberal Intellectual Thought." *Profession* 2006: 22–32.

Karafilis, Maria. "Crossing the Borders of Genre: Revisions of the *Bildungsroman* in Sandra Cisneros's *The House on Mango Street* and Jamaica Kincaid's *Annie John.*" *Journal of the Midwest Modern Language Association* 31.2 (1998): 63–78.

Karran, Kampta, ed. *Race and Ethnicity in Guyana.* Leeds, UK: Peepal Tree, 2000.

Katrak, Ketu. "Changing Traditions: South Asian Americans and Cultural/Communal Politics." *Massachusetts Review* 18.1 (2002): 75–88.

———. "South Asian American Literature." Cheung 192–218.

Kazal, Russell A. "Revisiting Assimilation: The Rise, Fall, and Reappraisal of a Concept in American Ethnic History." *American Historical Review* 100.2 (1995): 437–71.

Kershaw, Sarah. "For Schenectady, a Guyanese Strategy: Mayor Goes All Out to Encourage a Wave of Hardworking Immigrants." *New York Times* 26 July 2002: B1, B4.

Khan, Aisha. *Callaloo Nation: Metaphors of Race and Religious Identity among South Asians in Trinidad.* Durham, NC: Duke University Press, 2004.

Khandelwal, Madhulika S. *Becoming American, Being Indian: An Immigrant Community in New York City.* Ithaca, NY: Cornell University Press, 2002.

Kim, Elaine. "Beyond Railroads and Internment: Comments on the Past, Present, and Future of Asian American Studies." *Privileging Positions: The Sites of Asian American Studies.* Ed. Gary Y. Okihiro, Marilyn Alquizola, Dorothy Fujita Rony, and K. Scott Wong. Pullman: Washington State University Press, 1995. 1–9.

Kingston, Maxine Hong. *The Woman Warrior: Memoirs of a Girlhood Among Ghosts.* New York: Vintage, 1989.

Koltyk, Jo Ann. *New Pioneers in the Heartland: Hmong Life in Wisconsin.* Boston: Allyn and Bacon, 1998.

Koshy, Susan. "Category Crisis: South Asian Americans and Questions of Race and Ethnicity." *Diaspora: A Journal of Transnational Studies* 7.3 (1998): 285–320.

———. "The Postmodern Subaltern: Globalization Theory and the Subject of Ethnic, Area, and Postcolonial Studies." Lionnet and Shu-mei Shih 109–31.

———. *Sexual Naturalization: Asian Americans and Miscegenation.* Stanford, CA: Stanford University Press, 2004.

———. "Turning Color." *Transition* 6.4 (1996): 148–61.

Krishnan, R. S. "Cultural Construct and the Female Identity: Bharati Mukherjee's *Wife.*" *International Fiction Review* 25.1 (1998): 89–97.

Kristeva, Julia. *Revolution in Poetic Language.* Trans. Margaret Waller. New York: Columbia University Press, 1984.

Kulke, Eckehard. *The Parsees in India: A Minority as Agent of Social Change.* Munich: Weltforum Verlag, 1974.

Kurien, Prema. "Becoming American by Becoming Hindu: Indian Americans Take Their Place at the Multicultural Table." *Gatherings in Diaspora: Religious Communities and the New Immigration.* Ed. R. Stephen Warner and Judith G. Wittner. Philadelphia: Temple University Press, 1998. 37–70.

Lai, Him Mark, Genny Lim, and Judy Yung. *Island: Poetry and History of Chinese Immigrants on Angel Island, 1910–1940.* Seattle: University of Washington Press, 1991.

Lal, Vinay. *The Other Indians. A Political and Cultural History of South Asians in America.* Los Angeles: UCLA Asian American Studies Center Press, 2008.

Lallas, Demetrios J. "Salt of the Earth Country: A Genealogy of 'The American Dream.'" Ph.D. diss., University of Wisconsin, 2009.

Lee, Rachel C. *The Americas of Asian American Literature.* Princeton, NJ: Princeton University Press, 1999.

Leonard, Karen I. *Making Ethnic Choices: California's Mexican Americans.* Philadelphia: Temple University Press, 1992.

———. "South Asian Religions in the United States." Rajan and Sharma 91–114.

Leontis, Artemis. "The Diaspora of the Novel." *Diaspora* 2.1 (1992): 131–46.

Leviatin, David. "Beyond the Melting Pot and Back." Review of *The American Future: A History,* by Simon Schama. *Reviews in American History* 37 (2009): 296–302.

Lim, Shirley Geok-lin. "Immigration and Diaspora." Cheung 289–311.

Lim, Shirley Geok-lin, and Amy Ling, eds. *Reading the Literatures of Asian America.* Philadelphia: Temple University Press, 1992.

Ling, Amy. *Between Worlds: Women Writers of Chinese Ancestry.* New York: Pergamon, 1990.

Lionnet, Françoise. "Transnationalism, Postcolonialism or Transcolonialism? Reflections on Los Angeles, Geography, and the Uses of Theory." *Emergences: Journal for the Study of Media and Composite Cultures* 10.1 (2000): 25–35.

Lionnet, Françoise, and Shu-mei Shi. "Introduction: Thinking through the Minor, Transnationally." Lionnet and Shi 1–24.

———, eds. *Minor Transnationalism.* Durham, NC: Duke University Press, 2005.

Loomba, Ania. *Colonialism/Postcolonialism.* New York: Routledge, 1998.

Lorde, Audre. *Sister Outsider: Essays and Speeches.* New York: Crossing, 1984.

Low, Gail Ching-Liang. "In a Free State: Post-colonialism and Postmodernism in Bharati Mukherjee's Fiction." *Women: A Cultural Review* 4.1 (1993): 9–17.

Lowe, Lisa. *Immigrant Acts: On Asian American Cultural Politics.* Durham, NC: Duke University Press, 1996.

Luhrmann, T. M. *The Good Parsi: The Fate of a Colonial Elite in a Postcolonial Society.* Cambridge, MA: Harvard University Press, 1996.

Mahler, Sarah J. *American Dreaming: Immigrant Life on the Margins.* Princeton, NJ: Princeton University Press, 1995.

Maira, Sunaina. *Desis in the House: Indian American Youth Culture in New York City.* Philadelphia: Temple University Press, 2002.

Maira, Sunaina, and Rajini Srikanth, eds. *Contours of the Heart: South Asians Map North America.* New York: Asian American Writers' Workshop, 1996.

———. Introduction. Maira and Srikanth xvii–xxi.

Mani, Bakirathi. "Beauty Queens: Gender, Ethnicity, and Transnational Modernities at the Miss India USA Pageant." *positions: east asia cultures critique* 14.3 (2006): 717–47.

Mani, Lata. *Contentious Traditions: The Debate on Sati in Colonial India.* Berkeley: University of California Press, 1998.

Mankekar, Purnima. *Screening Culture, Viewing Politics: An Ethnography of Television, Womanhood, and Nation in Postcolonial India.* Durham, NC: Duke University Press, 1999.

Mannur, Anita. *Culinary Fictions: Food in South Asian Diasporic Culture.* Philadelphia: Temple University Press, 2010.

Martin, Denis-Constant. "The Choices of Identity." *Social Identities* 1.1 (1995): 5–20.

Martineau, Kim. "Guyanese Find Opportunity in Schenectady." *Times Union* (Albany, NY) 7 July 2002: B1.

maxconfus. "Re: 'Rumor.'" Online posting. port80cafe message board. 16 August 2002.

Maxey, Ruth. "'The Messiness of Rebirth as an Immigrant': Bharati Mukherjee's Changing Language of Migration." *South Asian Review* 26.2 (2005): 181.

———. "'Who Wants Pale, Thin, Pink Flesh?': Bharati Mukherjee, Whiteness, and South Asian American Writing." *Textual Practice* 20.3 (2006): 529–47.

Mazumdar, Sucheta. "The Politics of Religion and National Origin: Rediscovering Hindu Indian Identity in the United States." *Antinomies of Modernity: Essays on Race, Orient, Nation.* Ed. Vasant Kaiwar and Sucheta Mazumdar. Durham, NC: Duke University Press, 2003. 223–60.

McClintock, Anne. "'No Longer in a Future Heaven': Gender, Race, and Nationalism." McClintock et al. 89–112.

McClintock, Anne, Aamir Mufti, and Ella Shohat, eds. *Dangerous Liaisons: Gender, Nation, and Postcolonial Perspectives.* Minneapolis: University of Minnesota Press, 1997.

McDonald, Ian. "Tiger in the Stars." Benjamin et al. 271–76.

McFadden, Joanne. "Guyanese Community Spurs Schenectady Revitalization." *Business Review* (Albany, NY) 15 December 2003.

Mehta, Suketu. "So the Jains, They Have a Problem with Beef in the School Lunches. Who They Gonna Call?" *New York Times Magazine* 2 October 2005.

Melucci, Alberto. "Identity and Difference in a Globalized World." Werbner and Modood 58–69.

Michaels, Walter Benn. *Our America: Nativism, Modernism, and Pluralism.* Durham, NC: Duke University Press, 1995.

Miller, Anne. "Guyanese Courtship Resumes." *Times Union* (Albany, NY) 13 August 2006: D1.

Mishra, Vijay. *The Literature of the Indian Diaspora: Theorizing the Diasporic Imaginary.* New York: Routledge, 2007.

Mitchell, Katharyne. "Hybridity." *Cultural Geography: A Critical Dictionary of Key Concepts.* Ed. David Atkinson, Peter Jackson, David Sibley, and Neil Washbourne. London: I. B. Tauris, 2005. 188–93.

Mohanty, Chandra Talpade. "Under Western Eyes: Feminist Scholarship and Colonial Discourse." *Boundary 2: An International Journal of Literature and Culture* 12.3 (1984): 333–58.

Moore, Henrietta L. *The Subject of Anthropology: Gender, Symbolism and Psychoanalysis.* Malden, MA: Polity, 2007.

Moore, Kathleen. "Guyanese Population in Dispute." *Daily Gazette* (Schenectady, NY) 23 September 2009: A1+.

Mootoo, Shani. "Out on Main Street." *Out on Main Street & Other Stories.* Vancouver: Press Gang, 1993.

Morris, Rosalind C. "All Made Up: Performance Theory and the New Anthropology of Sex and Gender." *Annual Review of Anthropology* 24 (1995): 567–92.

Morrison, Toni. *Playing in the Dark: Whiteness and the Literary Imagination.* Cambridge, MA: Harvard University Press, 1992.

Mufti, Aamir, and Ella Shohat. Introduction. McClintock et al. 1–12.

Mukherjee, Bharati. "American Dreamer." *Mother Jones*. January–February 1997.

———. *Darkness*. New York: Fawcett Crest, 1985.

———. "Immigrant Writing: Give Us Your Maximalists!" *New York Times Book Review* 28 August 1988: 1, 28–29.

———. *Jasmine*. New York: Fawcett Crest, 1989.

———. *Wife*. 1975. New Delhi: Penguin, 1990.

Naficy, Hamid. *Accented Cinema: Exilic and Diasporic Filmmaking*. Princeton, NJ: Princeton University Press, 2001.

Narayan, Kirin. "Placing Lives through Stories: Second-Generation South Asian American." *Everyday Life in South Asia*. Ed. Diane P. Mines and Sarah Lamb. Bloomington: Indiana University Press, 2002. 425–39.

Narayan, Uma. *Dislocating Cultures: Identities, Traditions, and Third World Feminism*. New York: Routledge, 1997.

Nelson, Emmanuel S., ed. *Bharati Mukherjee: Critical Perspectives*. New York: Garland, 1993.

———, ed. *Writers of the Indian Diaspora: A Bio-Bibliographical Critical Sourcebook*. Westport, CT: Greenwood, 1993.

Ngai, Mae M. *Impossible Subjects: Illegal Aliens and the Making of Modern America*. Princeton, NJ: Princeton University Press, 2004.

Niranjana, Tejaswini. *Siting Translation: History, Post-structuralism, and the Colonial Context*. Berkeley: University of California Press, 1992.

Observant. "After Today's Article in the Gazette." Online posting. port80cafe message board. 27 July 2002.

Ong, Aihwa. *Flexible Citizenship: The Cultural Logics of Transnationality*. Durham, NC: Duke University Press, 1999.

Palumbo-Liu, David. *Asian/American: Historical Crossings of a Racial Frontier*. Stanford, CA: Stanford University Press, 1999.

Pat. "'RUMOR'—to Concerned." Online posting. port80cafe message board. 13 August 2002.

PatZ. "Re: Welcome Guyanese to this city." Online posting. port80cafe message board. 20 August 2002.

Peake, Linda, and D. Alissa Trotz. *Gender, Ethnicity and Place: Women and Identities in Guyana*. London: Routledge, 1999.

Pease, Donald E. *National Identities and Post-Americanist Narratives*. Durham, NC: Duke University Press, 1994.

Portes, Alejandro, ed. *The New Second Generation*. New York: Russell Sage Foundation Press, 1996.

Powell, Michael, and Michelle Garcia. "PA City Puts Illegal Immigrants on Notice." *Washington Post* 22 August 2006: A03.

Prashad, Vijay. "Desh: The Contradictions of 'Homeland.'" Maira and Srikanth 225–26.

———. *Everybody Was Kung Fu Fighting: Afro-Asian Connection and the Myth of Cultural Purity*. Boston: Beacon, 2002.

——. *The Karma of Brown Folk*. Minneapolis: University of Minnesota Press, 2000.

Pratt, Annis. *Archetypal Patterns in Women's Fiction*. Bloomington: Indiana University Press, 1981.

Puri, Shalini. *The Caribbean Postcolonial: Social Equality, Post-nationalism, and Cultural Hybridity*. New York: Palgrave Macmillan, 2004.

Purkayastha, Bandana. *Negotiating Ethnicity: Second-Generation South Asian Americans Traverse a Transnational World*. New Brunswick, NJ: Rutgers University Press, 2005.

Quayson, Ato. *Postcolonialism: Theory, Practice, or Process?* Malden, MA: Blackwell, 2000.

Radhakrishnan, R. "Conjunctural Identities, Academic Adjacencies." *Orientations: Mapping Studies in the Asian Diaspora*. Ed. Kandice Chuh and Karen Shimakawa. Durham, NC: Duke University Press, 2001. 249–63.

Rai, Amit. "'Start Narrative Here': Excess and the Space of History in Asian Diasporic Films." *South Asian Popular Culture* 1.1 (2003): 13–32.

Rajan, Gita. "Bharati Mukherjee." Nelson, *Writers of the Indian Diaspora* 235–42.

Rajan, Gita, and Shailja Sharma. "New Cosmopolitanisms: South Asians in the United States at the Turn of the Twenty-first Century." Rajan and Sharma 1–36.

——, eds. *New Cosmopolitanisms: South Asians in the U.S.* Stanford, CA: Stanford University Press, 2006.

——. "Theorizing Recognition: South Asian Authors in a Global Milieu." Rajan and Sharma 150–70.

Rangaswamy, Padma. *Namasté America: Indian Immigrants in an American Metropolis*. University Park: Pennsylvania State University Press, 2000.

Rastogi, Pallavi. *Afrindian Fictions: Diaspora, Race, and National Desire in South Africa*. Columbus: Ohio State University Press, 2008.

Ray, Sangeeta. *En-Gendering India: Woman and Nation in Colonial and Postcolonial Narratives*. Durham, NC: Duke University Press, 2000.

——. "The Nation in Performance: Bhabha, Mukherjee and Kureishi." Fludernik 218–38.

Report to the Secretary to the Government of India on the Condition of Indian Immigrants in Trinidad, British Guiana or Demerara, Fiji, Surinam/Dutch Guiana. Georgetown, Guyana: National Archives of Guyana, 1914.

Robbins, Bruce. "Introduction Part I: Actually Existing Cosmopolitanism." Cheah and Robbins 1–19.

Roediger, David R. *Working toward Whiteness: How America's Immigrants Became White; The Strange Journey from Ellis Island to the Suburbs*. New York: Basic Books, 2005.

Rogin, Michael. "Making America Home: Racial Masquerade and Ethnic Assimilation in the Transition to Talking Pictures." *Journal of American History* 79.3 (1992): 1050–77.

Ross, Robert L. "'Haunting Presence' and 'Broken Identities': The Immigrant Experience in Fiction." *South Asian Review* 18.15 (1994): 94–103.

———. "The Search for Community in Bapsi Sidhwa's Novels." Dhawan and Kapadia 71–79.

Rudrappa, Sharmila. *Ethnic Routes to Becoming American: Indian Immigrants and the Cultures of Citizenship.* New Brunswick, NJ: Rutgers University Press, 2004.

Rushdie, Salman. *Imaginary Homelands: Essays and Criticism, 1981–1991.* New York: Granta Books, 1991.

Rustomji-Kerns, Roshni, ed. *Living in America: Poetry and Fiction by South Asian American Writers.* Boulder, CO: Westview, 1995.

Safran, William. "Diasporas in Modern Societies: Myths of Homeland and Return." *Diaspora* 1.1 (1991): 83–99.

Said, Edward. *Orientalism.* New York: Vintage, 1979.

———. "Permission to Narrate." *Journal of Palestine Studies* 13.3 (1984): 27–48.

Samuelson, Robert J. *The Good Life and Its Discontents: The American Dream in the Age of Entitlement.* New York: Random House, 1995.

Sanchez, George. "'Go after the Women': Americanization and the Mexican Immigrant Woman, 1915–1929." *Unequal Sisters: A Multicultural Reader in U.S. Women's History.* Ed. Vicki Ruiz and Ellen DuBois. New York: Routledge, 1994. 284–97.

San Juan, E., Jr. *Racism and Cultural Studies: Critiques of Multiculturalist Ideology and the Politics of Difference.* Durham, NC: Duke University Press, 2002.

Schama, Simon. *The American Future: A History.* New York: HarperCollins, 2009.

Scheie, Timothy. "Addicted to Race: Performativity, Agency, and Césaire's *A Tempest.*" *College Literature* 25.2 (1998): 17–29.

Schein, Louisa. "Importing Miao Brethren to Hmong America: A Not-So-Stateless Transnationalism." Cheah and Robbins 163–91.

Schlote, Christiane. "Interpreters of Transnationalism: South Asian American Women Writers." *Amerikastudien/American Studies* 51.3 (2006): 387–409.

Schultheis, Alexandra W. *Regenerative Fictions: Postcolonialism, Psychoanalysis, and the Nation as Family.* New York: Palgrave Macmillan, 2004.

Serotta, Robert J. "Guyanese Helping to Make Schenectady Better." Letter. *Daily Gazette* (Schenectady, NY) 2 August 2003.

Sexton, Anne. "Cinderella." *Transformations.* Boston: Houghton Mifflin, 1971.

Shah, Purvi. "Redefining the Home: How Community Elites Silence Feminist Activism." *Dragon Ladies: Asian American Feminists Breathe Fire.* Ed. Sonia Shah. Boston: South End, 1997. 46–56.

Shankar, Lavina Dhingra. "The Limits of (South Asian) Names and Labels: Postcolonial or Asian American?" Shankar and Srikanth 49–66.

———. "Postcolonial Diasporics 'Writing in Search of a Homeland': Meena

Alexander's 'Manhattan Music,' 'Fault Lines,' and 'The Shock of Arrival.'" *Lit: Literature Interpretation Theory* 12.3 (2001): 285–312.

Shankar, Lavina Dhingra, and Pallassana R. Balgopal. "South Asian Immigrants before 1950: The Formation of Ethnic, Symbolic, and Group Identity." *Amerasia Journal* 27.1 (2001): 55–84.

Shankar, Lavina Dhingra, and Rajini Srikanth, eds. *A Part Yet Apart: South Asians in Asian America.* Philadelphia: Temple University Press, 1998.

Sharma, Rashmi. "Crossing the Dark Waters." *Living in America: Poetry and Fiction by South Asian American Writers.* Ed. Roshni Rustomji-Kerns. Boulder, CO: Westview, 1995. 11–26.

Sharpe, Jenny. *Allegories of Empire: The Figure of Woman in the Colonial Text.* Minneapolis: University of Minnesota Press, 1993.

———. "Gender, Nation, and Globalization in 'Monsoon Wedding' and 'Dilwale Dulhania Le Jayenge.'" *Meridians: Feminism, Race, Transnationalism* 6.1 (2005): 58–81.

Shohat, Ella, and Robert Stam. *Unthinking Eurocentrism: Multiculturalism and the Media.* London: Routledge, 1994.

Showalter, Elaine. *A Literature of Their Own.* Princeton, NJ: Princeton University Press, 1977.

Shukla, Sandhya. *India Abroad: Diasporic Cultures of Postwar America and England.* Princeton, NJ: Princeton University Press, 2003.

Sidhwa, Bapsi. *An American Brat.* Minneapolis, MN: Milkweed Editions, 1993.

———. *Cracking India.* Minneapolis, MN: Milkweed Editions, 1991. Originally published as *Ice-Candy-Man.* London: Penguin Books, 1989.

———. *The Crow Eaters.* London: Jonathan Cape, 1980.

———. "Why Do I Write?" Dhawan and Kapadia 27–34.

Sieg, Katrin. *Ethnic Drag: Performing Race, Nation, Sexuality in West Germany.* Ann Arbor: University of Michigan Press, 2002.

Sinclair, Upton. *The Jungle.* New York: Doubleday, Page, 1906.

Singh, Amardeep. "Deconstructing Question 9 on the 2010 Census." *Sepia Mutiny* weblog. 21 March 2010.

Singh, Jaspal Kaur. *Representation and Resistance: South Asian and African Women's Texts at Home and in the Diaspora.* Calgary: University of Calgary Press, 2008.

Sollors, Werner. *Beyond Ethnicity: Consent and Descent in American Culture.* New York: Oxford University Press, 1986.

———. Introduction. Sollors, *The Invention of Ethnicity* ix–xx.

———, ed. *The Invention of Ethnicity.* New York: Oxford University Press, 1989.

South Asian Journalists Association. "Fictional Desi TV Characters." *SAJAforum.org.* 3 January 2007.

Speek, Peter A. "The Meaning of Nationality and Americanization." *American Journal of Sociology* 32.2 (1926): 237–49.

Spivak, Gayatri Chakravorty. "Can the Subaltern Speak?" *The Post-colonial*

Studies Reader. Ed. Bill Ashcroft, Gareth Griffiths, and Helen Tiffin. London: Routledge, 1995. 24–28.
———. "Diasporas Old and New: Women in the Transnational World." *Textual Practice* 10.2 (1996): 245–70.
———. In Other Worlds: Essays in Cultural Politics. New York: Methuen, 1987.
———. "The New Subaltern: A Silent Interview." Chaturvedi 324–40.
Srikanth, Rajini. *The World Next Door: South Asian American Literature and the Idea of America.* Philadelphia: Temple University Press, 2004.
Stoneham, Geraldine. "'It's a Free Country': Visions of Hybridity in the Metropolis." *Comparing Postcolonial Literatures: Dislocations.* Ed. Ashok Bery, Patricia Murray, and Wilson Harris. New York: St. Martin's, 2000. 81–92.
Strock, Carl. "Who Heads Nativist Block in Schenectady?" Editorial. *Sunday Gazette* (Schenectady, NY) 18 August 2002: B1.
Takaki, Ronald. *A Different Mirror: A History of Multicultural America.* Boston: Little, Brown, 1993.
———. *Strangers from a Different Shore: A History of Asian Americans.* Boston: Little, Brown, 1989.
Thompson, Frank V. *Schooling of the Immigrant.* New York: Harper and Brothers, 1920.
Thunder in Guyana. Dir. Suzanne Wasserman. Women Make Movies, 2003.
Tomlinson, John. *Globalization and Culture.* Chicago: University of Chicago Press, 1999.
"Two Cities, Two Immigrant Landings." Editorial. *New York Times* 25 December 2002, late ed.: A22.
Van der Veer, Peter. "Introduction: The Diasporic Imagination." Van der Veer 1–16.
———, ed. *Nation and Migration: The Politics of Space in the South Asian Diaspora.* Philadelphia: University of Pennsylvania Press, 1995.
Vanita, Ruth. Introduction. *Queering India: Same-Sex Love and Eroticism in Indian Culture and Society.* Ed. Vanita. New York: Routledge, 2002. 1–11.
Vieira, Nelson H. "Hybridity vs. Pluralism: Culture, Race and Aesthetics in Jorge Amado." *Jorge Amado: New Critical Essays.* New York: Routledge, 2001. 231–51.
Von Burg, Ron, and Paul E. Johnson. "Yearning for a Past That Never Was: Baseball, Steroids, and the Anxiety of the American Dream." *Critical Studies in Media Communication* 26.4 (2009): 351–71.
Wald, Priscilla. *Constituting Americans: Cultural Anxiety and Narrative Form.* Durham, NC: Duke University Press, 1995.
Werbner, Pnina. *Imagined Diasporas among Manchester Muslims: The Public Performance of Pakistani Transnational Identity Politics.* Santa Fe, NM: School of American Research Press, 2002.
———. "Introduction: The Dialectics of Cultural Hybridity." Werbner and Modood 1–28.

———. "The Materiality of Diaspora—Between Aesthetic and 'Real' Politics." *Diaspora: A Journal of Transnational Studies* 9.1 (2000): 1.

Werbner, Pnina, and Tariq Modood, eds. *Debating Cultural Hybridity: Multicultural Identities and the Politics of Anti-racism.* Atlantic Highlands, NJ: Zed Books, 1997.

West, Cornel. *Race Matters.* Boston: Beacon, 1993.

Wickramagamage, Carmen. "Relocations as Positive Act: The Immigrant Experience in Bharati Mukherjee's Novels." *Diaspora: A Journal of Transnational Studies* 2.2 (1992): 171–200.

Williams, Patricia J. *Seeing a Color-Blind Future: The Paradox of Race.* New York: Farrar, Straus and Giroux, 1998.

Williams, Patrick. "Post-colonialism and Narrative." Herman et al. 451–56.

Williams, William Carlos. *In the American Grain.* New York: New Directions, 1925.

Wolcott, Harry F. "Making a Study 'More Ethnographic.'" *Representation in Ethnography.* Ed. John Van Maanen. Thousand Oaks, CA: Sage, 1995. 79–111.

Woodberry, Warren, Jr. "Immigrants Flock to an Upstate Haven." *New York Daily News* 22 June 2003: 7.

Woolf, Virginia. "Professions for Women." *Virginia Woolf: Women and Writing.* Ed. Michèle Barrett. New York: Harcourt Brace Jovanovich, 1979. 57–63.

Wu, Jean Yu-wen Shen, and Min Song, eds. *Asian American Studies: A Reader.* New Brunswick, NJ: Rutgers University Press, 2000.

Young, Robert J. C. *Colonial Desire: Hybridity in Theory, Culture, and Race.* New York: Routledge, 1995.

Zakaria, Fareed. "To Become an American." *Newsweek* 10 April 2006: 39.

Index

About the Author

anupama jain has taught at the University of Wisconsin-Madison, Union College, and Colby College. Her main academic interests are Anglophone and American narrative, postcolonial theory, utopianism, and social justice.